THE LION'S ROAR OF QUEEN ŚRĪMĀLĀ

A Buddhist Scripture
on the Tathāgatagarbha Theory

Prepared for the Columbia College Program of
Translations from the Oriental Classics

THE LION'S ROAR OF QUEEN ŚRĪMĀLĀ

A Buddhist Scripture
on the Tathāgatagarbha Theory

Translated, with Introduction and Notes by

ALEX WAYMAN
AND
HIDEKO WAYMAN

Columbia University Press
New York and London 1974

Alex Wayman, Professor of Sanskrit in the Department of Middle East Languages and Cultures and Professor in the Department of Religion at Columbia University, is the author of *Analysis of the Śrāvakabhūmi Manuscript* (1961), translator (in collaboration with F. D. Lessing) of *Mkhas grub rje's Fundamentals of the Buddhist Tantras* (1968), author of "Buddhism," in *Historia Religionum*, II (1971), and of *The Buddhist Tantras: Light on Indo-Tibetan Esotericism* (1973).

Hideko Wayman is a graduate of Tsuda College, Tokyo, in her native Japan and has an M.A. from the University of California, Berkeley.

Library of Congress Cataloging in Publication Data

Śrīmālāsūtra. English.

The lion's roar of Queen Śrīmālā.

Translation of the lost Sanskrit work made from a collation of the Chinese, Japanese, and Tibetan versions.

Bibliography: p. [133]–138

I. Wayman, Alex, tr. II. Wayman, Hideko, tr. III. Title.

BQ1792.E5W394 294.3′82 73–9673

ISBN 0–231–03726–0

Frontispiece

Queen Śrīmālā, from the Shōkō mandara, Hōryūji, Japan.

Photographed by Mr. Yūichi Yazawa of the Nara Museum.

This depiction of Queen Śrīmālā is the only one known in the world. It occurs in the upper right-hand corner of the Shōkō mandara painting, which represents Shōtoku Taishi's previous life, after-life, and his retinue. According to the legend, Shōtoku had lectured on the *Śrī-mālā-sūtra* to the Empress Suiko and had composed a commentary on the sūtra in the period A.D. 609–611. Later a cult arose based on Shōtoku Taishi's religious zeal, with the belief that Shōtoku was an incarnation of Queen Śrīmālā. The cult reached its peak during the Kamakura period. It was then that the painter Gyōson painted the mandara in 1253 at the request of Kenshin Tokugyō, scholar-monk, head of Shōryōin, Hōryūji. It is a National Treasure at the Shōsōin.

To

the Commentators

of yore and now

FOREWORD

The *Lion's Roar of Queen Śrīmālā* is one of the Translations from the Oriental Classics by which the Committee on Oriental Studies has sought to transmit to Western readers representative works of the major Asian traditions in thought and literature. Our intention is to provide translations based on scholarly study but written for the general reader rather than primarily for other specialists.

Considering the popularity and importance of the Śrī-Mālā Sūtra in Mahayana Buddhism, both in the Far East and in India, it is remarkable that no translation of it has appeared in a Western language. No doubt this task awaited the rather special combination of talents represented by Professor and Mrs. Wayman, who together have been able to deal with the many languages involved in its proper study. We are fortunate that the Waymans have persisted in this long and arduous project and have thereby achieved a milestone in Western study of the basic scriptures of Buddhism.

Wm. Theodore de Bary

CONTENTS

PREFACE

The *Śrī-Mālā-sūtra*, a composition of the Mahāsāṅghika sect, has had a remarkably successful career as a Mahāyāna Buddhist scripture. It became the chief scriptural authority in India for the theory that all sentient beings have the potentiality of Buddhahood and helped inspire the celebrated scripture called the *Laṅkāvatāra-sūtra*. It maintained its popularity as an influential Mahāyāna scripture in China and presumably was a source for the classic known as *The Awakening of Faith*. Through Korea, this work entered into the beginnings of Buddhism in Japan and has been important there down through the centuries. Its relative brevity obscures the numerous implications of relation with other Mahāyāna scriptures, which an eminent Chinese monk, Chi-tsang, attempted to make explicit in his commentary (see Appendix II). It is surprising that such an influential Buddhist work as the *Śrī-Mālā* has not yet been translated into a Western language. E. H. Johnston stated in the introduction to his edition of the *Ratnagotravibhāga*, "a translation of it into a European language is a desideratum for Buddhist studies."

The first draft of the translation was made in the autumn of 1962 at Madison, Wisconsin, by simultaneous comparison of several versions, the Tibetan with the Sino-Japanese. The work was discontinued due to our trip to India sponsored by the American Institute of Indian Studies (February, 1963, to January, 1964), and it was some time before we again had the opportunity to pursue the translation. Yet unaware, when we visited the Nāgārjunikoṇḍa art center and the site of Amarāvatī, we passed through an area of Andhra that may well have been a familiar district to the forever anonymous composer of the *Śrī-Mālā-sūtra*. Those two points along the Krishna River were in the third century A. D. the busy sites of Mahāsāṅghika activity.

The remaining work on the translation took place entirely at Columbia University in the City of New York. In the fall of 1966 Mr. Wayman was a visitor at this university and made corrections in the first draft by comparison with the Tibetan text. In the fall of 1967 Mr. Wayman joined the staff of Columbia. Professor Wm. Theodore de Bary encouraged us to contribute the *Śrī-Mālā* to the Translations from the Oriental Classics series of Columbia University Press, providing an incentive to complete the translation and annotation of this classic.

It is a pleasure to acknowledge the timely aid of other scholars. For some of our commentarial materials we are grateful to Dr. Shinsho Hanayama for supplying his edition of Shōtoku Taishi's commentary, and to Mr. Ryūshin Uryūzu for his presentation of the booklet *Shōmangyō gisho ronshū*. Professors Wm. Theodore de Bary, Burton Watson, and various others of the East Asian Languages and Cultures Department, Columbia University, made useful suggestions. During May, 1970, Mr. N. Aramaki arranged for Mr. Wayman's fruitful meeting in Kyoto with Professor A. Fujieda. In Tokyo Mr. Wayman had an instructive conversation with Professor A. Hirakawa. Mr. M. Mitsumori of the Hōryūji, Japan, cooperated with the kind permission of the Reverends Kaen Ōno and Ryōshin Takada, also of the Hōryūji, to arrange for the color photograph of the portrait of Queen Śrīmālā, the only such painting in the world. Professor Bunkyō Sakurabe kindly assented to our incorporation into Appendix II of his list of Texts cited by Chi-tsang. This is the list to which Mr. Shinjō Kawasaki has added further identifications. Above all, Mr. Kawasaki has been very cooperative, making many technical suggestions, especially of a bibliographic nature, and providing other valuable information for our work during his studies, under Mr. Wayman's direction, toward the doctorate at Columbia University. Finally, Miss Elisabeth Shoemaker of Columbia University Press contributed many editorial improvements and we are also grateful for her patience.

Alex Wayman and Hideko Wayman

New York City
June 1, 1971

TRANSLATORS' NOTE

Considering the *Śrī-Mālā*'s length, the translators have certainly devoted much effort toward a correct rendition into English, with the indispensable aid of published works, editions, parallel research, and the advice of colleagues. They feel that the protracted collaboration has avoided many pitfalls and discouragements that would beset the solitary translator. Mr. Wayman has prepared the various introductory sections and notes and is responsible for the final form of the translation. Mrs. Wayman, the cotranslator, has added to the introductions and annotations, supplied important data from the Sino-Japanese commentaries, and supervised preparation of the Glossary, Appendix, and Index.

Mrs. Wayman is a graduate of Tsuda College of Tokyo in her native Japan and subsequently earned an M.A. at the University of California, Berkeley. While Mr. Wayman was writing his doctoral dissertation, Analysis of the Śrāvakabhūmi Manuscript, she studied the *Śrāvakabhūmi* in Hsüan-tsang's Chinese translation as well as in the Japanese rendition. This experience impressed the translators with the exacting standard of Chinese translations attained in the T'ang dynasty, contrasting, as Buddhist specialists well know, with the freer translations of pre-T'ang times. Toward the end of the 1950s both translators contributed to the late Professor F. D. Lessing's planned Buddhist dictionary several thousand items from the *Gaṇḍavyūha* and other works with information on Sanskrit, Tibetan, Chinese, Japanese (in romanization), and English. Gradually, they gained confidence in their philological comparison of passages in these Asian languages.

When comparing the versions of the *Śrī-Mālā*, Mr. Wayman used for the Sanskrit fragments the collection made by Hakuju Ui; for the Tibetan translation he used both the Peking text from a xerox copy of the Japanese photographic edition in the University of Wisconsin Memorial Library and the Narthang edition accessible at Columbia University. Mrs. Wayman used for the Chinese versions the Guṇabhadra and Bodhiruci texts in the Taishō Tripitaka; and for the Japanese renditions, the text in both the Kokuyaku Issaikyō and Daizōkyō.

The translators soon noticed the numerous differences, mostly minor and negligible, between the Tibetan version and the pre-T'ang Guṇabhadra Chinese translation. There were also many seeming differences between that Chinese version of the Liu Sung dynasty and the T'ang translation by Bodhiruci, suggesting disagreement on certain important issues. However, extended considerations of such apparent divergences, with the help of the Tibetan and the Sanskrit fragments, suggest that the main differences in the two Chinese versions lie in alternate ways of expressing the same thing. Many of these variations may be due simply to a difference in time and place of the respective translations. Another possibility is that Guṇabhadra's Sanskrit text had a few material differences from the Sanskrit texts employed for the Bodhiruci and Tibetan translations.

Unfortunately, the original Sanskrit is extant only in the form of quotations, although these are usually of important sentences and therefore valuable in every case. Naturally, since there is insufficient Sanskrit for this original text to be taken as the basic one for translation purposes, the problem arose of which, if any, of the complete Asian versions should be accepted as the basic one, with differences in the other texts considered as variant readings. The translators acknowledge that one version should be allowed such a privileged status, unless there are reasons, which we now state, to justify an alternate procedure. The importance of the *Śrī-Mālā* does not reach its high point by exclusive reason of any of those particular versions. This scripture was highly esteemed in India in the form of the original Sanskrit, where it helped inspire the *Laṅkāvatāra-sūtra.* The Guṇabhadra version, the most popular of the Chinese ones, took a translation form in a committee project. All the Sino-Japanese commentarial tradition is based on it, but in large proportion this rises from textual difficulties peculiar to the Guṇabhadra text, difficulties which disappear when the sentence is translated by comparison of the versions. The Bodhiruci and Tibetan versions were translated in times of more exact translation stipulations and both were made from original Sanskrit texts which had some definite differences, but those two versions lack commentarial expansion. The Japanese versions are the living tradition of the *Śrī-Mālā* but are clearly secondary to the Chinese translations. Thus, none of those Asian versions looms over the others as a candidate for modern translation.

The translators felt that the important thing is to faithfully render the scripture into English by taking advantage of all the available versions, since they are all indeed authentic. But how? Having learned that the Taishō punctuation of the Chinese scriptures when made in the absence of the original Sanskrit must be observed with caution, the translators used the Tibetan version, because it is so literal, to define the boundaries of sentences, that is, their beginning and end. Extra remarks outside that boundary, such as sometimes occur in the Guṇabhadra version—not just a matter of punctuation— are not ordinarily included in the translation. However, even here, it was sufficient for the Guṇabhadra and the Bodhiruci versions to agree against the Tibetan for the translators to accept a modification of the boundary. Then, within the boundaries of sentences, as so defined, each of the versions contributed some of its structure and sense. Frequently the Sino-Japanese renditions were more intelligible than the Tibetan.

The translators' principle has been to reconstruct and render the original meaning of the scripture, as they came to understand it from the consensus of the versions. In dubious cases they adopted those readings which best conformed with the context and the rest of the work. This procedure has exploited whatever clarity is found in the various versions. The final version also has modifications suggested by the annotations and introductory materials, which led to the decision on chapters. The final English text can be read with the Tibetan or with each of the two Chinese versions and will be found to fit them quite well, give or take a minor divergence here and there. Thus, every reading of the translation is found in either Tibetan, Sanskrit fragments, or the two Chinese versions. Nevertheless, the synthetic translation comes out definitely closer to the Bodhiruci version than to the Guṇabhadra version.

The Bodhiruci text, like the Tibetan one, is found in the Mahāyāna Buddhist collection called the Ratnakūṭa; and here the *Śrī-Mālā* is in one piece without subdivisions. The translators have adopted the imposition, found in the Guṇabhadra version, of fifteen sections on the work. They have also provided four chapter headings under which the fifteen sections appear, and have furnished subheadings to permit easier comprehension by Western readers. The translators have not listed the many variations between the Asian renditions, since most of them are inconsequential. To maintain consistency, all translations, not only of the *Śrī-Mālā* text but of any other work cited, are their own, except in a few cases as noted.

INTRODUCTION

I. *Śrī-Mālā* as a Text

Literary History

Historical Setting of the Text

As a Mahāyāna scripture the *Śrī-Mālā* can be placed approximately soon after the early texts called Prajñāpāramitā-sūtras, of which the most important, such as the *Aṣṭasāhasrikā*, were written in the period c. 100 B.C.–A.D. 200. These early Mahāyāna scriptures contain the two-body theory of the Buddha, namely the "formal body" (*rūpa-kāya*), with which the Buddha appeared on earth, and the "dharma body" (*dharma-kāya*), the ultimate Buddha nature. These two are alluded to in the first of the scripture's main sections, when the queen praises the Lord with the lines, "Your bodily form and knowledge are unimaginable. Your Buddha nature does not perish; so it is right to take refuge in you, the *muni*." Later Mahāyāna scriptures such as the *Avataṃsaka* (c. 200–400) and the *Laṅkāvatāra* (4th century A.D.) subdivided the "formal body" into the *Saṃbhoga-kāya* and the *Nirmāṇa-kāya*.[1] The *Śrī-Mālā* evinces no knowledge of the three-body theory of the Buddha, but of course could be contemporary with the scriptures developing this theory. The time of the *Laṇkāvatāra* provides the *terminus ad quem*, since the latter sūtra cites the *Śrī-Mālā*.

A clue for more definite placement is the *Śrī-Mālā*'s glorification of the Buddhist queen and the stress on the "good daughter of the family" side by side with the "good son of the family." This points to a period when the prosperity of the Buddhist congregation depended heavily on the patronage of one or more Buddhist queens and contributions by ladies of high social rank. Although the history of India for these times is quite sketchy, the only known area that could apply is South India, especially the Andhra country where there are the celebrated Buddhist remains, Amarāvatī and Nāgārjunikoṇḍa. As is well known to Indian historians, after the fall of the South Indian Sātavāhana empire around A.D. 220, it was partitioned into several kingdoms including the Īkshvākus in

1 Louis de La Vallée Poussin, *La Siddhi de Hiuan-tsang*, Vol. II, appendix, "Les corps du Bouddha."

Andhradeśa. Nilakanta Sastri writes:

> The Īkshvākus ruled over the Krishna-Guntur region . . . Though seven kings are said to have ruled for fifty-seven years in all, only a few are known by name from inscriptions. . . . Vāsiṭhīputa Siri Chāntamūla, the founder of the line, performed the *aśvamedha* and *vājapeya* sacrifices. The reign of his son Vīrapurisadāta formed a glorious epoch in the history of Buddhism and in diplomatic relations. He took a queen from the Śaka family of Ujjain and gave his daughter in marriage to a Chutu prince. Almost all the royal ladies were Buddhists: an aunt of Vīrapurisadāta built a big stupa at Nāgārjunikoṇḍa for the relics of the great teacher, besides apsidal temples, *vihāras*, and *maṇḍapas*. Her example was followed by other women of the royal family and by women generally as we know from a reference to one Bodhisiri, a woman citizen.[2]

Referring to improvements of the Amarāvatī stupa at the mouth of the Krishna River during the first and second centuries of our era, Rowland says, "There are indications that the Buddhist establishments were supported by the queens of the ruling house, while the kings were followers of Hinduism."[3] Taking these facts into consideration, one may postulate that the *Śrī-Mālā* was composed partly to honor the eminent Buddhist ladies who were so responsible for this glorious period of South Indian Buddhism. Therefore, we tentatively place the composition of the *Śrī-Mālā* within the Īkshvāku rule of the third century A.D. This thesis suggests that other Tathāgatagarbha scriptures may have been written about the same time in this Krishna-Guntur region.

Bareau cites evidence that the Andhra Buddhism in the third century A.D. was principally of the late Mahāsāṅghika subsects, the Pūrvaśaila and Uttaraśaila. An inscription dated the fourteenth year of Māṭherīputa, an Īkshvāku king, mentions them. Also inscriptions of the second and third centuries A.D. have been found at Amarāvatī and at Nāgārjunikoṇḍa indicating the presence of those two subsects besides the subsect called Caitīya from which they historically issued. Although when the Chinese pilgrim Hsüan-tsang visited the area in the seventh century, Buddhism had obviously waned there, he still found 1,000 Mahāsāṅghika monks spread among twenty monasteries near Dhaṇyakaṭaka, an old name of Amarāvatī.[4]

If we grant the placement of the *Śrī-Mālā* in third-century Andhra, this information about the prevalence of the Mahāsāṅghika sect in that region suggests that the *Śrī-Mālā* is a Mahāyāna outgrowth of the later Mahāsāṅghika.

2 Nilakanta Sastri, *A History of South India*, p. 96.

3 Benjamin Rowland, *The Art and Architecture of India*, pp. 123–24.

4 André Bareau, *Les sectes bouddhiques du Petit Véhicule*, p. 99.

Fortunately, there is extant the *Mahāvastu*, a text of the Mahāsāṅghika subsect called Lokottaravādin. Comparison of this work with the *Śrī-Mālā* led to the discovery that the *Mahāvastu* contains passages that clarify some difficult terminology of the *Śrī-Mālā*, such as the "body made of mind" and its "inconceivable transference," as well as the implication of Bodhisattva stages involved in *Śrī-Mālā*'s allusion to renunciation of body, life force, and possessions. The very beginning of the *Mahāvastu* provides a set of Bodhisattva career-phases that neatly fits the chapter division of the first part of the *Śrī-Mālā*, which also contains various special tenets of the Mahāsāṅghikas. We therefore conclude that the *Śrī-Mālā* is a production of the Mahāsāṅghika sect in third-century Andhra.

The anonymous author of this Mahāyāna scripture naturally took as its heroine a Buddhist queen supposedly contemporary with the Buddha (6th cent. B.C.). But is she a historical personage? Her father and mother, King Prasenajit of Kosala and Queen Mallikā certainly are well authenticated as contemporaries of the Buddha. The king's name is written Pasenadi in the Pāli language. According to the Pāli tradition, Mallikā was the beautiful daughter of the chief garland maker of Kosala. One day she met the Buddha and respectfully offered him portions of sour gruel. The Buddha smiled and explained, in answer to Ānanda's question, that she would become the chief queen of Kosala that day. It happened that Pasenadi was returning from a battle with Ajātasattu, which he had lost. When Pasenadi entered the flower garden, Mallikā comforted him. In the evening he sent a chariot for her and anointed her chief queen. Malalasekera also informs us: "Mallikā had a daughter by Pasenadi; no mention is made of a son. He is said to have been disappointed on hearing that the child was a girl; but the Buddha assured him that women were sometimes wiser than men." A note identifies the daughter as probably the Vajirī (or Vajirā) mentioned as the king's only daughter in *Majjhima Nikāya* ii, 110. Under Malalasekera's entry "Vajirakumārī," we learn, "When peace was established between Pasenadi and Ajātasattu, Pasenadi gave Vajirā in marriage to Ajātasattu, and gave, as part of her dowry, the village in Kāsi which had been the cause of their quarrel."[5] The implication is that the series of battles between Pasenadi and Ajātasattu began before the birth of Vajirā and continued until she was of marriageable age—which is historically feasible. There is also a Vajirā, member of a sisterhood, whose verses are much cited in later times;[6] but the commentators do not link her to Pasenadi's daughter.

5 G. P. Malalasekera, *Dictionary of Pāli Proper Names*, II, 455, 456, 808.

6 Caroline Rhys Davids, tr., *The Book of the Kindred Sayings*, Part I, pp. 167–68.

However, Ayodhyā (Pāli: Ayojjhā), which the *Śrī-Mālā* makes the capital of Queen Śrīmālā and King Yaśomitra, is not associated with King Ajātasattu, whose capital was Rājagaha in Magadha. Furthermore, neither *Sirimālā nor *Yasomitta, the Pāli equivalents for Śrīmālā and Yaśomitra, are known from Pāli sources. It appears that the Ayodhyā setting of King Yaśomitra and Queen Śrīmālā is a fiction of the scripture composer.

The name Śrīmālā (glorious garland) given to the heroine of this scripture is obviously related to that of her mother Mallikā. It might refer to the incident in the garden where King Prasenajit first met her mother Mallikā (Daughter of the garland maker). Chi-tsang's commentary (p. 6) and the Mochizuki Dictionary (p. 2775-a) mention various theories, especially these two: At the time of her birth, people were overjoyed and offered garlands made of fine jewelry. The king, in admiration of her intelligence and virtue, called her "Śrīmālā" with the implication that other people only put on garlands while his daughter really was one, and therefore the best of garlands. This second theory is consistent with the scripture itself, which insists that the embracer of the Illustrious Doctrine is himself the embrace of the Illustrious Doctrine.

In conclusion, the scriptural account in its opening setting is half historical and half fictional.

The Title of the Scripture

These are the ways the sūtra is cited or referred to in Sanskrit works in their presumed chronological order:

1. In the *Laṅkāvatāra-sūtra: Śrīmālāṃ devīm adhikṛtya* (in connection with Queen Śrīmālā).
2. In the *Mahāyāna-Sūtrālaṃkāra: Śrīmālā-sūtra* (the Sūtra Śrīmālā).
3. In the *Ratnagotravibhāga: Āryaśrīmālā-sūtra* (the sūtra the noble Śrīmālā).
4. In Śāntideva's *Śikṣāsamuccaya: Śrīmālāsiṃhanāda-sūtra* (the sūtra lion's roar of Śrīmālā).

We notice some tendency to lengthen the title.

The Sanskrit title as preserved in transcription in the Tibetan canon appears to reflect the editing in India of the Ratnakūṭa collection at the time it was translated into Tibetan: *Ārya-Śrīmālādevīsiṃhanāda-nāmamahāyānasūtra* (The noble mahāyāna-sūtra called "Lion's roar of the Queen Śrīmālā"), in Tibetan, *Ḥphags pa lha mo dpal phreṅ gi seṅ geḥi sgra źes bya ba theg pa chen poḥi mdo.*

The Guṇabhadra translation into Chinese (Taishō V. 12–217, No. 353) has the lengthy title *Shêng-man-shih-tzŭ-hou i-ch'êng ta-fang-pien fang-kuang ching* (Śrīmālā's lion's roar – one vehicle – great correct means – correct far-ranging sūtra). According to Shōtoku Taishi's commentary (Introduction), the last two of the sixteen titles given in the final section of the sūtra were utilized in constructing this title. These two are as follows: "Kauśika, also retain it as 'Lion's roar of Queen Śrīmālā.' Also retain all explanations contained in this scripture as 'Eliminating all doubts, deciding the final meaning, and entering the One Vehicle path.'" Accordingly, we should understand in the Chinese title "One Vehicle – Great Means" to mean "Great Correct Means of the One Vehicle." The phrases "eliminating all doubts" and "deciding the final meaning" may have been reduced to the title segment "far-ranging Sūtra."

The Bodhiruci translation (Taishō V. 11-672, Nos. 310-48) in the Ratnakūṭa has for title simply *Shêng-man fu-jên hui* (Queen Śrīmālā's assembly). The term "assembly" is employed here in place of the word "sūtra" because each of the scriptures in the Chinese Ratnakūṭa is called an "assembly" and the *Śrī-Mālā* is the forty-eighth.

Furthermore, in Chinese commentarial literature Guṇabhadra's title is variously reduced in six different ways, the shortest being *Shêng-man ching* (= *Śrī-Mālā-sūtra*).[7]

Guṇabhadra's Chinese translation has been further translated into Japanese both by Kōyō Sakaino in the canon *Kokuyaku Daizōkyō* and by Seijun Hasuzawa in the canon *Kokuyaku Issaikyō*. In both cases the Chinese title is kept: *Shōman shishiku ichijō daihōben hōkō kyō*. Of course, reduced forms of this title are cited, the shortest being *Shōmangyō* (= *Śrī-Mālā-sūtra*).

It seems that as an early Mahāyāna sūtra of a particular sect, in the light of our third century A.D. placement, it was sufficient in the beginning to refer to this work as "The sūtra of Śrīmālā." But then the work passed out of the exclusive hands of the sect that had originated it and became revered by Mahāyānists generally. As it became more widely quoted and as it became part of this or that collection of scriptures, the title became lengthened.

The Text in Asian Countries

Importance in India. We have decided that the *Śrī-Mālā* was composed as a Mahāsāṅghika text in the third century A.D. in the Andhra region of South India. The trenchant brevity of the *Śrī-Mālā*, and its evident popularity, may have made it a key scripture in the wider canon of the Mahāsāṅghika sect.[8]

7 According to Ono, *Bussho kaisetsu daijiten*, p. 362-a, the six reference forms are: 1) Shêng-man ching, 2) Shih-tzŭ-hou ching, 3) Shêng-man shih-tzŭ-hou ching, 4) Shih-tzŭ-hou fang-kuang ching, 5) Shêng-man ta-fang-pien fang-kuang ching, 6) Shêng-man shih-tzŭ-hou-i ch'êng ta-fang-pien ching.

8 The Mahāsāṅghikas as a Hīnayāna sect had their *āgamas* (roughly equivalent to the Pāli *nikāyas*) called *Dīrgha*, *Madhyama*, *Saṃyukta*, *Ekottara*, and *Kṣudrapiṭaka*. Perhaps

The original Sanskrit has not survived except in quoted passages, mostly in the *Ratnagotravibhāga*, with a few sentences in Śāntideva's *Śikṣāsamuccaya*.[9] All of the *Ratnagotravibhāga*'s quotations from the *Śrī-Mālā* are extracted from what we have designated as Chapter Three. Since the *Śrī-Mālā* has a privileged position in the *Ratnagotravibhāga* as the most cited scripture, it appears that this chapter of the work constituted the fundamental required reading for students of the Tathāgatagarbha scriptures. The *Śikṣāsamuccaya* quotes only from Chapter Two of the *Śrī-Mālā*, whose eloquent statements on "Embrace of the Illustrious Doctrine" must have been appreciated by Mahāyānists who were not enamored of the "embryo of the Tathāgata" theory. This Tathāgatagarbha theory resembles the Hindu "ātman" doctrine despite the protestations to the contrary in the Tathāgatagarbha literature; and the *Śikṣāsamuccaya*, having quoted the *Śrī-Mālā*, is significantly silent about the "embryo of the Tathāgata."

Moreover, the *Laṅkāvatāra-sūtra* and the *Mahāyāna-Sūtrālaṃkāra-bhāṣya*—both celebrated texts of Indian Buddhism—refer explicitly to the *Śrī-Mālā*. The *Laṅkāvatāra* points either to Southern India or Ceylon for provenance, while the *Sūtrālaṃkāra-bhāṣya* is associated with the North Indian Asaṅga tradition; and so the *Śrī-Mālā* must have been appreciated by Buddhists in both the north and the south during the fourth century and its turn to the fifth. This is also borne out by the inclusion of *Śrī-Mālā* in the Ratnakūṭa collection.

The *Laṅkāvatāra* had been profoundly influenced by the *Śrī-Mālā*, partly for its "embryo of the Tathāgata" which the *Laṅkāvatāra* equates with the "store consciousness" (*ālaya-vijñāna*), and partly for its "three bodies made of mind" which the *Laṅkāvatāra* develops at length and in a manner inconsistent with the *Ratnagotravibhāga*. This indicates that the *Laṅkāvatāra* was composed outside of

---

this canon in Buddhist Sanskrit was the same as the one that was sacred to the Mahīśāsakas and was generously drawn upon by Asaṅga for materials in his *Yogācārabhūmi*. The *Mahāsāṅghika-vinaya* is preserved in Chinese (Taishō 22, No. 1425). W. Pachow and Ramakanta Mishra have published *The Prātimokṣa-sūtra of the Mahāsāṅghikas*. In the classification of five Buddhist sects by Lin Li-kouang, *L'Aide-Mémoire de la Vraie Loi*, p. 190, the Mahāsāṅghikas are said to have as their biography of the Buddha the *Mahāvastu*, which is extant in Buddhist Sanskrit. As reported by Bareau (*Les sectes*, p. 296), their Mahāyāna canon according to Paramārtha (mid sixth cent.) incorporated the *Prajñāpāramitā*, the *Avataṃsaka*, the *Mahāparinirvāṇa*, the *Śrī-Mālā*, the *Vimalakīrti*, and the *Suvarṇaprabhāsa*; and according to Hsüan-tsang included a *Dhāraṇī-piṭaka*. Besides, the *Śrī-Mālā* is naturally affiliated with the group called the *Tathāgatagarbha* sūtras, containing some other scriptures. That Mahāyāna canon would be mostly in existence by the time of *Śrī-Mālā* (3d cent. A.D.) or in the process of composition, and finished by the following century.

9 These quotations have been collected, arranged in the order of their appearance in the *Śrī-Mālā*, and published by H. Ui, *Hōshōron kenkyū*.

the Mahāsāṅghika circle which had given rise to the *Śrī-Mālā*, and was freely syncretizing the *Śrī-Mālā* with doctrines of other Buddhist sects. The fact that the *Ratnagotravibhāga* does not cite the *Laṅkāvatāra*, which may have already been written, is possibly due to a disagreement over interpreting the *Śrī-Mālā*.

The *Sūtrālaṃkāra-bhāṣya*, a fundamental work for the Asaṅga–Vasubandhu tradition, may have referred to the *Śrī-Mālā* only for "completeness' sake" in a survey of Mahāyāna doctrine. On the other hand, Paramārtha, who in the sixth century brought to China the story of Vasubandhu's life, includes an intriguing account of how Vasubandhu wrote various Mahāyāna commentaries, namely, on the *Śrī-Mālā*, the *Saddharmapuṇḍarīka*, and the *Vimalakīrti* (which constitute a triad very important in Japanese Buddhism) as well as on the *Avataṃsaka* and the *Nirvāṇa* (=*Mahāparinirvāṇa-sūtra*) (which join the *Śrī-Mālā* in importance about the Tathāgatagarbha theory), and on the *Prajñāpāramitā*.[10] But it seems that this story really applies to comments in the *Buddhagotraśāstra* attributed to Vasubandhu in Paramārtha's translation of it into Chinese; in any case, it shows that at that time the *Śrī-Mālā* was mentioned side by side with the most famous Mahāyāna scriptures.

The Prāsaṅgika school of Mādhyamika, represented principally by Candrakīrti, seems to ignore the *Śrī-Mālā*; and Śāntideva, who by Tibetan tradition is in this Mādhyamika lineage, quotes the *Śrī-Mālā* only for "Embrace of the Illustrious Doctrine," as is noted above. In the Svātantrika school of Mādhyamika, the *Śrī-Mālā* is quoted in Bhāvaviveka's *Prajñāpradīpa-mūlamadhyamakavṛtti*,[11] presumably composed in Mahāsāṅghika territory of Andhra.[12] Toward the end of the Indian Buddhist period, Abhayākaragupta, with general Mahāyāna syncretism under the banner of the Mādhyamika, cites the *Śrī-Mālā* in his *Munimatālaṃkāra*, as will be shown subsequently.

So far we have referred to other works to suggest *Śrī-Mālā*'s popularity. Let us turn to the text itself. There appear to be several reasons for the success of this scripture.

As a spiritual document—of which it is a shining example—it had to rise above its Mahāsāṅghika origins to embrace and exemplify the Buddhist religion. It does this by a consummate skill in touching upon the basic features of Buddhism, such as faith, the path, the goal; and in rendering decisions on some of the knotty and disputed points in Buddhist history, such as the status of the

10 J. Takakusu, "The Life of Vasubandhu by Paramārtha (A.D. 499–569)," 292.

11 As reported by Ryūshin Uryūzu, "The Tibetan Translation of the *Śrīmālā-Sūtra* and the Thought of *Śūnyatā*" (in Japanese), in *Shōmangyō gisho ronshū*, 203.

12 Thomas Watters, *On Yuan Chwang's Travels in India*, II, 220–23.

Arhat, the meaning of the Dependent Origination formula, and the threshold of Enlightenment. It has a masterful way of expressing clearly matters that ought to be clear, such as "Embrace of the Illustrious Doctrine"; and of alluding to profound matters, such as "Embryo of the Tathāgata," with suggestive and subtle language.

It is a forceful document on the lay Buddhist path; to be more precise, it portrays the bodhisattva path in a way that applies equally to layman or monk. Thus, in its interpretation of the six Perfections, it announces that a person who can speak for a long time without straying from the topic has "one-pointedness of mind" and it avoids mentioning that this is what others strive for with folded legs in monastic silence. It diplomatically does not assert the superiority of the lay bodhisattva over other bodhisattvas as does the *Vimalakīrti* when it makes its hero, the Bodhisattva Vimalakīrti, superior to Mañjuśrī. The lay bodhisattva is referred to as "good son of the family" and "good daughter of the family." It seems that these lay bodhisattvas had evolved an organization, called in certain Mahāyāna texts a *bodhisattvagaṇa*, that was separate from the monk *sangha*.[13] The *Śrī-Mālā* alludes to this organization in a revealing passage:

> Lord, at the time of decline of the Doctrine, when monks, nuns, and male and female laymen quarrel with each other to break up into many sects, whatever good son of the family or good daughter of the family delighting in the Doctrine which is without deceit or falsehood, for the sake of maintaining the Illustrious Doctrine, creates a bodhisattva group of those who have the Doctrine, would certainly be the good son of the family or good daughter of the family to obtain a prophecy from all the Buddhas because of that activity.

This separate organization may well go back historically to the original split in Buddhism about a century after the Buddha, between the orthodox establishment and the breakaway group called the Mahāsāṅghikas. The Mahāsāṅghikas appear in time to have come into league with the lay organizations which maintained and appropriately worshiped the Buddhist stūpa, and to have composed theological justifications, such as the supramundane nature of the Buddha. But they were a long time in securing literary works to rationalize their position as well as do the flood of works written in the monasteries to justify the life of contemplative retreat. When in the third century A.D. the *Śrī-Mālā* appeared to express the Mahāsāṅghika experience of centuries with religious sensitivity and maturity, it was naturally revered as a religious classic.

13 Akira Hirakawa, "The Rise of Mahāyāna Buddhism and Its Relationship to the Worship of Stūpas," 80–81.

Importance in China. The first translation into Chinese of the *Śrī-Mālā* was made by Dharmakṣema, a native of Central India. He began his translation activity in China in A.D. 414, working on the *Nirvāṇa Sūtra* at the school of Ku-tsang of the Northern Liang. His translation in A.D. 418 of Asaṅga's *Bodhisattva-bhūmi* is of capital importance for determining the dates of Asaṅga and his brother Vasubandhu, who apparently were Dharmakṣema's contemporaries. He was assassinated in 433. Dharmakṣema's translation of the *Śrī-Mālā* was no longer extant by the time of the Yüan dynasty.[14]

The second and most important Chinese translation was made by Guṇabhadra (d. A.D. 468), also a native of Central India. He became a specialist in the *Avataṃsaka-sūtra.* He lived in China during the Liu Sung dynasty, working at the school of Nanking from 435 until his death at the age of seventy-five. He was in charge of the translation of the *Śrī-Mālā* accomplished during his first year in China, in fact between August 14 and the end of the month, in 436.[15] Among his many other translations, of interest to our research are the *Laṅkāvasūtra*, the *Aṅgulimālīya-sūtra*, and the *Mahābherīhāraka-sūtra*, all important for the Tathāgatagarbha theory. Of course, an Indian could not be expected to learn Chinese well enough in one year to translate the *Śrī-Mālā.* The Japanese translation in the *Kokuyaku Issaikyō* (p. 83c-84a) records that Guṇabhadra recited the Sanskrit text;[16] Pao-yün (d. 449), a Chinese Sanskrit scholar who had studied in India, orally translated it into Chinese; and Hui-kuan (d. 443), an eminent scholar-disciple of Kumārajīva, wrote it down; and it seems that over one hundred monks read it through and made suggestions for the meanings and tones.

The third translation was made by Bodhiruci (672–727), a native of South India, who arrived in China in 693, during the T'ang dynasty, bringing with him the Sanskrit text of the Ratnakūṭa collection of individual Mahāyāna sūtras, which includes the *Śrī-Mālā* near the end. He translated the Ratnakūṭa between 706 and 713. He also translated the *Sukhāvatī-vyūha* and a number of works on Tantric ritual.[17]

Many Chinese commentaries were written on the *Śrī-Mālā*, possibly starting at Dharmakṣema's translation.[18] However, all the extant and definitely established commentaries were written on the basis of Guṇabhadra's translation,

14 Prabodh Chandra Bagchi, *Le Canon bouddhique en chine*, I, 212 ff.

15 *Ibid.*, pp. 378 ff.; Ui, *Hōshōron kenkyū*, p. 446.

16 Guṇabhadra's text might have differed from the Ratṇakūṭa version. This would account for his substitution at one point of the second group of persons, as is mentioned in note 86 to the translation.

17 Prabodh Chandra Bagchi, *Le canon bouddhique en Chine*, II, 540 ff.

18 Akira Fujieda, in "Hokuchō ni okeru 'Shōmangyō' no denshō," holds that the

and over twenty such books can be traced either in the Chinese commentaries or in the biographies of the eminent monks. Three contemporaries of Guṇabhadra are known to have written such commentaries. One of these, Fa-yao (died between 436 and 453), also commented on the *Mahāparinirvāṇa-sūtra*, the *Saddharmapuṇḍarīka-sūtra*, and the *Pañcaviṃśatisāhasrikā prajñāpāramitā*.[19] The fifth commentary on the Guṇabhadra version and now the earliest extant portion of any such commentary is a Tun-huang manuscript, namely the *Shêng-man i-chi*, Vol. 1, dated February 14, 504, of Northern Wei, which contains the fifteen-chapter division.[20] The fact that there are no commentaries on Bodhiruci's early eighth-century translation suggests that *Śrī-Mālā*'s popularity had declined prior to this time.

Of the various commentaries, three survived and influenced the literary tradition through the authority of their illustrious composers:

Shêng-man ching i-chi, 1 vol., by Hui-yüan (523–92), a T'ien-t'ai master who wrote more than fifty commentaries and books.

Shêng-man ching pao-k'u, 3 vols. and 6 vols., by Chi-tsang (549–623), who systematized and completed the San-lun school.

Shêng-man ching shu-chi, 2 vols., by K'uei-chi (632–82), the famous disciple of Hsüan-tsang.[21]

Of those three commentators, Chi-tsang (posthumous name: Chia-hsiang ta-shi) wrote the most outstanding encyclopedic commentary, which has influenced the study of the *Śrī-Mālā* in Japan even up to present times. Bunkyō Sakurabe translated Chi-tsang's work into Japanese in 1936 (the *Shōman hō-*

fragment, Stein No. 1649, Taishō Vol. 85–2763, is the earliest of seven Tun-huang *Śrī-Mālā* commentaries. It is presumably written in the latter part of the fifth century, has no indication of chapters, and is possibly a commentary on the Ḍharmakṣema translation. Fujieda bases his dating on the writing style and paper, for which see his article "The Tunhuang Manuscripts; a General Description," Part II, pp. 17–39.

19 Ui, *Hōshoron kenkyū*, p. 447.

20 Ui, *Saiiki butten no kenkyū*, pp. 275–302. It is Stein No. 2660, numbered 5623 in Giles, *Descriptive Catalogue of the Chinese Manuscripts from Tunhuang in the British Museum*.

21 Ono, *Bussho kaisetsu daijiten*, pp. 359–60. Regarding the Hui-yüan commentary, this is represented in the Pelliot collection of Tun-huang manuscripts; Mr. Shinjō Kawasaki has consulted Wang Chung-min's *Tun-huang i-shu tsung-mu so-yin* (General indexes to the Tun-huang manuscripts) and has found on p. 255 the author's statement that he personally perused this manuscript and found it to be the one by Hui-yüan (the T'ien-t'ai master). Fujieda, "Hokuchō ni okeru 'Shōmangyō' no denshō," counts this, Pelliot ch. 2901 and ch. 3308, as commentary No. 7, and mentions that this represents the latter part of the commentary which, combined with the incomplete portion previously printed in the Svastik edition of the Chinese canon, yields 80 percent of the original Hui-yüan commentary.

kutsu),[22] and this Japanese version is the one to which we refer as "Chi-tsang's commentary" or "Chi-tsang."

What is the explanation for *Śrī-Mālā*'s importance in Chinese Buddhism of that time? Three reasons occur to us: previous popularity in India, influence on other texts, and compatibility with Chinese thought.

By previous popularity we mean that when a Buddhist work was already celebrated in India, as our preceding discussion indicates was true of *Śrī-Mālā*, this encouraged its ready acceptance by the Chinese Buddhist community; and *Śrī-Mālā* was especially acceptable since the time of its introduction was the peak of Chinese Buddhism.

Textual influence on the *Laṅkāvatāra-sūtra* is obvious, and so when that sūtra became popular in China, particularly in circles of Ch'an Buddhism, this interest surely spread to the *Śrī-Mālā* which is accorded a prestigious mention in the *Laṅkāvatāra*.[23] Of greater importance is the presumed influence of *Śrī-Mālā* in the composition of *The Awakening of Faith*, a work of enormous popularity in China, starting, it is claimed, with its translation into Chinese in A.D. 550 by Paramārtha.[24] A thoroughgoing comparison between the *Śrī-Mālā* and *The Awakening of Faith* would not be relevant here, but one can easily find important passages in common by noting that the "Suchness" in *The Awakening of Faith* is equivalent to *Śrī-Mālā*'s "Tathāgatagarbha." We can assume that in China the two works were studied together in many quarters.

22 This is published in *Kokuyaku Issaikyō*, Wakan senjutsu, Kyōshobu, 11, 296 pages.

23 According to Philip B. Yampolsky, *The Platform Sutra of the Sixth Patriarch*, pp. 20–21, there was a tradition, apparently erroneous, that Guṇabhadra (the translator of both the *Śrī-Mālā* and the *Laṅkāvatāra*) was the teacher of Bodhidharma, the Ch'an Patriarch who founded the Laṅkāvatāra school in China.

24 Yoshito S. Hakeda, *The Awakening of Faith, Attributed to Aśvaghosha*, mentions, p. 113, n. 9, "The statement that the *Tathāgata-garbha* is of *śūnya* and *a-śūnya* is found in the *Śrīmālā Sūtra*, a fact which suggests that this text [i.e., *The Awakening of Faith*] developed the thought earlier expressed in that sūtra. T12. p. 221c." He also says, no. 12, "An almost identical expression can be found in the *Śrīmālā Sūtra*...: 'Oh, Lord, saṃsāra (birth and death) is grounded on the *Tathāgata-garbha*....' T12, p. 222b." Still other passages in *The Awakening of Faith* indicate the influence of *Śrī-Mālā*, especially the one on p. 57 of Hakeda's interpretation about the two kinds of permeation of the deluded mind, namely, the basic permeation which causes Arhats, Pratyekabuddhas, and Bodhisattvas to undergo the suffering of saṃsāra, and the other permeation which makes ordinary men suffer from their karma. Here the distinction is obviously that which the *Śrī-Mālā* makes between the inconceivable transference in saṃsāra of Arhats, Pratyekabuddhas, and Bodhisattvas who have attained power, as compared with the discontinuous transference in saṃsāra of ordinary persons. One may also notice on p. 65 in Hakeda the set "eternity, bliss, Self, and purity" which *Śrī-Mālā* shares with the *Mahāparinirvāṇa-sūtra* (cf. Takasaki, tr., *Ratnagotravibhāga*, pp. 298–99).

The last reason, congeniality to the Chinese way of thinking, is somewhat conjectural. A positive feature of compatibility is implied in an article by Thomé H. Fang,[25] containing remarks about the melting of the dharmas together in the Dharmadhātu. One can compare this with the doctrine of the *Śrī-Mālā* that when the Tathāgatagarbha is free from defilements it is accompanied by innumerable Buddha dharmas that are nondiscrete. The *Śrī-Mālā* is easily accommodated to the Chinese world view that the non-discrete absolute gives rise to the discrete phenomenal world. Besides, in a negative way, the *Śrī-Mālā* is singularly free from a feature dear to the Indian Buddhist mind and usually unappealing to the Chinese, of including long lists of Bodhisattva names or of presenting lists of technical terms with subvarieties of each. It should also be mentioned that every educated Chinese reader would probably notice in *Śrī-Mālā* a sentence reminding him of a Confucian saying, in Waley's words, "The Master said, To go too far is as bad as not to go far enough."[26] The *Śrī-Mālā* passage is of course: "their view goes too far from the meaning, or their view falls short of the meaning."

What are some evidences of *Śrī-Mālā*'s popularity in China? We have already observed that some of the commentaries on it were made by scholars of the highest eminence independently famous for their other works. Moreover, it is recorded that a most eminent monk of the (Liu-) Sung (420–78) named T'an-pin together with his disciple Sêng-tsung gave lectures on *Śrī-Mālā* about one hundred times, each time with an audience of more than 1,000.[27] The celebrated Emperor Wu-ti of the South Liang dynasty (502–57) seems to have devoted most of his commentarial labors, unfortunately lost, to the Prajñāpāramitā scriptures. However, he did not neglect the *Śrī-Mālā*, and even wrote a commentary on it.[28]

There are also good reasons for the fading of *Śrī-Mālā*'s influence. Probably it became overshadowed by *The Awakening of Faith*. The rival doctrines of Yogācāra were strongly upheld in Hsüan-tsang's school of the early T'ang dynasty. Perhaps of most importance, in the early eighth century the Chinese

25 "The World and the Individual in Chinese Metaphysics," *Philosophy East and West*, XIV. No. 2 (July, 1964).

26 This reference to the Confucian *Analects* was called to our attention by Professor Burton Watson of Columbia University. The saying is in Book XI, chap. XV, *The Analects of Confucius*, tr. by Arthur Waley (Vintage, ed., p. 156).

27 Hasuzawa, *Shōman shishiku*, p. 84-c.

28 Mikisaburō Mori, *Ryō no Butei: Bukkyō ōchō no higeki* [Wu-ti of the Liang; the tragedy of a Buddhist court]. We are grateful to Professor Mason Gentzler, formerly of Columbia University, for calling our attention to this book and loaning it. Also cf. Hasuzawa, *Shōman shishiku*, p. 84-c.

Ch'an sect turned for inspiration from the *Laṅkāvatāra-sūtra*, which is an ally of the *Śrī-Mālā*, to the *Prajñāpāramitā* scriptures.[29]

Importance in Japan. It is traditional that Jōgū or Prince Regent Shōtoku Taishi (574–622) wrote three commentaries known as "Commentaries on the Three Sūtras" (*sangyō gisho*). These are the *Shōmangyō gisho*, commentary on the *Śrī-Mālā*; *Yuimagyō gisho*, on the *Vimalakīrtinirdeśa*; and *Hoke gisho*, on the *Saddharmapuṇḍarīka*.[30] Some recent Japanese scholarship has challenged this tradition of authorship.[31] What do those scriptures have in common? Primarily, they are all scriptures of the Great Vehicle (Mahāyāna), whose saint is the bodhisattva. The *Śrī-Mālā* and the *Vimalakīrti* glorify the lay bodhisattva, in contrast to the monk bodhisattva; and the *Śrī-Mālā* and the *Saddharmapuṇḍarīka* (Lotus Sūtra) espouse the "One Vehicle," wherein Mahāyāna embraces all the vehicles. Aside from those obviously common features, the three works are markedly different in specific subject matter and in mode of presentation. Understandably, in Prince Shōtoku's time all three scriptures enjoyed great popularity in China, and this is sufficient reason for their being selected to play a paramount role in Japanese Buddhism. Since Buddhism was transmitted to Japan from Korea, it is interesting to note that three commentaries were written on the *Śrī-Mālā* alone by eminent Korean monks, Wŏnhyo (2 vols.), Tollyun (1 vol.), and Chŏng'u (1 vol.), all of the Silla dynasty (57 B.C.–A.D. 935).[32]

29 For this transition, cf. Chang Chung-yuan, *Original Teachings of Ch'an Buddhism*, pp. 3 ff.

30 Shinsho Hanayama, *A History of Japanese Buddhism*, pp. 11–12.

31 Nishi Giyū, "Yuimagyō gisho senjutsu no ito," in *Shōtoku Taishi Kenkyū* (1964), p. 143. However, Japanese scholarship on this matter has more recently been given a sensational turn by material exposed in Fujieda's article, "Hokuchō ni okeru 'Shōmangyō' no denshō" (1969). Fujieda's commentary No. 5 on the *Śrī-Mālā* is a Tunhuang manuscript of North China origin (Hokuchō) entitled *Shêng-man i-su pen-i*, a copy of which is in the Tōyō Bunko in Tokyo. Fujieda places it in the period 570–90. Fujieda and other Japanese scholars agree that Shōtoku's commentary on *Śrī-Mālā*, while very similar to this Tun-huang commentary, has subtle differences. In May, 1970, at Kyoto, Professor Fujieda told Mr. Wayman that he believes there is an intervening commentary between that work and Shōtoku's commentary. Then, at Tokyo, Professor Akira Hirakawa told Mr. Wayman that he believes the Chinese work was brought to Japan by an emissary and that the differences between the two commentaries stem from Shōtoku's occasional use of the Chinese characters in Japanese ways rather than in the strictly Chinese manner of understanding those characters. Fujieda (Hokuchō, p. 342) reports that Enjun Koizumi is carrying out a thorough comparison of the two commentaries.

32 Hasuzawa, *Shōman shishiku*, p. 84-c. Professor Gari Ledyard, Columbia University, has kindly furnished the Korean names for the characters. It is of interest that, according to Ui's *Bukkyō jiten*, Wŏnhyo (b. 617) studied under both Hsüan-tsang and K'uei-chi, and also wrote commentaries on the *Avataṃsaka*, *Laṅkāvatāra*, and *The Awakening of Faith*.

The Korean monk Hyeja (Japanese: Eji, d. 622) came to Japan in 595, the third year of Empress Suiko (593–628), and became the teacher of the Prince Regent Shōtoku.[33] In 615 he returned to Koguryŏ (37 B.C.–A.D. 668), bringing back to Korea Prince Shōtoku's commentary (possibly commentaries).[34]

Shōtoku Taishi is the name given to the prince upon his death; in life he was Umayado no ōji, the second son of Emperor Yōmei, and became prince regent in 592. Shōtoku was a contemporary of Chi-tsang, who outlived the prince by two years. The *Nihon shoki* records that Prince Shōtoku gave in the presence of the Empress Suiko the first lecture on the *Śrī-Mālā* in July, 606.[35] However, the date is not certain, because the *Jōgū shōtoku hō-ō tei setsu* records that it was in 598,[36] about three years after Shōtoku began studying under the Korean monk. The earlier date seems more in accordance with the Japanese tradition that Prince Shōtoku proclaimed Buddhism as the religion of the state in his "Seventeen-Article Constitution" of April 3, 604, because it is reasonable that he would try to impress the empress with the message of Queen Śrīmālā in order to lead up to and gain sanction for such a proclamation.

Among some other commentaries on the *Śrī-Mālā* written up to the end of the eighteenth century and preserved at the Hōryūji and other temples,[37] a commentary by a T'ang Chinese T'ien-t'ai monk named Ming-k'ung should be mentioned because his *Shêng-man ching i-su ssu-ch'ao*, 6 vols. (preserved under the Japanese title *Shōmangyō gisho shishō*), is a commentary on the one by Prince Shōtoku which was taken to China by eight Japanese monk-envoys, Kaimyō and others, in 772.[38] Ming-k'ung's commentary was brought back to Japan by Jikaku daishi (posthumous name, conferred by Emperor Junna), better known as Ennin (792–862), the third chief priest of the Enryakuji, who went to China in 838 and returned in 847.

Contemporary Japanese scholars have written many articles and books on the

33 This is the third year of Suiko: See Isamu Kanaji, *Shōtoku Taishi kyōgaku no kenkyū*, p. 9.

34 The data on the Korean monk Hyeja are furnished by Professor Ledyard from the *Honchō kōsō den*. The year of Hyeja's return coincides with the traditional year for the completion of Shōtoku Taishi's three commentaries, as stated in Saeki's *Shōmangyō kōsan*, pp. 13–14:

Age of Shōtoku	gisho	Inclusive dates of composition
38–40	Shōmangyō	April 8, 609–Jan. 25, 611
41–42	Yuimagyō	Jan. 15, 612–Sept. 15, 613
43–44	Hoke(kyō)	Jan. 8, 614–April 25, 615

35 Saeki, *Shōmangyō kōsan*, p. 13.

36 Ono, *Bussho kaisetsu daijiten*, p. 359d.

37 Saeki, *Shōmangyō kōsan*, pp. 9–10.

38 Hasuzawa, *Shōman shishiku*, p. 80-a.

Śrī-Mālā.[39] A number of these works are fine contributions to the understanding of this scripture.

What did the *Śrī-Mālā* mean to the Japanese after the period of its initial prestige conferred by sponsorship at the highest social level? Apparently on the basis of *Śrī-Mālā*'s passage, "The ultimate realization of the Dharmakāya is the One Vehicle," Hanayama writes, "What Prince Shōtoku worshiped was this Dharmakāya. And the Buddhism he put his faith in was the *Ekayana Buddhism*, i.e., the *One-Vehicle Buddhism*. In the practice of this Ekayana no distinction was made between layman and priest. He saw no need of our abandoning wife and children; no need to shut our own self deep in woods and sink in meditation."[40] This emphasis by the prince may very well have been influential in later Japanese Buddhism, especially in the teachings of Shinran Shōnin. Nevertheless, Queen Śrīmālā certainly does make distinctions between persons, as will be shown later in our Introduction.

In the light of later Japanese Buddhism, we can assume that the *Śrī-Mālā*'s clarification of Buddhist faith became of salient importance in Japan. Especially we should take note of the third kind of good son or daughter of the family mentioned in Chapter Four of the scripture, "who shrinks from gaining the knowledge of the profound Doctrine by himself, thinking, 'I cannot possibly know it; this meaning can only be understood by the Tathāgata himself,' and so keeping the Lord in mind, obtains the mental presence of the Lord." Here, "gaining by himself" is represented by characters pronounced *jijōju* (accomplished by himself) in Japanese. Hanayama's *Shōtoku Taishi* (p. 142) comments with the expressions *jibungyō* (practice by himself) and *tabungyō* (practice by another). Saeki[41] comments on the same passage with the expressions *jiriki* (self-power) and *tariki* (other-power). Thus, the *Śrī-Mālā* has a doctrine of faith easily assimilated to the all-important terminology of the Pure Land School, *jiriki* and *tariki*, but did not actually employ these terms.[42]

39 A noteworthy commentary is the one by Jōin Saeki, a former abbot of the Hōryūji, already referred to by its title of *Shōmangyō kōsan*. This makes many references to the writings of Chi-tsang and Prince Shōtoku. Hakuju Ui treats the *Śrī-Mālā* in his *Hōshōron kenkyū*, pp. 435–566. Shinshō Hanayama has written many studies on the *Śrī-Mālā* commentary (the *Shōtoku Taishi gyosei Shōmangyō gisho*). Senior scholars and promising younger ones contributed essays on *Śrī-Mālā* to form a book *Shōmangyō gisho ronshū* (Articles on the *Shōmangyō gyosei gisho*). Jōjun Hasuzawa's introduction to his *Śrī-Mālā* version in the *Kokuyaku Issaikyō* has been useful.

40 Hanayama, *A History of Japanese Buddhism*, p. 13.

41 Saeki, *Shōmangyō kōsan*, p. 311.

42 The Chinese characters for *jiriki* and *tariki* are in the early translation by Dharmakṣema of the *Bodhisattvabhūmi*. There they are in a context of four kinds of power for generating the Mind of Enlightenment; cf. in translation, Alex Wayman, "The

Importance in Tibet. The *Śrī-Mālā* was translated into Tibetan by the Indian pandits Jinamitra and Surendrabodhi working with the prolific Tibetan translator Ye śes sde. The translation can be assigned to the early ninth century (by 815, and possibly a few years earlier). The sūtra is located next to last in the *Dkon-brtsegs* (Skt.: Ratnakūṭa) collection of the Kanjur (translation of the Buddhist scriptures); and this accounts for its consistency, except for a few notable spots, with the Bodhiruci translation into Chinese where the *Śrī-Mālā* is also part of the Ratnakūṭa collection. Accordingly, we can assume that these two translations from Sanskrit are regularly and literally close to the original text. Two enterprising Japanese who spent some years in Tibet each translated the Tibetan text into the Japanese language: Ekai Kawaguchi's translation was published in 1924; Tōkan Tada's in 1936.

The Tibetan version of the *Śrī-Mālā* does not appear to have had much influence of itself in Tibet. This is due to the prevalent reliance of Tibetan Buddhism on the authoritative commentarial tradition. In this case, there is of course the handbook on the Tathāgatagarbha theory, the *Ratnagotravibhāga*, as it is now titled in E. H. Johnston's Sanskrit edition, or the *Uttaratantra* (T. *rgyud bla ma*) as it is titled in the eleventh-century Tibetan translation by Sajjana and the great translator Blo ḷdan śes rab. This treatise is honored in Tibetan tradition as one of the "five books of Maitreya" (T. *byams chos sde lṅa*), which according to tradition Asaṅga obtained from Maitreya in the Tuṣita heaven. As a matter of fact, Asaṅga probably had nothing to do with the *Ratnagotravibhāga*. All learned Tibetan monks would have studied this text along with the other Maitreya books, principally the *Mahāyāna-Sūtrālaṃkāra* and the *Madhyāntavibhāga*.

Because of the importance of the *Uttaratantra*, the many citations therein of the *Śrī-Mālā* would naturally be observed by the attentive Tibetan reader. But this is as far as a Tibetan would ordinarily go with this particular sūtra. Of course, if anyone wanted to specialize in the Tathāgatagarbha theory, as did the Jonaṅpa sect of Tibet, it would be necessary for him to read the sūtra itself rather than rely on quotations, even though these quotations are among the most important sentences of the *Śrī-Mālā*.

Bodhisattva Practice According to the Lam-Rim-Chen-Mo," *The Tibet Society Newsletter*, 1, no. 2 (July-December 1967), 87. The two terms were employed by Tan-luan (476–524), founder of the Ching-t'u (Pure Land) school in China, and accordingly came into Japan with the Pure Land sect called Jōdo. Shinran Shōnin does not quote the *Śrī-Mālā* in his *Kyōgyōshinshō*, according to the Index in Kosho Yamamoto, tr. *The Kyogyoshinsho*.

The Structure of the Śrī-Mālā

Chapter Divisions

Neither the Bodhiruci translation into Chinese nor the Tibetan translation contains any chapter divisions. It is clear that the original Sanskrit text was a continuous stretch without marked subdivisions. The Guṇabhadra translation into Chinese includes chapter divisions amounting to fifteen which are based on the sixteen titles listed in the Epilogue of the sūtra (see, in Appendix I, Table: The Chinese sectional titles of *Śrī-Mālā*).[43] The earliest extant Chinese commentary on the Guṇabhadra translation, the Tun-huang manuscript Stein No. 2660, copied February 14, 504, has similar chapter divisions.

While the titles listed at the end of the sūtra are obviously relevant to sectional divisions, their imposition on the Guṇabhadra Chinese rendition left certain problems. To be explicit: while they led to numerous subsections (Nos. 6–13 in one part of the scripture), they allotted only one subsection each to "Embrace of the Illustrious Doctrine" and "One Vehicle" even though a perusal of these two stretches indicates various shifts of subject matter of the type which occasions the other subsections. As a result, the Chinese chapter division yields some lengthy undivided stretches and then numerous small chapters. We also observe that the "One Vehicle" section appears to have two subdivisions "not final meaning" and "final meaning" which are not alluded to in the list in the Epilogue.

This consideration gives rise to the question of whether the original Sanskrit text contained transitional sentences which would enable the reader to observe the structure of the scripture prior to coming to the end of it. Now it happens that there are such sentences in the text as presently available. We refer to the kind of division suggested by sentences about "eloquence" (*pratibhāna*). There are five such sentences, indicating the inspired portion of the scripture, and further inspirations. The first three are in the section "Embrace of the Illustrious Doctrine," namely: (1) "Then Queen Śrīmālā implored the Lord with these words: 'Furthermore, when teaching in the scope of the great aspirations, may the Tathāgata's power make me eloquent!' " (2) "May the Tathāgata's power make me also eloquent to teach the far-ranging meaning!" (3) "May

43 According to Hasuzawa, *Shōman shishiku*, p. 87–b, the Taishō text was based only on the Koryō (Korai) edition, which has the chapter divisions.

the Tathāgata's power make me also eloquent to teach the great meaning!" When we ponder these sentences in relation to the content of this section, we conclude that they constitute ascending levels and thereby relate what are called "the three all-inclusive aspirations" to subsections of the section "Embrace of the Illustrious Doctrine."

The fourth "eloquence" sentence heads the "One Vehicle" section: (4) "Queen, you must preach eloquently the embrace of the Illustrious Doctrine that was held by all the Buddhas and was explained by me." This shows that the sequel, a little over half the entire sūtra, is presented from the standpoint of complete Buddhahood. Many titles listed at the end of the *Śrī-Mālā* provide subsections in the portion immediately after its designated "One Vehicle" section.

The final occurrence inaugurates a switch to the queen as the bearer of the message: (5) "May the Tathāgata's power make me eloquent for still further explanations of the faultless meaning!" This confirms the queen's eloquence subsequent to the departure of the Lord, that is, for the time after she returns to the world—as Chi-tsang's commentary mentions—to uphold and spread the Doctrine. We conclude that even without the final list and the traditional chapter divisions in China this rather brief scripture has enough internal structure to permit an intelligent perusal. Although the final list cannot substitute for the internal structural evidence, it is indispensable for making clear the important aspects of the scripture.

Furthermore, of the sixteen titles listed at the end of the scripture, the sixteenth is suggestive of the scripture's own intention of major divisions. The two Chinese renditions agree in the sentence, "Also retain all explanations contained in this Scripture as 'Eliminating all doubts, deciding the final meaning, and entering the One Vehicle Path.'" The Tibetan version differs somewhat: "Also retain all explanations contained in this Scripture as 'Deciding the cause, (also) the final meaning, and the sole resort.'" By accepting a compromise between the two versions, we arrive at the suggestive sentence: "Also retain all explanations contained in this Scripture as 'Eliminating all doubts, deciding the cause, clarifying the final meaning, and entering the One Vehicle.'" These four phrases admirably head four main divisions of the sūtra.

Taking into account those findings, we have attempted an approach different from that of the Sino-Japanese commentarial traditions. We have decided on a chapter division which includes the traditional chapter headings as subsections under the new chapter titles. A further justification stems from our historical remarks that the *Śrī-Mālā* was evidently composed in Andhra at a time when the Mahāsāṅghika sect was strong in that area of India. At the beginning of the

Mahāvastu, the "Vinaya" of the Lokottaravādin subsect of the Mahāsāṅghika, there is a mention of four career-phases of Bodhisattvas. They are the "natural career-phase" (*prakṛti-caryā*), the "aspiration career-phase" (*praṇidhāna-caryā*), the "conforming career-phase" (*anuloma-caryā*), and the "nonregressing career-phase" (*anivartana-caryā*). Each of these is illustrated in the former lives of Gautama Buddha. They seem to fit much more easily the situation in *Śrī-Mālā* than does the terminology of the Bodhisattva career which Dayal presents from other works.[44] For example, the *Śrī-Mālā*'s sections "Ten Great Vows" and "The All-inclusive Aspirations" do not fit the classical terminology of "generating the mind of enlightenment" (*bodhicittotpāda*).[45]

By comparing the illustrations near the beginning of the *Mahāvastu* with the progress of material in the *Śrī-Mālā*, and superimposing the four titles mentioned near the end of the scripture as our compromise between the Chinese and the Tibetan, it is reasonably simple to establish the following chapters, preceded by the Prologue and followed by the Epilogue:

Chapter One: "Eliminating All Doubts." 1. Praises of the Infinite Merit of the Tathāgata, and 2. Ten Great Vows. These are both the "natural career-phase" involving the planting of virtuous roots in the presence of a Buddha.

Chapter Two: "Deciding the Cause." 3. Three All-inclusive Aspirations. This is the "aspiration career-phase." 4. Embrace of the Illustrious Doctrine. A. Teaching in the Scope of the Great Aspirations, and B. Teaching the Far-ranging Meaning. These two are the "conforming career-phase." C. Teaching the Great Meaning. This is the "nonregressing career-phase." That finishes the career-phases of the Bodhisattva, namely, the causal part, aimed at the fruit, which is complete Buddhahood.

Chapter Three: "Clarifying the Final Meaning." 5. One Vehicle (subdivided by internal indications). 6. The Boundless Noble Truths through 13. Intrinsic Purity of the Mind (based on the same titles as in the Chinese chapter divisions).

Chapter Four: "Entering the One Vehicle Path." 14. The True Son of the Tathāgata and 15. The Lion's Roar of Queen Śrīmālā.

44 Har Dayal, *The Bodhisattva Doctrine*, especially chapter III, "The Thought of Enlightenment."

45 As in Dayal (*ibid.*). The Tibetan word for "vow" is here *yid dam* (=Skt. *samādāna*), which means a vow in the sense of a commitment in the present. The Tibetan word for "aspiration" is here *smon lam* (=Skt. *praṇidhāna*), which means an aspiration regarding the future.

Following is the summary of our chapter divisions combined with the first fifteen titles from the Epilogue:

Chapter One. Eliminating All Doubts

1. Praises of the True and Infinite Merit of the Tathāgata
2. The Inconceivably Great Vows

Chapter Two. Deciding the Cause

3. The Great Aspiration Which Includes All Aspirations
4. Teaching the Inconceivable Embrace of the Illustrious Doctrine

CAUSE

Chapter Three. Clarifying the Final Meaning

5. Teaching the Entering the One Vehicle
6. Teaching the Boundless Noble Truths
7. Teaching the Tathāgatagarbha

8–9. Teaching the Dharmakāya; Teaching the Hidden Purport of the Meaning of Voidness

10. Teaching the One Truth

11–12. Teaching the Permanent, Steadfast, Calm, Eternal; and the One Refuge; Teaching the Wayward Stage

13. Teaching the Hidden Purport that the Mind Is Intrinsically Pure

Chapter Four. Entering the One Vehicle Path

14. Teaching the True Son of the Tathāgata
15. Lion's Roar of Queen Śrīmālā

EFFECT

"Eliminating All Doubts" is the cause of "Entering the One Vehicle Path"; "Deciding the Cause" is the cause of "Clarifying the Final Meaning." The translators have combined titles 8 and 9 because of their conceptual continuity, and have combined titles 11 and 12 because of their reversed position in the text.[46]

46 The fact that the topics of sections 11 and 12 actually occur in the body of the *Śrī-Mālā* in the reverse order demonstrates that they should be considered one section. Presumably in the original Sanskrit text the words of these two sectional titles formed one long compound.

Synopsis of the Scripture

Prologue. The scripture opens in Śrāvāstī. King Prasenajit and his Queen Mallikā move to interest their daughter Queen Śrīmālā in the Buddha's Doctrine.

Chapter One. Eliminating All Doubts. 1. Śrīmālā evokes the Buddha, who approaches in his inconceivable body. She praises his two bodies which are the bodily form and the knowledge body. The Lord prophesies that Queen Śrīmālā will attain the incomparable right perfected enlightenment. 2. Queen Śrīmālā takes ten great vows, the first five constituting Hīnayāna ethics, the second five, Mahāyāna ethics. The most important one is the tenth vow, to embrace the Illustrious Doctrine and never to forget it. By performance of a Truth Act, the retinue is relieved of all doubts.

Chapter Two. Deciding the Cause. 3. Queen Śrīmālā forms three great aspirations: to always comprehend the Illustrious Doctrine; to teach unweariedly the Illustrious Doctrine; and to protect and uphold the Illustrious Doctrine without regard to body, life force, or possessions. These three comprise all Bodhisattva aspirations. 4. She prays for the Tathāgata's power to make her eloquent when teaching in the scope of the great aspirations; also when teaching the far-ranging meaning. With her first scope of eloquence, she teaches that the embrace of the Illustrious Doctrine gives rise to the Great Vehicle. That the good son or daughter of the family who embraces the Illustrious Doctrine supports four burdens greater than the four burdens of earth, namely (1) getting ordinary persons to try to achieve the perfections of gods and men; (2–4) getting certain persons to join the Vehicle of Disciples, or the Vehicle of the Self-Enlightened, or the Great Vehicle. That the persons who rely on that good son or daughter of the family gain four precious things superior to the four kinds of jewels, namely (1) the merit for the perfections of gods and men; (2–4) the virtuous root for approaching the Vehicle of Disciples, or the Vehicle of the Self-Enlightened, or the Samyaksambuddha. With the scope of her second eloquence, she teaches that the embrace and the embracer of the Illustrious Doctrine are the same. She explains that when the good son or daughter of the family has the Perfection of Giving, or of Morality, or of Forbearance, or of Striving, or of Meditation, or of Insight, it is the maturation of others and those others are installed in the Illustrious Doctrine. The queen then prays for the Tathāgata's power to make her eloquent when teaching the great meaning. With the scope of her third eloquence, she teaches that the embracer and the embrace of the Illustrious Doctrine are the same. She explains that the good son or daughter of the family who renounces his body obtains the body of a

Buddha; who renounces his life force lives in the wondrous activity of the Buddha's Doctrine; who renounces his possessions is honored by all sentient beings; and thus is the embrace of the Illustrious Doctrine.

Chapter Three. Clarifying the Final Meaning. 5. The queen eloquently preaches the embrace of the Illustrious Doctrine that was held by all the Buddhas. The "Illustrious Doctrine" is a term for the Great Vehicle. The religious life and ordination belong to Tathāgata-hood. The Arhats and the Pratyekabuddhas with fear take refuge in the Lord. What they call "nirvāṇa" is a means belonging to the Tathāgatas, because the Arhats and the Pratyekabuddhas do not have all merits, have measurable and conceivable merit, have a remainder of faults, and so are far away from the nirvāṇa-realm. Concerning the liberation of Arhats and Pratyekabuddhas, there are two kinds of passing away—discontinuous passing away of ordinary sentient beings, and the inconceivable transference of the Arhats, Pratyekabuddhas, and Bodhisattvas who have attained power. The Arhats and the Pratyekabuddhas have neither eliminated all defilements nor avoided all rebirth. There are four static kinds of defilement, which generate all the mobile defilements. The greatest power of defilement is the unconscious nescience entrenchment; although static it is different from the four static kinds. The Arhats and the Pratyekabuddhas can eliminate the four static kinds, but they and even Bodhisattvas in their last life cannot eliminate the nescience entrenchment, which is eliminated on the Buddha stage. The Arhats and the others all have a remainder of the four Noble Truths to experience. They have a fractional nirvāṇa, but are without the single taste of nirvāṇa. When all the defilements and secondary defilements are eliminated, one obtains the inconceivable Buddha natures and as a Tathāgata-Arhat-Samyaksambuddha utters the Lion's Roar with final meaning. The vehicles of the Disciples and the Self-Enlightened are included in the Great Vehicle. "Great Vehicle" is an expression for the Buddha vehicle, and so the three vehicles are counted as one vehicle (*ekayāna*). The Tathāgata is the imperishable refuge. The Saṃgha is the refuge with temporal limitation. The sentient beings who take refuge in the Tathāgata have faith flowing from true nature; the faith leads them to the Dharma and to the Saṃgha for refuge. Thus the Tathāgata is himself the three refuges. 6. The four Noble Truths do not belong to the Disciples and the Self-Enlightened, for these persons do not have the supramundane knowledge of the nonprogressive Noble Truths. The four Truths belong to the Tathāgatas, who eliminate the store of all defilements by inconceivable voidness knowledge. 7. The Tathāgatagarbha is covered by the defilement store; when liberated from this store it is the Dharmakāya of the Tathāgata. Accordingly, there are both the Create and the Uncreate explanations of the Noble Truths. The Create explanation has intellectual limitation by reason of the defilements; the Uncreate explanation is without intellectual limitation by reason of elimination of all defilements. 8–9. The cessation of suffering is the Tathāgata's Dharmakāya, or Tathāgatagarbha freed from defilement by the two kinds of voidness knowledge of the Tathāgatas, namely, the Tathāgatagarbha is void of the stores of defilement, and the Tathāgatagarbha is not void of the Buddha natures. 10. The Noble Truth "Cessation of Suffering" is the true refuge. The other three Noble Truths, namely, "Suffering," "Source of Suffering," and "Path," are not the true refuge. 11–12. Immature ordinary persons have the wayward views of two extremes. When they think, "The constructions are impermanent," it is their nihilistic view and when they think, "Nirvāṇa is permanent," it is their eternalistic view. This is because they have four wayward ideas: that the impermanent is permanent, suffering is pleasure, nonself is self, the impure is pure. The Disciples and the Self-Enlightened do not have these four wayward ideas and so have "pure knowledge," which, however, does not know the Tathāgata's Dharmakāya. The sentient beings with faith that the Tathāgata has permanence, pleasure, self, and purity are called sons of the Lord. The Lord pointed out the mundane four resorts so that persons would be brought further toward the supramundane refuge. 13. The Tathāgatagarbha is the base either of nondiscrete constructed Buddha natures or of discrete constructed defilements. The Tathāgatagarbha experiences suffering, is the reason for aspiration towards nirvāṇa, and the reason for "cyclical flow" (*saṃsāra*); it is not a "self." There are two difficult doctrines: that consciousness is intrinsically pure, and that intrinsically pure consciousness can be defiled.

Chapter Four. Entering the One Vehicle Path. 14. By two discipleship levels, a third with a knowledge in the precincts of the Dharma involving five visions, and a fourth reaching certainty in the two difficult doctrines, the Disciples can then enroll others in the Great Vehicle. 15. The queen gains eloquence for further explanations of the faultless meaning. She explains three kinds of good son or daughter of the family: the one with the profound Dharma through introspection; the one with a knowledge in the precincts of the Dharma; and the one who with humility gains the mental presence of the Lord. Some other persons falsely explain the Dharma. The Lord praises the queen and departs. Queen Śrīmālā converts King Yaśomitra to the Great Vehicle. As queen she converts the women in the capital, and as king he converts the men.

Epilogue. The Lord arrives at the Jetavana in Śrāvastī and explains the scripture to Ānanda and to Indra. The Lord instructs them on remembering the scripture by fifteen titles and on remembering the entire scripture under four headings. He entrusts the scripture to Indra. All assembled there rejoice.

II. Classification of Persons

The Characters in the *Śrī-Mālā*

Again and again the *Śrī-Mālā* refers to sets of persons in ways that intimately relate to its religious message. Sometimes these sets are significantly mentioned in contrast. This scripture is genuinely interested in all sentient beings since they are all held to have the potentiality of Buddhahood called "embryo of the Tathāgata."

In brief, the characters are classified as "ordinary persons," "disciples" (*śrāvaka*), "the self-enlightened" (*pratyekabuddha*) of two kinds, Arhats ("worthy ones" or "who have destroyed the adversary"), Bodhisattvas "recently entered in the Great Vehicle" and Bodhisattvas "who have attained power" or "who are in their last life," "good sons of the family" and "good daughters of the family," and finally the Buddha who is called Bhagavat ("The Lord"), "Tathāgata" ("Thus-gone"), "Samyaksambuddha" ("Complete Buddha") or more fully "Tathāgata-Arhat-Samyaksambuddha."

Among those, the "ordinary persons" are those without friendly guides, who do not hear the Illustrious Doctrine. In contrast, the Disciples have such a friendly guide in their progress, and the Self-Enlightened manage by themselves. These two, called "noble" (*ārya*) are characters in the Hīnayāna ("lesser vehicle"). Bodhisattvas are beings who have the double aim of enlightenment for themselves and benefit for others. They are characters in the Mahāyāna ("great vehicle"). These Bodhisattvas can be either laymen or monks, and the laymen are called "good sons of the family" and "good daughters of the family." Finally, the Buddha is the great person who is the fruition of the path, who has given rise to the Three Jewels.

Śrī-Mālā has a set of "Disciples, the Self-Enlightened, and Bodhisattvas newly entered in the Great Vehicle" and another set of "Arhats, the Self-Enlightened, and Bodhisattvas who have attained power." By the Buddhism of "three vehicles" these two sets would be related as persons in progress and in fulfillment, as follows (see below, "Persons in Stages" for the order of attainment):

In progress:	In fulfillment:
Disciple	Arhat
Self-Enlightened One (first kind)	Self-Enlightened One (second kind)
Bodhisattva newly entered	Bodhisattva who has attained power

Traditionally, the Disciple attained fruition as an Arhat by comprehension of the four Noble Truths and by a meditative achievement called the "diamond *samādhi*" (*vajropama-samādhi*).[47] While the term "Self-Enlightened One" (*pratyekabuddha*) is not employed consistently in Buddhist books, the *Śrī-Mālā* is evidently following the tradition that there are two kinds, the first one called *khaḍgaviṣāṇakalpa* (living a lonely life) and the second one, *pratyekajina* (self-victorious). Abhayākaragupta (*Muni*, p. 229–4), explains the two as the one becoming enlightened without recourse to other persons, and the one who teaches the Doctrine without recourse to words.[48] Henceforth we shall translate the first term into English as "Self-Enlightened one" and refer to the second kind by the Sanskrit term "Pratyekabuddha." The "Bodhisattva newly entered in the Great Vehicle" is in the scope of the queen's first two (of three) aspirations, especially with the practice of the Perfections (*pāramitā*) and the practice of maturing the sentient beings by preaching and teaching. The "Bodhisattva who has attained power" is in the scope of the queen's third aspiration, and referred to in other works as the Bodhisattva of the eighth and higher stages, i.e. the last three of the ten Bodhisattva stages.

The queen considers the Bodhisattva superior in both what we label the "in progress" set and the "in fulfillment" set. For the "in progress" set, the queen says: "even a little embrace of the Illustrious Doctrine of the Great Vehicle, because of its expanse, is superior to all the virtuous Dharmas of the Vehicle of the Disciples and the Self-Enlightened." For the "in fulfillment" set, she says: "The Arhats and the Pratyekabuddhas are far away from the nirvāṇa-realm," but does not include the "Bodhisattva who has attained power." Still, all three of the latter group are said equally to have a "body made of mind" (*manomaya-kāya*). By "Nirvāṇa-realm" the queen refers to the Complete Nirvāṇa of the Buddhas.

The *Śrī-Mālā* makes it clear that the lay Bodhisattvas called "good son of the family" and "good daughter of the family" are those who embrace the Illustrious Doctrine in various degrees. They contrast with the "heretics" who pose as knowing the Doctrine and who broadcast false information about it. However, the scripture does not make a separate category of these "heretics" or explain whether they overlap other categories such as "ordinary persons" and "Disciples."

47 See n. 77 to the translation.

48 Cf. Alex Wayman, "The Sacittikā and Acittikā Bhūmi and the Pratyekabuddhabhūmi [Sanskrit texts]," *Journal of Indian and Buddhist Studies* (Tokyo), 7 (no. 1, 1960), 375–79. The *pratyekajina* is said by Asaṅga to teach the Doctrine in a corporeal manner, that is, by magical displays. The term also occurs in the Lotus Sūtra (*Saddharmapuṇḍarīka*).

Persons on Stages

The theory of the path is basic to every Buddhist sect, and the divergent interpretations lend the stamp of individuality to a particular school of thought. The *Śrī-Mālā* has its own theory, presumably as a Mahāyāna outgrowth of the later Mahāsāṅghika sect which teaches a rudimentary doctrine of ten Bodhisattva stages in the *Mahāvastu*. The *Śrī-Mālā* has nuances due to centuries of scholastic exegesis and disagreements, and consequently the discussion we are now undertaking encounters difficulties at every turn.

Although we shall have to cite abstruse passages which serve to deepen the discussion, we promise to clarify them. The first of these knotty passages is the reference to our scripture in the *Mahāyāna-Sūtrālaṃkāra* prose commentary on verse XI, 59, as follows: "In connection with staying in three states, the Lord said in the *Śrīmālāsūtra*, 'Having become a Disciple, he becomes a Self-Enlightened one, and then a Buddha.'" Now the ascribed citation is not in the *Śrī-Mālā* text in any extant version. We must assume that it is an interpretation, and so must decide whether it is a correct interpretation. In the *Mahāyāna-Sūtrālaṃkāra* context, the three states are (1) that of a Disciple of the Buddha, who has seen the truth but has not attained the goal; (2) that of the Self-Enlightened one, striving in meditation by himself because there was no Buddha when he was born; (3) that of the one who, abandoning the body of birth, adopts a Nirmāṇa-kāya (creative body) and attains enlightenment.[49] From our preceding outline of characters, it follows that the "Self-Enlightened one" is the first kind. We are forced to the striking conclusion that the *Mahāyāna-Sūtrālaṃkāra* understands the *Śrī-Mālā* to teach, explicitly or implicitly, that one proceeds through the "in progress" set in the order Disciple, Self-Enlightened one, and Bodhisattva newly entered; and then subsequently passes through the "in fulfillment" set by three stages of a body made of mind belonging in series to the Arhat, Pratyekabuddha, and Bodhisattva who has attained power; and with this special body now called a Nirmāṇa-kāya then advances to the state of a complete Buddha. While this sequence would not have occurred to us by the mere reading of the *Śrī-Mālā*, there is nothing in the text which conflicts with such an interpretation. Indeed, it seems to accord with the "One Vehicle" position of the *Śrī-Mālā*.

The next difficult passage concerns the description of the difference between persons on different stages by way of the differing manifestation of "Thusness" (*tathatā*). This is the terminology of the *Ratnagotravibhāga* (I, 45, 46):

49 Sylvain Lévi, ed., *Asaṅga: Mahāyāna-Sūtrālaṃkāra*, p. 70.

> This embryo of the Victor is taught by the seers of reality to be in sentient beings according as Thusness is different in ordinary persons, the noble ones, and Saṃbuddhas.
> Ordinary persons are wayward; opposite to them are those who have seen the truth; noumenally free from waywardness and devoid of phenomenal imagination are the Tathāgatas.

Here the lowest stage is of course the "ordinary person." He has the four wayward ideas which take the impermanent as permanent, suffering as pleasure, nonself as self, and the impure as pure. According to the *Śrī-Mālā*, when he holds "All constructions are impermanent," this is simply his nihilistic view since his mental frame is faulty because of going astray regarding the five personality aggregates. Opposite to him are the two "Noble ones," the Disciples and the Self-Enlightened, who have learned to contemplate the impermanent as impermanent, and so on, and thus when they hold "All constructions are impermanent," they have seen the truth. But as they dwell on these four aspects of saṃsāra—impermanence, suffering, nonself, and impurity—they are ascribed noumenal waywardness and do not reach the nirvāṇa-realm which has permanence, pleasure, self, and purity. The Tathāgatas, noumenally free from waywardness and devoid of imagination concerning saṃsāra, realize the nirvāṇa-realm that way.

The description in terms of Thusness is based on an obscure passage in the *Śrī-Mālā:* "Lord, this Tathāgatagarbha is the embryo of the Illustrious Dharmadhātu, the embryo of the Dharmakāya, the embryo of supramundane dharma, the embryo of the intrinsically pure dharma." The *Ratnagotravibhāga* understands these expressions as the different manifestations of Thusness which for various reasons are not recognized by persons as being present in themselves. The *Ratnagotravibhāga* (pp. 76–77, alluding to the preceding p. 74) assigns these unappreciated Thusness aspects as follows:

(1) The embryo of the Illustrious Dharmadhātu is not accessible to ordinary persons, who fall into the belief in a real personality; because the embryo of the Illustrious Dharmadhātu is the realm without flux that is the cessation of a real personality.

(2) The embryo of the Dharmakāya and the embryo of supramundane dharma are not accessible to the Disciples and the Self-Enlightened, who adhere to waywardness; because they contemplate the ideas of impermanence, suffering, nonself, and impurity (of saṃsāra) instead of the permanence, pleasure, self, and purity of the Tathāgatagarbha (=nirvāṇa).

(3) The embryo of the intrinsically pure dharma is not accessible to the

Bodhisattvas newly entered in the Great Vehicle, whose thoughts are distracted by voidness; because they seek the "voidness door of liberation" for destruction of modes-of-being, and do not understand voidness as the Tathāgatagarbha which is void of defilement and not void of Buddha natures (according to *Śrī-Mālā*'s interpretation).[50]

The commentary of the *Ratnagotravibhāga* is reasonably clear as far as it goes, but no mention is made of how the manifestation of Thusness occurs in the Arhats, Pratyekabuddhas and Bodhisattvas who have attained power.

The *Śrī-Mālā* does not explain specifically the type of defilement found in those persons on the various stages of concealing the "embryo of the Tathāgata" or Thusness. This is somewhat detailed in the *Ratnagotravibhāga* (p. 67) on the basis of the *Tathāgatagarbha-sūtra*. The defilement of ordinary persons is the outbursts of lust, hatred, and delusion; these are like the seed which conceals the tree, and are eliminated by vision. The defilement of the two noble ones is the dormant state of lust, hatred, and delusion; this is like the tattered garment over the image of the Buddha, and is eliminated by practice. The defilement in the stream of consciousness of an Arhat—and so also in that of a Pratyekabuddha and of a Bodhisattva who has attained power—is comprised of the nescience entrenchment like the earth, instigates the embodiment as a pure body made of mind, and is destroyed by the Tathāgata's enlightenment knowledge.

In *Śrī-Mālā*'s terminology of defilement, there are two degrees of persons. Those with discontinuous transference include ordinary persons, Disciples, Self-Enlightened ones, and Bodhisattvas newly entered, as they have not eliminated the four "static kinds of defilement" accompanied by innumerable mobile defilements. Those with inconceivable transference are the Arhats, Pratyekabuddhas, and the Bodhisattvas who have attained power, as they have eliminated the four static kinds of defilement, but have not eliminated the nescience entrenchment called "static kind in attraction to (supramundane) gestation."

As to the progress of a Bodhisattva, whether lay or monk, the *Śrī-Mālā* does not use the specific language of ten stages, but both the Chinese and the Japa-

50 This clarifies a passage by Tsoṅ-kha-pa quoted in Ruegg, *La théorie*, p. 101: "en effet, dans le *Śrīmālāsiṃhanadasūtra* il est dit: 'Par rapport au *vyavadāna-bīja (rnam par byaṅ ba'i sa bon)* il est dit que tous les êtres animés sont munis du *tathāgatagarbha*.'" Ruegg properly observes that this citation is not in the sūtra. However, Tsoṅ-kha-pa apparently meant the Tathāgatagarbha as the "embryo of the intrinsically pure *dharma*," which amounts to the "seed of purity" *(vyavadāna-bīja)*. As to the "voidness door," the three standard "doors to liberation" are listed in the *Mahāvyutpatti* (Nos. 1542–1544): "voidness" *(śūnyatā)*, "signless" *(ānimitta)*, and "wishless" *(apraṇihita)*.

nese commentaries take for granted this implication of the *Śrī-Mālā* and occasionally discuss points in terms of these Bodhisattva stages. These ten divide into two groups of five, because starting with the sixth the Bodhisattva has an opportunity to enter nirvāṇa. They also divide into groups of seven and three, because starting with the Eighth Stage ("Motionless") the Bodhisattva is called "nonregressing." Various statements of the queen can be subsumed under those ten stages in line with both the five-five and the seven-three divisions. Thus the queen's three aspirations imply stages. The first aspiration, to comprehend the Illustrious Doctrine in all lives, is the lowest, as the initial entrance into the Great Vehicle; here there are the "Bodhisattvas newly entered in the Great Vehicle," apparently prevalent from the First through the Fifth, Sixth, or Seventh Stages. The second, to teach the Doctrine to the sentient beings without rest or weariness, is certainly the practice of the six Perfections on the first seven stages. The third, to protect and to uphold the Illustrious Doctrine without regard to body, life force, or possessions, points to the Bodhisattvas who have attained power, starting with the Eighth Stage.

The foregoing has clarified some important aspects of the stages, but at the same time has introduced some further difficult concepts such as "inconceivable transference." Certain conclusions given above without proof will be justified as we attempt more clarification by way of special treatment: (1) Stages of the "bodies made of mind," (2) the last three Bodhisattva stages, and (3) Stages of the lay Bodhisattva.

1. *Stages of the "bodies made of mind."* Now we must take up a most difficult phrase in the *Śrī-Mālā*, "the arising of these three bodies made of mind in three stages." The three bodies made of mind are explained by the queen as belonging to the Arhat, the Pratyekabuddha, and the Bodhisattva who has attained power. This raises two problems: What is a "body made of mind"? What are the three stages?

As to the first problem, we observe that, according to the *Śrī-Mālā*, the Arhat, and the others, with this "body made of mind" has an "inconceivable transference." This kind of transference is clarified in the *Mahāvastu* where it poses the question of why the Buddha's mother experiences no pain when she is delivered of her glorious son through her right side, and goes on to explain, "Tathāgatas come forth with a form that is made of mind. That is why her side is not rent and why she does not feel it."[51] Ancient Buddhist meditation theory held that by an advanced meditation technique a monk can contemplate a duplicate form of himself within his body and draw it forth, as was stated in the

51 Dr. Radhagovinda Basak, ed., *Mahāvastu Avadāna*, I, 266.

Pāli canon in the *Dīgha-nikāya* (i. 77):

> Here a monk creates a body from this [his] body having form mind-made, with all limbs and parts, not deprived of senses. Just as if a man were to pull out a reed from a sheath, he would know: "This is the sheath, this is the reed. The sheath is one thing, the reed is another. It is from the sheath that the reed has been drawn forth."[52]

Also, in the Buddhist genesis myth preserved in the Pāli canon and in the *Mahāvastu*, the beings at the outset of redevelopment of inferior worlds are said to be made of mind (*manomaya*) and further described as being self-luminous and wherever they wish to be, as well as feeding on joy and living in pleasure.[53] These passages give a general idea of the body made of mind. Moreover, the *Śrī-Mālā* speaks of three bodies made of mind, and accordingly the *Ratnagotra-vibhāga* (p. 50) states: "In this case, saṃsāra is an expression for the three bodies made of mind in the nonfluxional realm, with their reflected image in the three realms . . . ." This difficult remark is clarified by observing that the *Śrī-Mālā* has involved Buddhist saints in an exegesis of the celebrated Buddhist formula of Dependent Origination (*pratītya-samutpāda*), which stands for *saṃsāra* in twelve members: (1) nescience (*avidyā*), (2) motivations (*saṃskāra*), (3) perception (*vijñāna*), (4) name-and-form (*nāma-rūpa*), (5) six sense bases (*ṣaḍāyatana*), (6) contact (*sparśa*), (7) feelings (*vedanā*), (8) craving (*tṛṣṇā*), (9) indulgence (*upādāna*), (10) gestation (*bhava*), (11) birth (*jāti*), (12) old age and death (*jarā-maraṇa*). The *Daśabhūmika-sūtra* labels them as either defilement (*kleśa*), action (*karma*), or suffering (*duḥkha*): "Among them, nescience, craving, and indulgence form a group by way of defilement; motivations and gestation form a group by way of action; the rest form a group by way of suffering.[54] This important set of data can be tabulated as follows:

Dependent Origination

Defilement:	(1) nescience	(8) craving and (9) indulgence
Action:	(2) motivation	(10) gestation

52 As is quoted in Vajirañāṇa's *Buddhist Meditation in Theory and Practice*, p. 440. Furthermore, in the *Aṅguttara-nikāya* (Book of fours)—cf. A. D. Jayasundere, *The Book of the Numerical Sayings* (Madras, 1925), Part II, p. 235—this may be the "mind body" which realizes the "eightfold deliverance."

53 Basak, ed., *Mahāvastu*, I, 441–42.

54 P. L. Vaidya, ed. *Śikṣāsamuccaya of Śāntideva*, pp. 123 lines 21–22, which so quotes the *Daśabhūmika-sūtra*.

Suffering:	(3) perception, along with	(11) birth, along with
	(4) name and form,	(12) old age and death
	(5) six sense bases,	
	(6) contact,	
	(7) feelings	

To show the relevance of this information on Dependent Origination, it will be necessary to refer to note 56 to the translation, where we show that the *Śrī-Mālā* has redesignated the classical four kinds of "indulgence" (No. 9) as the four static kinds of defilement. The Arhats, Pratyekabuddhas, and Bodhisattvas who have attained power have eliminated the four static kinds which are the condition for "gestation" (No. 10) leading to birth (No. 11) in the three realms. Instead, these Arhats, and the others, have a "body made of mind," a saintly variety of "perception" (No. 3) projected by the nescience entrenchment (No. 1) and by a saintly variety of "motivations" (No. 2), namely the nonfluxional action (*anāsrava-karma*). Therefore, in the above-cited passage, the "three bodies made of mind" are all referable to a special case of "(3) perception," and "their reflected image in the three realms" is referable to a special case of "(11) birth." That is to say, as has been pointed out, the body made of mind is a duplicate of the coarser body. The body made of mind is assigned to the "nonfluxional realm," and its reflected image in a coarser body is assigned to the fluxional "three realms." The three realms appear not to be the standard set—realm of desire, realm of form, and formless realm—but rather the pre-Buddhist set of underworld, earth surface, and atmosphere. The latter set seems to be indicated by the same Buddhist genesis myth mentioned above, where the "body made of mind" starts among the gods of the "realm of form." The sequel shows, "Then this great earth came into being like a lake of water," and the myth portrays the "great earth" as the stage for the reflection of that mental body into coarser forms.

As to the second problem about the three stages, the Chi-tsang commentary on the *Śrī-Mālā* (p. 173) gives various interpretations of the three without necessarily committing itself to any. For example, it mentions the *Laṅkāvatāra-sūtra*'s account of three bodies made of mind arranged along the ten Bodhisattva stages, with a theory that the first such body is prevalent on the first five stages, the second in the sixth and seventh stages, and the third in the eighth and higher stages; but properly treats this solution with reserve. It gives another interpretation that is consistent with the *Ratnagotravibhāga*, which continues the passage previously cited from this work, as follows:

And that is chiefly established in the [Sixth] Bodhisattva Stage called

"Facing" (*Abhimukhī*), by reason of the unhindered contemplation of the Perfection of Insight facing the supernormal faculty of flux-extinction, and by reason of the contemplation of Great Compassion facing away from realizing that [supernormal faculty] in order to protect all the sentient realm.

But why is the Sixth Bodhisattva Stage mentioned in this connection when the commentarial traditions agree that the "Bodhisattva who has attained power" is in the Eighth Stage? The explanation seems to depend on the *Daśabhūmika-sūtra* because according to this sūtra all three stages, Sixth, Seventh, and Eighth, have some mention of the Bodhisattva's refraining from entering nirvāṇa and continuing to face saṃsāra.[55] And why does the *Ratnagotravibhāga* associate these bodies made of mind with a Bodhisattva stage since the Arhats and Pratyekabuddhas are not Bodhisattvas? The answer seems to be that the "One Vehicle" theory of the *Śrī-Mālā* requires the Bodhisattva stages to incorporate even the progress of the Arhats and Pratyekabuddhas. Wherever these Arhats and Pratyekabuddhas are placed, i.e., the Sixth Bodhisattva Stage according to the *Ratnagotravibhāga*, the Bodhisattva would be superior by reason of his Bodhisattva vow. But since the Bodhisattva who has attained power belongs to the Eighth Stage, it is reasonable to assign the Arhats and Pratyekabuddhas to the Sixth and Seventh Stages, respectively.

In illustration, early Buddhism holds that the Arhat attains the flux-extinction (in Pāli, *āsava-kkhaya*), while the Bodhisattva doctrine of the *Mahāvastu* holds that the Bodhisattva would not advance from the Sixth to the Seventh Stage if he were eager to have the meditative attainment of cessation of ideas and feelings,[56] in short, if he were satisfied with the Arhat attainment. Instead he continues to face saṃsāra by reason of his Great Compassion, and so passes beyond the Arhat attainment to the Seventh Stage. Again, the Pratyekabuddha, who teaches the Doctrine without recourse to words, appears to be described by certain statements about the Bodhisattva on this stage. Dayal explains from the *Bodhisattvabhūmi*, "His words, deeds and thoughts are now independent of *nimitta* (cause and motive)," and from the *Daśabhūmika-sūtra*, "He discerns the thoughts and feelings of others."[57] However, the Bodhisattva on this Stage is certainly superior to the silent Pratyekabuddha, because according to the *Mahāvastu*[58] the Bodhisattva must here employ powerful eloquence.

55 See Har Dayal, *The Bodhisattva Doctrine*, pp. 289–90.
56 Basak, ed., *Mahāvastu*, I, 149.
57 Har Dayal, *The Bodhisattva Doctrine*, pp. 281 and 290.
58 J. J. Jones, tr., *The Mahāvastu*, I, 105.

In short, it seems that the three bodies made of mind refer to the upward progress from the Sixth to the Eighth Bodhisattva Stage, where in the Sixth and the Seventh the Bodhisattva shares this body made of mind with the Arhat and Pratyekabuddha respectively. Of course, this role of the Sixth Stage is consistent with the division of the ten stages into two groups of five. The emphasis on the Eighth Bodhisattva Stage, to which the *Mahāyāna-Sūtrālaṃkāra* evidently refers with its allusion to a Nirmāṇa-kāya with which one advances to enlightenment, is consistent with the division of the ten stages into the first seven and the last three.

2. *The last three Bodhisattva Stages.* For the last three stages, there is a most important passage in the *Mahāvastu* which should be quoted in full because of our thesis that the *Śrī-Mālā* is an outgrowth of the Mahāsāṅghika sect, of which the *Mahāvastu* is a preeminent work:

> When this was said, the venerable Mahā-Kāśyapa asked the venerable Mahā-Kātyāyana. "O son of the Victor, starting from what stage are these Jātaka tales[59] related by the Victor to be assigned?" The venerable Mahā-Kātyāyana replied, "O *dhutadharmadhara*,[60] these Jātaka tales start from the Eighth Stage." "Starting from what stage do the Bodhisattvas renounce all they possess and make austere sacrifice?" "Starting from the Eighth Stage the Bodhisattvas are to be honored with the honor due a Samyaksambuddha. On this point it is said: "Starting from the Eighth Stage, the Bodhisattvas, born from the Victor's heart, are to be regarded as Samyaksambuddhas. For after that, they do not regress."[61]

We shall see that the remark about renouncing all they possess, to start with the Eighth Stage, directly ties in with the position of the *Śrī-Mālā*.

The *Ratnagotravibhāga* (on I, 2) quotes the *Dhāraṇīśvararājasūtra* to show that the arising of the Three Jewels in the life of Śākyamuni is also the prototype for the last three Bodhisattva stages: "The Lord was completely enlightened to the equality of all natures, well set into motion the Wheel of the Doctrine, and is the trainer of the host of innumerable disciples." Here the Buddha sitting under the Tree of Enlightenment is the conventional representation of the Eighth Bodhisattva Stage; the Wheel of the Doctrine, the Ninth; and the host (*gaṇa*),

59 "Jātaka tales" are narrations of the glorious previous lives of the Buddha as a Bodhisattva. There are many of these in the *Mahāvastu* itself.

60 The expression *dhutadharmadhara* means "one who holds the nature of a purified man," hence a saint. For more information, see Franklin Edgerton, *Buddhist Hybrid Sanskrit Dictionary*, 285, column B.

61 Basak, ed., *Mahāvastu*, I, 122–23.

the Tenth. Rgyal tshab rje's commentary on the *Ratnagotravibhāga* (= *Uttaratantra*), as cited by Obermiller, explains the last three Bodhisattva stages as containing the "proximate cause of the Three Jewels": "The Bodhisattva on the 8th Stage is called 'the Buddha in the conventional sense—*aupacāriko buddhaḥ* = *saṅs-rgyas-btags-pa-pa*,' inasmuch as he has obtained the controlling power over the elements. The 9th and 10th Stages, respectively, contain the proximate causes of the Jewel of the Doctrine and that of the Congregation."[62] These three Bodhisattva stages would then be the meaning of Queen Śrīmālā's remarks about the good son or daughter of the family who makes three renunciations for the sake of making persons embrace the Illustrious Doctrine. The queen explains that in such a case the renunciation of body yields the body of a Buddha, which is presumably the *Sūtrālaṃkāra*'s "Nirmāṇa-kāya" on the Eighth Stage, although the Guṇabhadra and Bodhiruci translations agree in assigning the Dharmakāya here. The renunciation of life force places the Bodhisattva "in the wondrous activity of the Buddha's Dharma," hence on the Ninth Stage. The renunciation of possessions makes the Bodhisattva "honored by all sentient beings," and this is consistent with the Tenth Stage, where he is surrounded by the Congregation (*saṃgha*). In the summary of the *Ratnagotravibhāga* (I, 3):

> From the Buddha comes the Doctrine, and from the Doctrine the Noble Congregation.
>
> In the Congregation is the embryo whose goal is fulfilling the realm of knowledge; and fulfilling that knowledge is the supreme enlightenment accompanied with (Buddha) natures of Powers, and so on, which perform the aims of all the sentient beings.

The last three Bodhisattva stages are also the basis—according to the *Ratnagotravibhāga* (p. 58)—for *Śrī-Mālā*'s statement that the Arhats and the Pratyekabuddhas are "far away from the nirvāṇa-realm." That is to say, they do not see the four kinds of merit (*guṇa*) which are inseparable from the nirvāṇa-realm. These four are presented in four paragraphs in *Śrī-Mālā*, in each of which it is repeated that what is called "nirvāṇa"—referring to the fractional nirvāṇa—is a means belonging to the Tathāgata. The *Ratnagotravibhāga* assigns the foundation of these merits to the successive Bodhisattva Stages, Eighth, Ninth, and Tenth, and the Buddha Stage, as follows: Eighth = merits of all (best) aspects; Ninth = immeasurable merits; Tenth = inconceivable merits; and Buddha Stage = completely pure merits. In the light of the preceding subsec-

62 E. Obermiller, tr., *The Sublime Science of the Great Vehicle to Salvation*, offprint from *Acta Orientalia*, IX (1931), 116, note.

tion, assigning the Arhats and Pratyekabuddhas to respective sharing of the Sixth and Seventh Bodhisattva stages—but surpassed on each stage by the Bodhisattva—it is reasonable to say that they are far away from the Buddha Stage. But the Bodhisattva who has attained power, and who is therefore on the Eighth or higher Stage, cannot be "far away" from the supreme enlightenment accompanied by the Buddha natures.

3. *Stages of the lady Bodhisattva.* Since the *Śrī-Mālā* glorifies the queen, it is interesting to observe its position on female capabilities. It was general in Buddhist scriptures to place an upper limit on the spiritual progress of women. For example, the Lotus Sūtra maintains (chap. XI, "Apparition of a Stūpa") that a woman cannot occupy any of the five ranks, to wit, Brahma, Indra, protector of one of the four quarters, universal emperor (*cakravartin*), or non-regressing Bodhisattva; and makes consistent remarks elsewhere.[63]

The theory of female limitation went hand in hand with the view that a woman by reason of her merit and devotion can have a transmutation of her sex into that of a male, and in this mode continue the progress to the supreme goal.[64] For example, Abhidharma texts speak of the four ascetic levels concluding with the "supreme mundane natures."[65] Vasubandhu's *Abhidharmakośa* observes that both men and women can engage in the four degrees, but that when a woman masters the supreme mundane natures, she loses her female sex attribute and is converted into a "male."[66] The *Vimalakīrtinirdeśa* somewhat rebels against this theory in the episode of the Devī, to whom Śāriputra suggests a change of sex. The goddess teaches Śāriputra the lesson that the beings who appear as women are no more women than is Śāriputra when, by her magic, he adopted the form of a woman.[67]

The *Śrī-Mālā* is more positive than the *Vimalakīrti* in rejecting this theory of female limitation, and becomes the preeminent scripture for pleading the case for the ladies. This is seen in the queen's constant use of the term "good daughter of the family" along with "good son of the family" as a Bodhisattva on every spiritual level. This terminology is used even for the Bodhisattva who

63 *Lotus Sūtra* (tr. Kern), chaps. VIII, "Destiny of the Five Hundred Monks," and XXII, "Ancient Devotion of Bhaishajya-rāja."

64 See Étienne Lamotte, *L'Enseignement de Vimalakīrti*, pp. 280–81, for references to the literature.

65 The four are known as the "four degrees conducive to penetration" (*nirvedhabhāgīya*), namely, warmth, summits, forbearances consistent with the truth, and supreme mundane natures. A description of them is not relevant here.

66 Louis de La Vallée Poussin, *L'Abhidharmakośa de Vasubandhu* (1925), chap. VI, p. 171.

67 Lamotte, *L'Enseignement de Vimalakīrti*, pp. 280–83.

has renounced "body, life force, and possessions," which our preceding discussion indicates to be a reference to the last three Bodhisattva stages. When the *Śrī-Mālā* allows that a good daughter of the family, by renouncing possessions (having previously renounced body and life force) is endowed with uninterrupted, permanent, and inconceivable merits that are unshared by other sentient beings, it apparently makes her equivalent in the terminology of other scriptures to a Bodhisattva of the Tenth Stage.

Granted that the *Śrī-Mālā* permits women such status, the question arises: What status does the sūtra intend Queen Śrīmālā to have? Prince Shōtoku's commentary on the *Śrī-Mālā* introduced the interpretation that the queen is a Bodhisattva of the Seventh Stage, inspired by the Tathāgata to be eloquent even about the higher stages, but also able to express that doctrine which ordinary persons can grasp.

However, the scripture itself has some indications. In section 13, the Lord is made to say, "Queen, you as well as the Bodhisattvas possessed of the great Dharma are able to hear these two Doctrines. Queen, the rest, the Disciples, accept the two Doctrines only through faith in the Tathāgata." The "Bodhisattvas possessed of the great Dharma" are evidently those elsewhere referred to as having attained power, hence on the Eighth or higher Stages in the ten-stage terminology. The passage shows that the queen is not in that group, and so is beneath the Eighth Stage.

A further evidence is found in Chapter Four when the queen mentions the three kinds of good son or daughter of the family. She herself seems to fit the third kind: "who shrinks from gaining the knowledge of the profound Dharma by himself, thinking, 'I cannot possibly know it; this meaning can only be understood by the Tathāgata himself,' and so keeping the Lord in mind obtains the mental presence of the Lord."

Finally, the Prologue of the sūtra represents the queen in a situation consistent with the "Bodhisattva newly entered in the Great Vehicle." It does not seem to have been the intention of the sūtra to suggest an exalted status for Queen Śrīmālā. The problem of her Bodhisattva Stage seems immaterial to the message of the *Śrī-Mālā*, which teaches that the queen has been inspired to have eloquence about the entire Bodhisattva path and about the "One Vehicle" as it was understood by the Tathāgata, because the queen has obtained the mental presence of the Lord.

III. Doctrine of *Śrī-Mālā*

Vehicle and Nirvāṇa

One Vehicle

The theory of "One Vehicle" is so important in *Śrī-Mālā* that in the original text prior to the imposition of chapter divisions fully half of the entire scripture, namely, our Chapter Three, "Clarifying the Final Meaning," can be considered as the development of "One Vehicle" theory.

According to the *Śrī-Mālā*, the "One Vehicle" (*ekayāna*) is the Great Vehicle (*mahāyāna*) which incorporates all vehicles. The *Śrī-Mālā* agrees with the Lotus Sūtra that the "Great Vehicle" is the Buddha Vehicle which has discovered and taught all Buddhist truth. Another important agreement with the Lotus Sūtra is the application of "One Vehicle" to the nirvāṇa doctrine. The two scriptures agree that there is only one complete nirvāṇa, which belongs to the Tathāgatas; but that there are also partial nirvāṇas which are shown by the Tathāgatas as a means for promoting persons spiritually.[68] The *Śrī-Mālā* takes the "embryo of the Tathāgata" (*Tathāgatagarbha*) as the basis of "One Vehicle." That "embryo" potentiality is not predestined to various enlightenments; rather all sentient beings arrive at an identical enlightenment or nirvāṇa, because their "species" (*gotra*) is precisely that "embryo of the Tathāgata." Accordingly, the theory of One Vehicle rivals the Prajñāpāramitā exegesis of radically different paths and fruits for the Disciples, the Self-Enlightened, and the Bodhisattvas.[69]

68 *Lotus Sūtra*, chaps. VII, "Ancient Devotion," and VIII, "Destiny of the Five Hundred Monks." In the *Śrī-Mālā*, the Tibetan expression for "partial *nirvāṇa*" is *yan lag gi mya ṅan las ḥdas*, which probably has the original Sanskrit of *aṅganirvāṇa*. The same Tibetan expression occurs in Asaṅga's *Samāhitabhūmi* portion of the *Yogācārabhūmi*, for which his explanation (PTT Vol. 109, p. 269–5 to p. 270–1) should here be cited: "Dhyāna [meaning the four standard *dhyāna* of Buddhist meditation] is called 'one's partial *nirvāṇa*' (*tadaṅganirvāṇa*); it is also called 'a sort of *nirvāṇa*' (*paryāyanirvāṇa*). It is 'one's partial *nirvāṇa*' because one's *nirvāṇa* is partial by eliminating only the side of defilement and because one lacks the side of certainty; and it is 'a sort of *nirvāṇa*' because it is not the complete *nirvāṇa*." Mr. Wayman maintains in the Introduction that the *Śrī-Mālā* is a product of the Mahāsāṅghika sect and also maintains in *Analysis of the Śrāvakabhūmi Manuscript* (pp. 25–29) that Asaṅga belongs to the Later Mahīśāsaka sect. The apparent agreement about a "partial *nirvāṇa*" is consistent with André Bareau's finding (*Les sectes*, p. 292) of a remarkable doctrinal agreement of the Mahīśāsaka with the Mahāsāṅghika as well as with the Andhaka who are the Mahāsāṅghika of South India.

69 This exegesis is clearly portrayed by the *Abhisamayālaṃkāra* and affiliated commentarial literature; cf. E. Obermiller, *The Doctrine of Prajñā-pāramitā as Exposed in the Abhisamayālaṃkāra of Maitreya*, reprint from *Acta Orientalia*, Vol. XI, 1932.

Śrī-Mālā's section on "One Vehicle" quickly gets to the heart of the matter with the important phrase "mundane and supramundane virtuous natures," and the section itself exemplifies the meaning in various ways. The *Śrī-Mālā* contrasts those who distinguish superior and inferior natures (*dharma*) (and who do not attain the nirvāṇa-realm) with those who experience the single taste of wisdom and liberation (and who do attain the nirvāṇa-realm). Again, the *Śrī-Mālā* uses the expression "supramundane knowledge" for the nonprogressive form of the four Noble Truths, and by implication classifies as "mundane knowledge" the progressive form of the four Noble Truths whereby one understands natures as superior, middling, and inferior. In the case of resorts, the *Śrī-Mālā* speaks of four mundane resorts[70] which the Lord taught so as to lead beginners in the right direction, and contrasts those resorts with the supramundane resort, the Truth as Cessation of Suffering.

The expressions "mundane" (*laukika*) and "supramundane" (*lokottara*) are ancient in their Pāli forms (*lokiya* and *lokuttara*). However, their use in the Theravādin Buddhism as well as in Asaṅga's Yogācāra system especially based on the Mahīśāsaka school, is quite different from what we find in the *Śrī-Mālā*. For example, in the *Saṃdhinirmocana-sūtra*, the basic scripture of the Yogācāra, the "Maitreya chapter" contains the passage, "Maitreya, one should understand that all the virtuous natures—mundane and supramundane—of either the Disciples, Bodhisattvas, or Tathāgatas, are the fruit of calming (*śamatha*) and clear vision (*vipaśyanā*)" (as cited in Tsoṅ-kha-pa's *Lam rim chen mo*, beginning of *śamatha* [calming of the mind] section). In Asaṅga's exposition, the mundane fruits of "calming" are the meditative attainments of the four Dhyāna levels; the supramundane fruits of "clear vision" are the result of pondering the four Noble Truths.[71] The disagreement is immediately apparent: Asaṅga considers the contemplation of the four Noble Truths to be the supramundane path, whereas the *Śrī-Mālā* has both a mundane and a supramundane "four Noble Truths." Besides, the *Śrī-Mālā* maintains that the Disciples and the Self-Enlightened ones have not eliminated all the secondary defilements on calming and clear vision; hence, in their case, these two procedures are not completely pure and cannot yield the supramundane natures.

The difference between the two approaches lies in the fact that Asaṅga and his ancient tradition employ the terms "mundane" and "supramundane" to apply to various objective domains, while the *Śrī-Mālā* employs those terms for

70 The four resorts are listed in n. 95 to the translation.

71 This is the topic of the Fourth Yogasthāna of Asaṅga's *Śrāvakabhūmi*; cf. Alex Wayman, *Analysis of the Śrāvakabhūmi Manuscript*, pp. 125 ff.

the varying subjective consciousness. When the terms have objective application, such language as "I shall proceed by either the mundane or the supramundane route" can be employed[72]. The "mundane route" turns out to be aimed at "freedom from passion" by meditative ascension through the four Dhyāna heavens of the "realm of form" with consequent endowment of the "five supernormal faculties." The "supramundane route" amounts to realizing the four Noble Truths by pondering certain characteristics of each one, with consequent endowment of the sixth supernormal faculty, "knowledge of flux destruction." In contrast, the *Śrī-Mālā* includes all the religious paths in its One Vehicle; none is superior or inferior from the standpoint of the nirvāṇa-realm or Tathāgata's Enlightenment, accompanied by nondiscrete Buddha natures; and from this nirvāṇa standpoint both the above-mentioned routes are supramundane. But again, from the graded saṃsāra-standpoint accompanied by discrete defiled natures, both those routes are mundane. The *Śrī-Mālā* insists that as long as consciousness is defiled everything is mundane. And according to the Mahāsāṅghika *Mahāvastu*, everything the Tathāgata does—walking, eating, and so forth—is supramundane.[73]

Nirvāṇa and Enlightenment

There is an historical evolution in the concept of nirvāṇa." "Nibbāna" is the Pāli language equivalent of the Sanskrit word "nirvāṇa." In the Abhidharma tradition, nibbāna (later referred to as the Hīnayāna nirvāṇa) contrasts with the phenomenal world (*saṃsāra*). It is usually identified with *pratisaṃkhyā-nirodha* (cessation through understanding each element), which Vasubandhu's *Abhidharmakośa* explains as an unconditioned (or unconstructed, *asaṃskṛta*) fruit of the ascetic life or human agency. The freedom from all phenomenal taints, and even from the subtle forces of sublime meditation itself, is called nirvāṇa without remainder. The one who attains this nirvāṇa is called the Arhat.

The development of early Mahāyāna thought in the form of the Prajñāpāramitā scriptures eroded the clear contrast between nirvāṇa and saṃsāra, so that Nāgārjuna (2d cent. A.D.) could write in his famous *Madhyamaka-kārikā* (XXV, 20):

> Where is the limit of saṃsāra,
> there is the limit of nirvāṇa;
> Not the slightest thing
> whatsoever is between them.

72 *Ibid.*, p. 125.
73 J. J. Jones, tr., *The Mahāvastu*, I, p. 132.

The implication of the *Śrī-Mālā* as understood by the *Ratnagotravibhāga* is to explain nirvāṇa and saṃsāra in a manner whereby they can be mixed (*saṃsṛṣṭa*, "brought forth together") in a "pure and impure state," where purity is the participation of nirvāṇa and impurity the participation of saṃsāra. In our previous discussion of stages of the bodies made of mind, we observed that, in the theory of Bodhisattva stages, the Sixth, Seventh, and Eighth are each a stage in which the person is delicately balanced between nirvāṇa and saṃsāra in the sense that he could enter a quiescent nirvāṇa but stays in saṃsāra in pursuance of his Bodhisattva vow. The Bodhisattva has reached the very state from which the Arhat passes into fractional nirvāṇa but the Bodhisattva avoids that supposed escape and starts a new spiritual life toward the lofty goal of the nirvāṇa-realm which is the Revelation-Enlightenment.

The *Śrī-Mālā* does not deny the early view of Buddhism that the Arhat reaches the unconstructed nirvāṇa, but does deny that this attainment is complete or constitutes the final release from the phenomenal world (*saṃsāra*). Toward the end of the scripture we learn that the one having "knowledge in the precincts of the Dharma" has the "vision of the sleep of the Arhats," a remark consistent with earlier information that the Arhats, the Pratyekabuddhas, and even Bodhisattvas in their last life have a remainder to cultivate of the path leading to the cessation of suffering, and so the Arhats have a remainder of rebirth. Only the Tathāgatas realize the nirvāṇa-realm in the ultimate sense.

The *Śrī-Mālā* insists that what the Arhats believe to be nirvāṇa is in fact a means belonging to the Tathāgatas. The *Ratnagotravibhāga* (p. 56) says that this statement of the *Śrī-Mālā* refers to the *parinirvāṇa* of the Arhats and Pratyekabuddhas: it is a means to keep them from retreating (*avivartana-upāya*), which is a means the complete Buddhas who are sovereign over *dharmas* utilize; it is like the magical city in the midst of a forest appearing to travelers weary from a long journey. This explanation is consistent with the queen's "One Vehicle" theory, since the followers of the Buddhist path are all included in the Great Vehicle, and need only take the Bodhisattva vow to continue beyond the Arhat attainment as Bodhisattvas who have postponed the entrance into the quiescent nirvāṇa. This new theory of nirvāṇa required a metaphysical formulation, and the *Śrī-Mālā* may well be the preeminent early scripture which appropriately states the case.

The *Śrī-Mālā* summarizes its view of nirvāṇa and saṃsāra by positing a constructed and an unconstructed nirvāṇa as well as a constructed and an unconstructed saṃsāra. The *Ratnagotravibhāga* (p. 8) explains, "The 'unconstructed' (*asaṃskṛta*) should be understood as the opposite of the 'constructed.' Here, the 'constructed' (*saṃskṛta*) is said for whatever thing one recognizes as having birth (*utpāda*), continuation (*sthiti*), and destruction (*bhaṅga*)." The closest the *Śrī-Mālā* comes to explaining that passage about nirvāṇa and saṃsāra is when it reports that the Tathāgatagarbha transcends the constructed realm and is the base of constructed Buddha natures as well as the base of external constructed natures that are defilement stores. This confirms that the constructed nirvāṇa is the constructed Buddha natures and that the constructed saṃsāra is the constructed defilement stores. The *Śrī-Mālā* also maintains that the truth Cessation of Suffering is unconstructed; this in effect equates the unconstructed nirvāṇa with the Truth Cessation of Suffering. Only the unconstructed saṃsāra is left unexplained in the *Śrī-Mālā*, although this text implies a connection here with the Tathāgatagarbha, which experiences suffering.

The *Ratnagotravibhāga* (p. 50) quotes that *Śrī-Mālā* passage on the two kinds of both nirvāṇa and saṃsāra, but seems to take for granted that its readers already understand these on an elementary level, for it launches into a subtle discussion about the three bodies made of mind. It represents the "constructed" and the "unconstructed" in terms of the agent by which the body made of mind is both impure and pure, the impurity from saṃsāra and the purity from nirvāṇa. Thus, it explains regarding those three bodies that their saṃsāra is by reason of their being impelled by nonfluxional roots, and that their nirvāṇa is by reason of their not being impelled by fluxional action (*karma*) and defilement (*kleśa*).

The *Śrī-Mālā* means that the unconstructed nirvāṇa is accompanied by the constructed nirvāṇa, and the unconstructed saṃsāra is accompanied by the constructed saṃsāra. There is a special case for bodies made of mind belonging to the Arhats, Pratyekabuddhas, and Bodhisattvas who have attained power. Their constructed saṃsāra is gestation by reason of the nescience entrenchment as the defilement and by reason of nonfluxional action. Their unconstructed nirvāṇa is the freedom from the four static defilements but it is still fractional, a limited vision (like the Zen Buddhist *Satori*), because these persons have not yet gained the innumerable Buddha natures constituting the constructed nirvāṇa.

Now that we understand what the *Śrī-Mālā* means by nirvāṇa, we can appreciate the identification of nirvāṇa with enlightenment. The *Ratnagotravibhāga* appeals to this scripture to illustrate the fifth of its seven "diamond topics," namely, enlightenment as explained by the queen: "Lord, 'incomparable rightly completed enlightenment' is an expression for the nirvāṇa-realm." Here "enlightenment"—the fifth "diamond topic"—is the unconstructed nirvāṇa, which is accompanied by the Buddha natures—the sixth "diamond topic." The *Ratnagotravibhāga* (p. 56) explains the identification of enlightenment with nirvāṇa as follows: "What is called Buddhahood through the Revelation-Enlightenment toward all natures (*dharma*) and [the best of] all aspects, and what is called nirvāṇa through the elimination of impurity along with its flux when there is the great Revelation-Enlightenment—these two are inseparable and indivisible because nondual in the nonfluxional realm."

The *Śrī-Mālā* is not the only Mahāyāna scripture that identifies nirvāṇa-realm with enlightenment. One of the scriptures affiliated with the Tathāgata-garbha literature, called *Jñānālokālaṃkāra-sūtra*, takes a similar position when it states (Narthang, Kg., Mdo, Ga, 446a-5 ff.): "Mañjuśrī, enlightenment is the inseparable ground. Of that, what is the 'ground' and what is the 'inseparable'?" The passage continues with thirteen explanatory pairs of synonymous nature. Thus, when nirvāṇa is the "ground," then it is quiescent as "inseparable"; when enlightenment, it is inactive; when the unconstructed, it is incessant; when Thusness, it is nameless; when the Dharmadhātu, it is abodeless; when true limit (*bhūtakoṭi*), it is not different.

That emphasis on "inseparable ground" is consistent with the remark in the *Śrī-Mālā*, "Therefore the nirvāṇa-realm has a single taste (*ekarasa*). That is to say, the tastes of wisdom and liberation are identical."

TATHĀGATAGARBHA

The Tathāgatagarbha Theory and Scriptures

The Tathāgatagarbha theory is anticipated by the ancient doctrine held by some old Buddhist sects, especially the Mahāsāṅghika, that consciousness is intrinsically pure and defiled by adventitious defilements, and that there is a substratum consciousness (*mūlavijñāna*).[74] The next stage in the development of the theory is found in the Mahāyāna scriptures such as the *Avataṃsaka*, where it is taught that the Buddha's divine knowledge pervades sentient beings, and that its representation in an individual sentient being is the substratum consciousness. When this intrinsically pure consciousness came to be regarded as an element capable of growing into Buddhahood, there was the "embryo (*garbha*) of the Tathāgata (=Buddha)" doctrine, whether or not this term is employed.[75]

74 André Bareau, *Les sectes*, pp. 67–68, 72; also Appendix, p. 277. See Lamotte, *L'Enseignement de Vimalakīrti*, pp. 51–54, for early views on the "pure mind."

75 In the present work, the word *garbha* in the term *tathāgatagarbha* is rendered "embryo" in the sense of causal potentiality for becoming the Tathāgata. The principal meanings of the Sanskrit word *garbha* are "womb," "interior," and "embryo." The "womb" interpretation is prevalent in Chinese translations of the term

In the *Mahāvastu*, the "Vinaya" of a Mahāsāṅghika subsect, it is written, regarding the mother of a Buddha, "Today, O queen, you will give birth to a good youth (*sukumāra*) of immortal embryo (*amara-garbha*), who destroys old age and illness, celebrated and beneficial in heaven and on earth, a benefactor of gods and men."[76]

The scriptures authoritative for the "embryo of Tathāgata" theory in Buddhism are known principally from the treatise edited by E. H. Johnston under the title *Ratnagotravibhāga-Mahāyānottaratantra-śāstra*, and referred to in its Tibetan translation by a portion of that title, *Mahāyānottaratantra-śāstra* or in abbreviation as the *Uttaratantra*. The only scripture alluding to the doctrine by its own title is the *Tathāgatagarbha-sūtra*. Other works concerned with various aspects of the theory are the *Ārya-Śrīmālā-sūtra*, the *Mahāparinirvāṇa-sūtra* (its Tathāgatadhātu chapter), the *Ārya-Aṅgulimālīya-sūtra*, the *Anūnatvāpūrṇatvanirdeśaparivarta* (in Chinese but not Tibetan), and the *Mahābherīhāraka-sūtra*. In addition, certain works are closely related in subject matter, even when not expressly employing the term "embryo of the Tathāgata," and so are utilized in the *Ratnagotravibhāga*. Here there are the *Dhāraṇīśvararājaparipṛcchā* (= *Tathāgatamahākaruṇānirdeśa-sūtra*), the *Jñānālokālaṃkāra-sūtra*, and the *Sāgaramatiparipṛcchā*.[77]

None of the Tathāgatagarbha scriptures had its own Indian commentary known by translation into Chinese or Tibetan,[78] although as was observed earlier

---

tathāgatagarbha beginning with those scriptures which identify this term with the *ālayavijñāna*, a term usually rendered as "store consciousness," where the "store" is understood to be a store of seeds remaining from past actions. The Chinese of the *Śrī-Mālā* employs this "womb" rendition. However, the *Śrī-Mālā* and its associated śāstra, the *Ratnagotravibhāga*, are silent on the term *ālayavijñāna*. The Tibetan translation, *sñiṅ po*, which means "heart," "pith," "essence," seems to agree with the "interior" interpretation of *garbha*. It should be emphasized that neither the Tibetan nor the Chinese translations of the term *tathāgatagarbha* as found in the *Śrī-Mālā* clarifies the intention of the unknown author of the *Śrī-Mālā*. This is because the translators of the Buddhist canon use standard or stereotyped equivalents for certain Sanskrit technical terms in text after text. While the Asian renditions of Sanskrit terms are sometimes suggestive, in the end we must learn how a given term is employed in the particular text being studied. For more information about the term *ālayavijñāna*, see Ruegg, *La théorie*, pp. 499–516.

76 Basak, ed., *Mahāvastu* I, 266.

77 Cf. Takasaki, *A Study*, pp. 34–35; also Ferdinand D. Lessing and Alex Wayman, eds. and trs., *Mkhas grub rje's Fundamentals of the Buddhist Tantras*, pp. 49, 97.

78 While the Tibetan Jonaṅpa school included the *Avikalpapraveśadhāraṇī* in the group, and this work has a commentary by Kamalaśīla translated into Tibetan, examination of the work and its commentary in the Narthang Kanjur and Tanjur discloses no reason for counting it as a Tathāgatagarbha scripture. And of course the Jonaṅpa's inclusion of the *Saṃdhinirmocana-sūtra* was properly rejected by the Gelugpa, per Mkhas grub rje's work as referred to in the preceding note.

Paramārtha attributed such a commentary to Vasubandhu. It seems that none of the scriptures counted in the group aimed at presenting a complete, coherent picture of the Tathāgatagarbha doctrine, and so the author of the *Ratnagotravibhāga* (Discrimination of the jewel species) found it necessary to write a comprehensive treatise for the topic rather than to compose a commentary on one particular scripture.

Those are not the only scriptures which employ the term "Tathāgatagarbha." Both the *Laṅkāvatāra-sūtra* and the *Ghanavyūha-sūtra* employ the term, but identify it with the "store consciousness" (*ālaya-vijñāna*), avoided in the *Ratnagotravibhāga*. Presumably that is why these two sūtras are not included among the standard "Tathāgatagarbha scriptures." Besides, both the *Candrottarādārikā-sūtra* and the *Samādhirāja-sūtra* apparently refer to the Tathāgatagarbha,[79] but not with sufficient emphasis to be included in the group of such scriptures.

Also, the Tathāgatagarbha doctrine is associated with the theory of stages (*bhūmi*), particularly as set forth in the *Mahāvastu* and the *Daśabhūmika-sūtra*. This is the implication of *Śrī-Mālā*, and the *Mahābherīhāraka-sūtra* (Narthang Kg, Mdo, Tsa, 203a) expressly mentions the Seventh, Eighth, and Tenth stages.

Synonyms and Alternate References to the Tathāgatagarbha

Abhayākaragupta (*Muni*, p. 205–2) provides these synonyms for the "embryo of the Tathāgata": "species intrinsically abiding" (*prakṛtistha-gotra*), "support" (*niśraya* and *pratisaraṇa*), "cause" (*hetu*), "holder" (*ādhāra*), "place of adherence" (*pratyupasthāna*), "antecedent" (*pūrvaṃgama*), "base" (*pratiṣṭhā*), "seed" (*bīja*), "element" (*dhātu*), and "the self-existent" (*svabhāva*). The *Śrī-Mālā* has the set "support, holder, base" (*niśraya, ādhāra, pratiṣṭhā*; original Sanskrit in *Ratnagotravibhāga*, p. 73).

Some other terms from the list are found in the *Ratnagotravibhāga*. This text is based on what it calls the "seven adamantine topics," which are (1) Buddha, (2) Dharma, (3) Saṃgha, (4) Element (*dhātu*), (5) Enlightenment (*bodhi*), (6) Merit (*guṇa*), and (7) Act (*karma*). The first three are of course the Three Jewels of Buddhism, here treated as effects or fruits. The fourth, "element," is the "embryo of the Tathāgata" and is "what is to be enlightened" as the "cause" (*hetu*) or the "seed" (*bīja*) of supramundane natures for originating

79 For the *Candrottarādārikā-sūtra*, cf. Nakamura, "A Critical Survey," p. 66; and for the *Samādhirāja-sūtra*, cf. Guenther, *Sgam. Po. Pa: The Jewel Ornament of Liberation*, p. 2.

the Three Jewels. The remaining three adamantine topics are (5) Enlightenment, (6) its ancillaries, which are the immaculate Buddha natures, and (7) the activity of the Buddha as the Tathāgata acts said to number thirty-two. The last three topics are the condition (*pratyaya*) for originating the Three Jewels by purifying the embryo.[80] Abhayākaragupta (*Muni*, p. 229), while referring to the "seven adamantine topics," explains the "cause" as "cause for achieving" (*upādāna-kāraṇa*) and the "condition" as "associative condition" (*sahakāri-pratyaya*).[81] The Sanskrit term for the "cause" shows that it is the material cause for achieving (as clay for the pot). Hence, the associative conditions are to be considered as the purifying agents of that "material" (as the working over and treating of the clay).[82]

The term "Thusness" (*tathatā*) is also employed in a qualified way for the Tathāgatagarbha. According to the *Ratnagotravibhāga* (I, 23), Thusness defiled is the Tathāgatagarbha, and Thusness undefiled is Enlightenment. The *Śrī-Mālā* states, "Lord, 'incomparable rightly completed enlightenment' is an expression for the nirvāṇa-realm. 'Nirvāṇa-realm' is an expression for the Dharmakāya of the Tathāgata." In the *Śrī-Mālā* there are two main conditions for the "embryo of the Tathāgata": either covered by defilements, when it is called only "embryo of the Tathāgata"; or free from defilements, when the "embryo of the Tathāgata" is no more the "embryo" (potentiality) but the Tathāgata (=the Dharmakāya) (actuality).

There are four stock terms applied to the Tathāgatagarbha in *Śrī-Mālā* and affiliated scriptures: "permanent" (*nitya*), "steadfast" (*dhruva*), "calm" (*śiva*), and "eternal" (*śāśvata*). This terminology is especially applied to the Tathāgatagarbha in conditions free from defilement. For example, the *Mahābherīhāraka-sūtra* states at one point (Narthang, Mdo, Tsa, 191b-4): "Kāśyapa, accordingly at the time one becomes a Tathāgata, a Buddha, he is in nirvāṇa, and is referred to as 'permanent,' 'steadfast,' 'calm,' 'eternal,' and 'self' (*ātman*)." The same sūtra states (Tsa, 148b-3, 4): "These Disciples, Self-Enlightened ones, and Bodhisattvas newly entered in the Mahāyāna are incapable of understanding the *parinirvāṇa* of the Buddha Lords as permanent, steadfast, calm, and eternal."

80 E. H. Johnston, ed., *The Ratnagotravibhāga Mahāyānottaratantraśāstra*, text (I, 23, 26) and commentary.

81 The Sanskrit words are based on the Skt. -Tib. equivalences of *Mahāvyutpatti*, No. 4491 and 4492.

82 Cf. Takasaki, *A Study*, pp. 150–52, for the illustration of purification in the case of a precious stone.

The *Anūnatvāpūrṇatvanirdeśaparivarta* supplies reasons for using the four terms:

This Dharmakāya, Śāriputra, is permanent, by reason of being the unalterable true nature with boundless natures (*dharma*). This Dharmakāya, Śāriputra, is steadfast, by reason of being the steadfast refuge at the uttermost limit. This Dharmakāya, Śāriputra, is calm, by reason of being the nondiscursive true nature with nondual natures. This Dharmakāya, Śāriputra, is eternal, by reason of being the unfabricated true nature with indestructible natures.[83]

Queen Śrīmālā also stresses that the Dharmakāya as the purified Tathāgatagarbha has the four exclusive attributes of permanence, pleasure, self, and purity, which are conventionally the four wayward views. According to the *Ratnagotravibhāga* (pp. 31–3), these four fruits issue from the four kinds of Bodhisattva practice, to wit: permanence through contemplation of great compassion (*mahākaruṇā*), pleasure through contemplation of the *samādhis* Gaganagañjā and so on (usually four in number), self through contemplation of Perfection of Insight (*prajñā-pāramitā*), and purity through contemplative conviction (*adhimukti*) in the Doctrine of the Great Vehicle.

Universality of Tathāgatagarbha

A striking feature of the Tathāgatagarbha scriptures is their theory about the universality of Buddhahood potentiality. The *Ratnagotravibhāga* (p. 25) states: "Now, with reference to 'Thusness' (*tathatā*) when stained, it was said, 'All sentient beings have the embryo of the Tathāgata.' " The *Ratnagotravibhāga* (p. 26) presents three senses in which it is said that all sentient beings have the embryo of the Tathāgata: (1) the Tathāgata's Dharmakāya permeates all sentient beings; (2) the Tathāgata's "Thusness" is omnipresent (*avyatibheda*) in them; (3) the Tathāgata's species (*gotra*) occurs in them.

The first sense is derived from the *Tathāgatotpattisaṃbhavanirdeśa* chapter of the *Avataṃsaka-sūtra* as cited in the *Ratnagotravibhāga* (p. 22): "There is no sentient being in the class of sentient beings in whom the Tathāgata's Knowledge (*jñāna*) does not penetrate at all."[84] The second sense is set forth in the *Mahāyāna-Sūtrālaṃkāra* (IX, 37): "Although without distinction in any (being),[85]

83 Johnston, ed., *Ratnagotravibhāga*, text p. 54.

84 Takasaki, *A Study*, p. 189, has determined the scriptural source of the passage, but as usual our translation is from the original Sanskrit.

85 Note that the *Mahāyāna-Sūtrālaṃkāra* does not apparently accept the differing manifestation of Thusness as set forth in our introductory section "Persons on Stages" on the basis of the *Śrī-Mālā*.

'Thusness,' having gone to purity, is the state of 'Thus-gone' (Tathāgata). Therefore, its embryo belongs to all body-holders (*dehin*)." The third sense is given by the *Tathāgatagarbha-sūtra* as quoted in the *Ratnagotravibhāga* (p. 73): "Good son of the family, this is the true nature of the *dharmas:* whether Tathāgatas arise or do not arise, these sentient beings always have the embryo of the Tathāgata."

The *Śrī-Mālā* stresses the difficulty of appreciating the presence of the embryo: "The Tathāgatagarbha is something not seen before or understood before by any Disciple or Self-Enlightened one. It has been seen directly and understood by the Lord." The *Ratnagotravibhāga* mentions as the reason the fact that the embryo is in the condition of defilement and cites two scriptural passages, so far not identified:

> Just as gold is not seen when covered by pebbles and sand and is seen by due purification, likewise the Tathāgata in the world.[86]
> Intrinsically pure, endowed with steadfast nature; covered without by the beginningless sheath which although not originally real, has a limit—it is not seen, like gold covered (by pebbles and sand).[87]

According to the *Ārya-Aṅgulimālīya-sūtra* (Narthang Kg., Mdo, Ma, 248b-2 ff.), it can be seen directly beginning with a Bodhisattva of the Tenth Stage: "Accordingly, only the Bodhisattvas who have reached the Tenth Stage can see by themselves that there is the element of Self in their own bodies." But according to the *Śrī-Mālā*, only the Lord understands it.

Naturally the doctrine of an element of Buddhahood being present in all sentient beings led in some quarters to a viewpoint that all sentient beings are already Buddhas. Hence we read in the *Ārya-Aṅgulimālīya-sūtra* (Narthang Kg., Mdo, Ma, 310a-3 ff.):

> Mañjuśrī Kumārabhūta said the following to [the good son of the family] Aṅgulimālīya: "What is the sense of the 'Tathāgatagarbha' explanation? If there is the embryo of the Tathāgata in all sentient beings, would not all sentient beings be Buddhas no matter if all those sentient beings kill, tell lies, drink to intoxication, engage in unlawful sex, steal, and commit all unvirtuous deeds?" . . . The Lord spoke: "Indeed, the embryo of the Tathāgata is in all sentient beings; but being surrounded by myriads of defilements, it abides like a lantern within a flask."

86 Johnston, ed., *Ratnagotravibhāga*, p. 6, in Prākrit.
87 *Ibid.*, p. 37, in Sanskrit.

The Gelugpa school of Tibet treats this topic in terms of the distinction between a Buddha and a Complete Buddha, referred to respectively as "awakened" (*buddha*) and "expanded" (*vibuddha*). If "embryo of the Tathāgata" had meant the same as "Intrinsic-nature Body" (equivalent to Dharmakāya) and were in the stream of consciousness of all sentient beings, these would all be "expanded" from the outset, and so could not be "awakened" (as we would say of a lotus that if it were already full-blown it could not reach the stage of bud-opening). On the other hand, if there were no embryo of the Tathāgata in their streams of consciousness, there would be no cause (*hetu*) for their becoming "fully expanded" after being "awakened."[88]

By our previous indications, the embryo of the Tathāgata is the material cause, which is sometimes the finished product, just as clay is always clay and is sometimes a pot. And while that embryo is the cause of the Three Jewels, it does not reach fulfillment by itself, because three associate conditions are necessary, as has been stated: enlightenment, merit, and act.

Voidness Knowledge of the Tathāgatagarbha

This is the most difficult aspect of the Tathāgatagarbha doctrine and our conclusions here have a bearing on how to translate certain disputed sentences in the *Śrī-Mālā*.

It has already been pointed out that when the Tathāgatagarbha is free from adventitious defilements, it is the Dharmakāya. Now, Abhayākaragupta (*Muni*, p. 232-2, 3) mentions the position of Vasubandhu that the Dharmakāya is of two kinds, constructed and unconstructed (*saṃskṛta* and *asaṃskṛta*). Also Tsoṅ-kha-pa contrasts an "unconstructed Dharmakāya" with a "Knowledge Dharmakāya."[89] In the terminology of the Tathāgatagarbha doctrine, the unconstructed Dharmakāya is "Thusness undefiled"; and the constructed Dharmakāya, evidently also the Knowledge Dharmakāya, is the set of Buddha natures, which are the Ten Powers, Four Confidences, and so on. The *Śrī-Mālā* reserves the term "Dharmakāya" for the unconstructed kind. The queen mentions that it is accompanied by constructed Buddha natures more numerous than the sands of the Ganges, but does not call these the "constructed Dharmakāya" or "Knowledge Dharmakāya." We have seen in a prior section that the queen calls them the "constructed nirvāṇa."

88 *Mkhas grub rje's Fundamentals . . .*, pp. 49 ff.

89 Tsoṅ-kha-pa, *Zab lam nā-roḥi chos drug gi sgo nas ḥkhrid paḥi rim pa "Yid ches gsum ldan,"* PTT, Vol. 161, pp. 12–13. Here the "unconstructed Dharmakāya" is identified with the objective clear light (*yul gyi ḥod gsal*) and the "knowledge Dharmakāya" is identified with the subjective clear light (*yul can gyi ḥod gsal*). The term "clear light" is employed with its tantric meaning.

Both the Tathāgatagarbha and its ultimate condition of Dharmakāya are credited with knowing in the sense of experiencing. Along these lines, the *Śrī-Mālā* teaches that the Tathāgatagarbha experiences suffering, and alone has "aversion toward suffering as well as longing, eagerness, and aspiration towards nirvāṇa." The *Mahābherīhāraka-sūtra* (Narthang Kg., Mdo, Tsa, 183b-2) holds that defilements distort this experiencing power: "Just as a film over a man's eyes gives a yellow or a blue obscuration, so it is with defilements. The embryo of the Tathāgata is certainly like an eye."

Again, the *Anūnatvāpūrṇatvanirdeśa* introduces a factor of knowledge:

> Śāriputra, that which has been taught by the Tathāgata to be the Dharmakāya, that is this, possessing nondiscrete *dharmas*, and possessing the merit of knowledge that it is not separate, namely, from Tathāgata natures more numerous than the sands of the Ganges.[90]

The point of that passage is that the Dharmakāya is not only not separate from Tathāgata natures but also knows that it is not separate from them. This feature of nonseparate natures along with knowledge occurs in a disputed context of the *Śrī-Mālā*. The translation problem especially devolves about two sentences which are found in sections 8–9 of the *Śrī-Mālā*: "The Dharmakāya and the Meaning of Voidness." They happen to be quoted in the *Ratnagotravibhāga* (p. 55, 76) in striking disagreement with the form of the Tibetan translation of the *Śrī-Mālā-sūtra:*

> / tata ucyate / śūnyas tathāgatagarbho vinirbhāgair muktajñaiḥ sarvakleśakośaiḥ / aśūnyo gaṅgānadīvālikāvyativṛttair avinirbhāgair amuktajñair acintyair buddhadharmair iti /

The Ratnakūṭa version of the *Śrī-Mālā*, both Tibetan and Bodhiruci Chinese, contains these sentences in a form whereby one would understand the original Sanskrit to read **amuktajñaiḥ* and **muktajñair* where the *Ratnagotravibhāga* has respectively *muktajñaiḥ* and *amuktajñair*. In their uninflected forms, the Sanskrit expressions *muktajña and amuktajña* are adjective compounds, and *-jña* here as final member has a standard meaning of "knowing" (something or about something), whence *muktajña* ("knowing that it is liberated or dropped off") and *amuktajña* ("knowing that it is not liberated or not dropped off"). In the *Śrī-Mālā*'s two sentences, the compound *-jña* agrees with *buddhadharma* (Buddha natures) or with *sarvakleśakośa*.

90 Johnston, ed., *Ratnagotravibhāga*, p. 2; the passage is cited as authority for the sixth adamantine topic, "merits."

The solution of the difficulty comes by noticing that the Sanskrit word *mukta* has been translated differently by the Guṇabhadra and the Bodhiruci versions. Ui has shown that the Guṇabhadra Chinese text of *Śrī-Mālā* has rendered the word *mukta* by a character meaning "dropped off" (but this text omits an equivalent to the "knowing").[91] On the other hand, the Bodhiruci text renders *mukta* as "liberated," as does the Tibetan version. Accepting Ui's suggestion that the Guṇabhadra version agrees with the *Ratnagotravibhāga* wording of the sentences, we would translate the two sentences as follows:

> Lord, the Tathāgatagarbha is void of all the defilement-stores, which are discrete and knowing as dropped off.
>
> Lord, the Tathāgatagarbha is not void of the Buddha natures, which are nondiscrete, inconceivable, more numerous than the sands of the Ganges, and knowing as not dropped off.

We would translate the Ratnakūṭa form of the sentences as follows:

> Lord, the Tathāgatagarbha is void of all the defilement-stores, which are discrete and knowing as not liberated.
>
> Lord, the Tathāgatagarbha is not void of the Buddha natures, which are [nondiscrete,] inconceivable, more numerous than the sands of the Ganges, and knowing as liberated.

In fact, both translations suffer from obscurity: "knowing as dropped off" is as opaque as "knowing as not liberated."

We appeal to the *Ratnagotravibhāga* (II, 23), which mentions two levels of the Tathāgata's knowledge:[92]

> [His] knowledge (*jñāna*) is held to be without flux by reason of cessation of defilements together with impregnations; and held to be pervasive because neither attached nor impeded.

91 Hakuju Ui, *Hōshōron kenkyū*, pp. 463–64. The translation of the Sanskrit sentence has also been discussed in the article by Ryūshin Uryūzu, "Shōmangyō no chibetto-yaku to kūshisō." A Western treatment is in David Seyfort Ruegg, *La théorie*, "Avinirbhāga, sambaddha et amuktajña comme épithètes des qualités de l'Absolu," pp. 257–361.

92 Of these two levels, the first, as pointed out in our earlier introductory material, pertains to the body made of mind belonging to the Bodhisattva who has attained power and who is thus on the pure and impure stages which are the last three Bodhisattva stages. The second aspect pertains to the Buddha stage. Concerning the flux (*āsrava*) mentioned in the first half of the verse as well as a number of times in

Accordingly, in the above translation of the *Ratnagotravibhāga* form of the sentences, where *mukta* is rendered "dropped off," the meaning is that the Lord's knowledge pervades the defilement-stores with the knowing that they are dropped off from the Tathāgatagarbha, and pervades the Buddha natures with the knowing that they are not dropped off from the Tathāgatagarbha. On the other hand, in the above translation of the Ratnakūṭa form of the sentences, where *mukta* is rendered "liberated," the meaning is that the Lord's knowledge pervades the defilement-stores with the knowing that they are not in the state of liberation, and pervades the Buddha natures with the knowing that they are in the state of liberation. In this light, even though the *Ratnagotravibhāga* and the Ratnakūṭa disagree in the literal wording of the sentences, it is possible to understand them in a mutually consistent manner. The real difference is in the translation of the word *mukta*.

But then it might be asked, which is the earlier—the form of the sentences in the Ratnakūṭa or the form cited by the *Ratnagotravibhāga*? This is a difficult question, but two sorts of consideration for reply occur to us. As the consideration of context, we notice that the *Ratnagotravibhāga* does not cite the two sentences on account of the expressions *muktajña* and *amuktajña* but for the sake of other expressions in those sentences. That is, it quotes (at p. 55) one of the sentences to show "the meaning that the Buddha natures are non-discrete" (*buddhadharmāvinirbhāgārthaḥ*), and (at p. 76) both sentences in a discussion about defilement and voidness. However, the *Śrī-Mālā* itself at that place in the scripture speaks about two voidness knowledges of the Tathāgata. The queen clarifies these two as belonging not to the Tathāgatagarbha but exclusively to the Tathāgata, who thus knows the Tathāgatagarbha. In the two sentences revealing these two knowledges, the disputed phrases are the only expressions that contain any word meaning "knowledge" or "knowing." It follows that the *Śrī-Mālā* context, while somewhat obscure, does indeed apply to the disputed phrases; and this fact does suggest a priority for the Ratnakūṭa wording of the sentences. As the consideration of doctrine, it seems to us that the Ratnakūṭa interpretation of *mukta* as "liberated" stresses religious values, while the other interpretation of *mukta* as "dropped off" or "detached" is contrary to a famous verse included by the *Ratnagotravibhāga* (p. 76):

---

the present work, there are four kinds in a traditional list (Edgerton, *Buddhist Hybrid Sanskrit Dictionary*, p. 122): that of desires (*kāma*), of generation (*bhava*), of nescience (*avidyā*), and of views (*dṛṣṭi*). The knowledge that these fluxes have ceased (*āsrava-kṣayajñāna*) is the sixth in the traditional list of six supernormal faculties (*abhijñā*). Edgerton also (*Dictionary*, p. 122) cites *Lalitavistara* 351.1, *śuṣkā āśravā na puna śravanti*, which means, "the fluxes, dried up, flow no more."

So there is nothing to be removed
and nothing to be added;
Reality should be seen as Reality,
and the seer of Reality is liberated.[93]

Therefore, we have accepted the Ratnakūṭa reading in our translation of the *Śrī-Mālā*.

Tathāgatagarbha and Ālayavijñāna

Two works that were very influential in Chinese Buddhism, the *Laṅkāvatāra-sūtra* and *The Awakening of Faith* identify the Tathāgatagarbha with the *ālayavijñāna* (store consciousness). The *Laṅkāvatāra-sūtra* (pp. 222–223) has a remarkable passage appealing to Queen Śrīmālā's authority:

Mahāmati, if there were no Tathāgatagarbha referred to as *ālayavijñāna*, then, in the absence of the Tathāgatagarbha referred to as *ālayavijñāna*, no evolution, no deterioration would take place. But evolution and deterioration belong to both the immature and the noble ones. Also, while abiding in a pleasant state during the present life and future noble destiny due to their inner consciousness, the yogins do not cast off their burden and are hard to deflect. Mahāmati, this domain of Tathāgatagarbha "*ālayavijñāna*" is intrinsically pure, but is impure because it has been defiled by the adventitious defilements going with the discursive views of all the Disciples, Self-Enlightened ones, and heretics. Not so the Tathāgatas! They have direct perception of that domain, like a myrobalan fruit [manifesting (itself)] on the palm of the hand.[94] This, Mahāmati, I revealed in connection with Queen Śrīmālā and I empowered other Bodhisattvas of subtle, wise, and pure discrimination [to know] that there is the Tathāgatagarbha referred to as *ālayavijñāna*, along with seven perceptions (*vijñāna*), for the sake of revealing the egolessness

93 Takasaki, *A Study*, pp. 300–1, repeats the nine occurrences of the verse reported by La Vallée Poussin in *Mélanges chinois et bouddhiques*, I, 394; and adds to the list the mention of the verse in the *Buddhagotraśāstra*.

94 The word "myrobalan" stands both for a certain tree indigenous to India and for its fruit. There are three varieties of myrobalan, known in Sanskrit as *vibhītakī* (Terminalia belerica), *harītakī* (Terminalia chebula), and *āmalakī* (Phyllanthus emblica), the berry-type fruits of which are employed in traditional Indian medicine which ascribes to them wondrous healing properties, as discussed in Alex Wayman, "Notes on the Three Myrobalans," *Phi Theta Annual* (Oriental Languages Honor Society, Berkeley), no. 5 (1954–55), pp. 63–77. The myrobalan also figures as a stock illustration, as in this passage of the *Laṅkāvatāra-sūtra,* for the creative power of thought, which in high levels of meditative praxis can materialize the unseen worlds in the manner of the myrobalan berry concretized upon the palm of the hand.

of *dharmas* to the Disciples attached to its evolution. The Tathāgata realm that was revealed when I empowered Queen Śrīmālā is not a realm accessible to the Disciples, Self-Enlightened ones, heretics, and logicians.

Despite this identification of the two terms, in India they were distinguished as cardinal doctrines of rival schools of thought. According to the *Śrī-Mālā* and consistent tradition, the permanent Tathāgatagarbha is both the reason for phenomenal life (*saṃsāra*) and the aspiration toward and attainment of nirvāṇa. Asaṅga and his followers of the Yogācāra school teach that the *ālayavijñāna* is responsible for phenomenal life and ceases when there is "nirvāṇa without remainder." Asaṅga mentions that the persons who lack the *ālayavijñāna* are the Arhat, the Pratyekabuddha, the nonregressing Bodhisattva, and the Tathāgata.[95] According to *Śrī-Mālā* all these beings have the Tathāgatagarbha, with the difference that only the Tathāgata both sees and understands it. It is plain that when the *Laṅkāvatāra-sūtra* identifies the two terms, this scripture necessarily diverges in the meaning of one or both of the terms from the usage of the term Tathāgatagarbha in the earlier *Śrī-Mālā* or of the term *ālayavijñāna* in the subsequent Yogācāra school. Johnston, in the Foreword (p. xiii) to his edition of the *Ratnagotravibhāga*, takes note of that *Laṅkāvatāra-sūtra* passage "which is avowedly based on the *Āryaśrīmālāsūtra*," and concludes, as we are forced to do, "The difference between the two doctrines is as obvious as the fact there is some genetic relationship between them."

A direct relationship between the two doctrines is established by their both citing this verse from among the few verses preserved of the lost *Mahāyāna-Abhidharma-sūtra*:

> The element from beginningless time is the substratum of all the dharmas. Owing to its existence, there is every [phenomenal] destiny as well as the attainment of nirvāṇa.[96]

In the *Ratnagotravibhāga*, the "element" (*dhātu*) is explained as the Tathāgatagarbha, while in Asaṅga's Yogācāra school the "element" is explained as the *ālayavijñāna*.

The most challenging sentence in the above passage from the *Laṅkāvatāra-sūtra* is the one containing "the Tathāgatagarbha referred to as *ālayavijñāna*,

95 *Viniścaya-saṃgrahaṇī*, PTT, Vol. 110, p. 238–3.

96 As is pointed out by Takasaki, *A Study*, p. 290, this verse, which is cited in the *Ratnagotravibhāga*, p. 62, is also quoted in the *Mahāyānasaṃgraha-bhāṣya* of Vasubandhu and in Sthiramati's commentary on Vasubandhu's *Triṃśikā*. A discussion of the verse from the Vijñānavādin standpoint is found in Louis de La Vallée Poussin, *Vijñaptimātratāsiddhi*, I (Paris, 1928), 169–72.

along with seven perceptions." This is evidently intended as a solution for *Śrī-Mālā*'s obscure passage about a sixfold group of perceptions (*vijñāna*) and a further perception, unnamed by the scripture, in all constituting the seven momentary natures. In the Yogācāra-type terminology of the *Laṅkāvatāra*, the seven momentary natures are the "evolving perceptions" (*pravṛtti-vijñāna*), namely the five based on the outer sense, the sixth perception based on the mind itself, and the seventh one called the "defiled mind" (*kliṣṭa-manas*). Previously ("Stages of the 'Bodies Made of Mind' ") we have shown how the doctrine of Dependent Origination is essential to understanding the *Śrī-Mālā*. Now we can further suggest that the queen's terminology of an undefined *vijñāna* is consistent with early Buddhist terminology of Dependent Origination, the famous twelve-membered formula in which an undefined *vijñāna* is the third member. While the Chinese and Japanese commentaries that we utilized did not, when commenting on that passage of the *Śrī-Mālā*, mention what we take as a solution, we are reasonably certain that the queen intends the further *vijñāna* to be that member of Dependent Origination, momentary in its application to the ordinary person who has "discontinuous passing away," and intends the sixfold group to constitute the *vijñāna* as one of the five personality aggregates.

However, there is no reason for identifying the Tathāgatagarbha with the third member of Dependent Origination, and to the extent that the Yogācāra school identifies this member with the *ālayavijñāna*, to that extent the *ālayavijñāna* must diverge from the Tathāgatagarbha. Indeed, in the Yogācāra school, the *ālayavijñāna* was understood to be the equivalent of the "appropriating consciousness" (*ādāna-vijñāna*) of a celebrated verse in the scripture *Saṃdhinirmocana:*

> The "appropriating consciousness," profound and subtle, proceeds with all seeds like a violent stream. I did not teach it to the spiritually immature, lest they would imagine it to be a self.[97]

While Asaṅga was apparently silent about assigning his *ālayavijñāna* (=*ādāna-vijñāna*) to a member of Dependent Origination, his later school definitely implies the identification with the third member and thus seals the difference with the

97 For this verse, see *ibid.*, pp. 173–74, where it is mentioned as being quoted by Sthiramati on the *Triṃśikā* as well as in the *Yogaśāstra*. It is also quoted in Candrakīrti's *Madhyamakāvatāra* (PTT, Vol. 98, p. 136–1) and in Abhayākaragupta's *Muni* (PTT, Vol, 101, p. 265–5). The earliest quotation of it would be in Asaṅga's *Mahāyānasaṃgraha*, chap. I, p. 4; cf. Étienne Lamotte, *La Somme du Grand Véhicule d'Asaṅga*, pp. 14–15.

Tathāgatagarbha.[98] If the Yogācāra school had identified the third member of Dependent Origination with their "defiled mind" (*kliṣṭa-manas*), this would have left their *ālayavijñāna* free to approach the Tathāgatagarbha in usage. Perhaps Yogācāra, like the school of the *Laṅkāvatāra-sūtra*, had such a view when it identified the two doctrines.

However, the *Laṅkāvatāra-sūtra* and the *Ratnagotravibhāga* are not necessarily at odds in the usage of two important terms, the *āśraya-parāvṛtti* in the former and the *āśraya-parivṛtti* in the latter. The *Laṅkāvatāra* (p. 81) teaches that there is a "revolution of the basis" (*āśraya-parāvṛtti*), referring to the *ālayavijñāna*, in the Eighth Stage of the Bodhisattva, where according to the implication of the *Śrī-Mālā* one obtains the body of a Buddha. The *Ratnagotravibhāga* (p. 21) teaches that there is a "reversion of the basis" (*āśraya-parivṛtti*), referring to the Tathāgatagarbha, in the Buddha Stage, where according to the *Śrī-Mālā* the Tathāgatagarbha is accompanied by the innumerable Buddha natures. The *Śrī-Mālā* does not employ either of those two terms and does not directly say that the Tathāgatagarbha reverts to a pregenetic condition of Dharmakāya. This is part of the mystery of the Tathāgatagarbha; and the *Śrī-Mālā* concludes, "The Lord alone has the Eye for it."

98 Asaṅga in his *Mahāyānasaṃgraha* (*idem*) identifies the "appropriating consciousness" (*ādāna-vijñāna*) with his *ālayavijñāna*. It is called "appropriating consciousness" because it appropriates and holds together the material organs in all embodiments (*ātmabhāva*). Vasubandhu's commentary (*La Somme* . . . ,) chap. I, p. 15, takes the decisive commentarial step by explaining its role at the time of rebirth (*pratisaṃdhi-bandha*) as being the "stream of consciousness" (*saṃtāna-vijñāna*). Consistent with this position, Vasubandhu in his commentary *Pratītyasamutpādādi-vibhaṅga-nirdeśa* (PTT, Vol. 104, p. 286–4) explains that the *vijñāna* being reborn is not the group of six *vijñānas* (*ñiṅ mtshams sbyor ba na rnam par śes pa gaṅ yin pa de rnam par śes paḥi tshogs drug ma yin pas*); and since he has this discussion in his commentary on *vijñāna* as the third member of Dependent Origination, it is obvious that he intends this third member called *vijñāna* to be the *ādāna-vijñāna* of the *Saṃdhinirmocana-sūtra* verse.

THE LION'S ROAR OF QUEEN ŚRĪMĀLĀ

A Mahāyāna Scripture

Translated from the Tibetan, Chinese, and Japanese renditions, and Sanskrit fragments

PROLOGUE

This is what I once heard.[1] The Lord was dwelling in the Jetavana of Anāthapiṇḍika's park[2] in Śrāvastī.[3] King Prasenajit of Kosala[4] and his Queen Mallikā had believed in the Buddha's Doctrine for only a short time. Now they engaged in conversation.

"O great king, our daughter Queen Śrīmālā is profound and clever. If she were just to see the Buddha, she would understand the Doctrine with little difficulty and she would have no doubts about the Buddha's teaching."

1 More literally: "Thus by me it was heard upon an occasion." This translation includes the expression *ekasmin samaye* (upon an occasion), the time component, with the first sentence, rather than as customary with the second sentence by the rendition "once" in "Once the Lord was dwelling . . ." See John Brough, " 'Thus Have I Heard . . .'," *Bulletin of the School of Oriental and African Studies*, XIII (Part 2, 1950), 416–26. Another learned article, by Dr. N. H. Samtani, "The Opening of the Buddhist Sūtras," *Bhāratī* (Bulletin of the College of Indology, No. 8, Part II, 1964–65), pp. 47–63, shows that the Pāli commentator Buddhaghosa was aware of both interpretations based on punctuation and seems to have favored the modern punctuation which includes the *ekasmin samaye* with the second sentence. These researches indicate that the early Buddhist scriptures intended the time component to go with the second sentence, while Mahāyāna texts reinterpreted the punctuation to accentuate the first sentence. *Śrī-Mālā*'s Epilogue expands the words "was heard" in this manner: "Having embraced this scripture in the presence of the Lord, and having learned it by heart, . . ." Accordingly, the initial sentences of the *Śrī-Mālā* have been understood in the Mahāyāna manner, justifying acceptance in this case of Brough's suggestion.

2 According to Bimala Churn Law, *Indological Studies*, Part IV, pp. 123 ff., Prince Jeta laid out the grove which was the first permanent center of Buddhism. The banker Sudatta paid for the monastery. The Buddha called the monastery Jetavana in honor of the prince, and called the place Anāthapiṇḍika (also Anāthapiṇḍada [who gives alms to the helpless]) in honor of the banker who was called by that name because of his generosity.

3 At the time of the Buddha, Sāvatthī (Skt. Śrāvastī) was the capital of Kosala. On the ancient location is the modern Sāheṭh-Māheṭh, on the borders of the Gonda and Bahraich districts of Oudh (U.P.); cf. Law, *Indological Studies*, Part IV, p. 123.

4 Kosala is second in the traditional list of the sixteen Mahājanapadas, or states. In the Buddha's time Kosala had subjugated Kāsī (the district of modern Benares); it was northwest of Magadha, with which it had conflicts; cf. G. P. Malalasekera, *Dictionary of Pāli Proper Names*.

King Prasenajit said to Queen Mallikā: "We should send a message to Queen Śrīmālā to arouse her interest."

Queen Mallikā replied: "Yes, this is the time."

Then King Prasenajit and Queen Mallikā composed a letter praising the infinite merit of the Tathāgata and sent it by a court official named Chandra.[5] He proceeded to Ayodhyā,[6] then to the ladies' quarters of the palace, bowed to Queen Śrīmālā, exchanged salutations, and handed Queen Śrīmālā the letter.

CHAPTER ONE

Eliminating All Doubts

1. Praises of the Infinite Merit of the Tathāgata

The queen, with joyful respect to her father and mother, touched her head with it, and read it, then stating, "The letter has an auspicious meaning." Convinced of the meaning, she touched it with her head, deeply moved with wonder, and spoke these verses before her retinue and Chandra:

> It is said that the voice of a Buddha is most rare in the world. If this saying be true, I must serve thee.
>
> If the Lord Buddha may come for the sake of the world, may he, with compassion, come here on behalf of the teaching for me!

At that very instant, the Lord approached in the space [in front], and she saw the inconceivable[7] body of the Buddha seated there, emitting

5 The Tibetan gives his name in longer form, *yid brtan pa zla ba lta bu*, perhaps *Candrāpta (trustworthy as the moon).

6 Ayodhyā on the banks of the Sarayū was also called Sāketa, and there is a theory that Ayodhyā and Sāketa were adjoining cities. In older times Sāketa was the capital of Kosala. Cf. Law, *Indological Studies*, Part III, pp. 7–8. Ayodhyā is associated with the "solar race of kings," starting with the legendary King Īkṣvāku. It is the capital city in the Hindu epic *Rāmāyaṇa*. In classical times, it was here that Asaṅga converted his brother Vasubandhu to the Mahāyāna, and Vasubandhu composed Mahāyāna commentaries and died.

7 "Inconceivable" in Tibetan and Bodhiruci; "incomparable" in Guṇabhadra.

pure light rays.[8] Queen Śrīmālā and her retinue respectfully bowed with folded hands at their heads, and she praised the best of speakers:

> Lord, there is nothing comparable to your bodily form and glory.[9] I bow to you, the Lord of the world, matchless and incomparable.
>
> Your bodily form and knowledge are unimaginable. Your Buddha nature does not perish; so it is right to take refuge in you, the *muni*.[10]
>
> With matchless skill you have overcome the faults of body and mind.[11] I bow to you, King of the Doctrine, who have acquired the stage without loss.[12]
>
> You are the Lord with knowledge body, who has comprehended all the knowable. I bow to you who have attained the ultimate of all the Buddha natures.

8 Chi-tsang (pp. 40–41) explains that this pure light is not the oval of light around the Buddha's body or his head halo, but is the light rays issuing from his pores and limbs; and he explains that these light rays remove the darkness and defilement of sentient beings.

9 Shōtoku Taishi (pp. 22–23) mentions that "bodily form" is the *rūpa-kāya* (Form Body) and "glory" the Dharmakāya. Hence, these are the two Buddha bodies according to the Prajñāpāramitā scriptures and the works of Nāgārjuna.

10 *Muni* is a title of the Buddha, often translated into English as "sage," and rendered into Tibetan as "capable one." It frequently occurs as part of the Buddha's name, Śākyamuni (capable one of the Śākya clan). An equivalent to *muni* is lacking in the two Chinese renditions.

11 The Tibetan interposes "speech," which is not in either Chinese version. According to Shōtoku Taishi (p. 23), the faults of mind are the three poisons, which are lust, hatred, and delusion, as well as the four wayward ideas that are listed elsewhere in the *Śrī-Mālā*. He mentions (pp. 23–24) another interpretation apparently agreeing with the Tibetan text regarding "speech," namely that there are three sins of mind, four of speech, and three of body (see n. 18, below).

12 Shōtoku Taishi (p. 24) explains that this is the stage of diamond mind which cannot be conquered by the two māras called "son of the gods" and "defilement," but which has not been freed of the other two māras called "personality aggregates" and "death," and so is called "stage difficult to conquer." This is the Fifth Bodhisattva Stage, in Sanskrit *Sudurjayā*; and Har Dayal, *The Bodhisattva Doctrine*, p. 288, cites Candrakīrti's explanation of the name "difficult to conquer" as referring to the inability of the "son of the gods" māras to conquer that Stage. Another interpretation advanced by Shōtoku Taishi is that it is the Buddha Stage which the four māras cannot conquer. Saeki (p. 40) states that this stage of diamond mind is the stage preceding the Buddha Stage; therefore, although he does not specifically mention it, this is the Tenth Bodhisattva Stage where the Bodhisattva is referred to as "King of the Doctrine." The Tibetan "stage without loss" seems to agree with Guṇabhadra's "difficult-to-conquer stage" while the Bodhiruci version differs with "inconceivable stage."

Homage to you, the infinite. Homage to you, beyond comparison. Homage to you, whose nature is matchless. Homage to you, whose form is limitless.[13]

May the Lord now protect me and quicken the seed of enlightenment.[14] May the *muni* benefit me in this and subsequent lives.

The Lord spoke forth: "Queen, in your former lives I have made you practice toward enlightenment; and in future lives I shall assist you." Queen Śrīmālā prayed: "Whatever the merit I have performed in this and in other lives, by that merit, Lord, may I always see you, assisting me."

Thereupon, Queen Śrīmālā along with all her lady attendants and entire retinue bowed to the feet of the Lord. The Lord prophesied to Queen Śrīmālā amid the assembled group that she would attain the incomparable right perfected enlightenment.

"Queen, by reason of your virtuous root[15] formed of the merits accumulated by praising the genuine qualities of the Tathāgata, you, for incalculable aeons, will experience perfect sovereignty among gods and men. In all your lives you will not fail to see me. Just as you now praise me face to face, so you will continue praising. And you will also make offerings to innumerable Buddha Lords.

"After 20,000 aeons you will become the Tathāgata-Arhat-Samya-

13 This is a thesis of the Mahāsāṅghikas and of their Lokottaravādin subsect (Bareau, *Les sectes bouddhiques*, pp. 58–59, 76). Paramārtha (*ibid*, p. 59) explains three ways in which the body of the Buddha is limitless: 1) limitless in measure, i.e. limitless in greatness or smallness; 2) limitless in number, i.e. limitless in its multiple and simultaneous appearances to sentient beings; 3) limitless in causes, i.e. limitless in the various virtuous roots serving as causes for the natures (*dharma*) that constitute the body of the Buddha.

14 Śāntideva's *Śikṣāsamuccaya* (London, 1922; Cecil Bendall and W. H. D. Rouse, trs., pp. 8–9) gives a number of illustrations of how the thought of enlightenment is aroused by various external stimuli and sometimes by Tathāgatas (=Buddhas) in disguise.

15 According to the *Abhidharma-kośa* (de La Vallée Poussin, tr., Chapter II, p. 160), there are three virtuous roots: absence of greed, absence of hatred, absence of delusion (=insight). These are the roots of the universal virtuous elements in every virtuous consciousness, namely, faith, striving, indifference, modesty, shame, absence of greed, absence of hatred, non-injury, catharsis, carefulness.

ksambuddha Samantaprabha. At that time, in your Buddha land[16] there will be no evil destiny.[17] Besides, at that time the sentient beings will stay on the path of ten virtuous actions;[18] those beings will not have sickness or old age or disagreeable disturbances; and even the names of the path of unvirtuous actions will not be mentioned.

"Any sentient being born in that Buddha land will surpass the Paranirmitavaśavartin deities[19] in pleasure; glory of shape and color; splendor in the sense objects of form, sound, odor, smell, tangibles; and ecstasy of that sentient being in all enjoyments.

16 For the theory of Buddha lands or fields, and their ruling Buddhas, see J. J. Jones, tr., *Mahāvastu*, I, 95–99. This discussion occurs under the heading of the "Sixth Bhūmi" or Sixth Bodhisattva Stage. The implication that a sixth-stage Bodhisattva is associated (for the first time) with some Buddha field is a Mahāsāṅghika addition to the theory about the "bodies made of mind" belonging to the Arhats, Pratyekabuddhas, and Bodhisattvas who have attained power, which start on the Sixth Stage, for which see above, Introduction. Saburō Iyenaga, in his *Jōdai Bukkyō shisō kenkyū*, p. 126, extensively discusses the theory that Shōtoku believed in the Amida type of pure land, by consideration of his commentary on the *Vimalakīrti*. It is surprising that Iyenaga does not mention there the *Śrī-Mālā*, or Shōtoku's commentary on it, since the *Śrī-Mālā* has this description of a Buddha land, and implies that beings with "inconceivable transference" are born there.

17 The "five destinies" of ancient Buddhism include three evil destinies: animals, hungry ghosts (*preta*), and hellish beings. Good destinies are gods and men. When the list is increased to six, it is by addition of the class of *asuras* (demigods) who fight with the gods. According to Lin Li-kouang, *L'Aide-Mémoire de la Vraie Loi*, p. 24, the *asuras* are of two kinds, those which are a privileged type of *preta*, and those which are included among the animals.

18 The path of ten virtuous actions is always explained as the abstention from the path of unvirtuous actions, three of body, four of speech, and three of mind. The evils performed with the body are killing, stealing, and obscene behavior; those with the speech are lies, slander, harsh language, and frivolous talk; those with the mind are covetousness, malice, and wayward views. For more information, see, for example, Lin Li-kouang, *ibid.*, pp. 246–53. But the two Chinese translations omit reference to the ten.

19 The Paranirmitavaśavartin deities constitute the highest of the six classes of "passion deities" in the "realm of Desire" (*kāma-dhātu*) according to Buddhist mythology. The other five are the Cāturmahārājakāyikas, Trāyastriṃśas, Yāmas, Tuṣitas, and Nirmāṇaratis. They are apparently called "passion deities" because they engage in sexual commerce while always preserving their sexual power. The Paranirmitavaśavartin deities agree with the Nirmāṇaratis in non-tantric Buddhism (cf. Lin Li-kouang, p. 55), obtaining their satisfaction by hearing and smelling; in tantric Buddhism (cf. Lessing and Wayman, *Mkhas grub rje's Fundamentals of the Buddhist Tantras*, pp. 168–69) the Paranirmitavaśavartin deities obtain their joy by gazing.

"Queen, any sentient beings born in that Buddha land will also be installed in the Great Vehicle. Accordingly, Queen, at that time the beings who have created virtuous roots will all gather in that Buddha land."

While Queen Śrīmālā was hearing the sublime prophecy, uncountable gods and men were inspired to be born in that Buddha land. And the Lord prophesied that all of them would be born in that world-region.

2. Ten Great Vows

Thereupon, Queen Śrīmālā, having heard the prophecy about herself directly from the Lord, joined her hands in salutation and made ten great vows:

(1) "Lord, from now on, and until I attain enlightenment, I hold to this first vow, that I shall not permit any thought of violating morality.

(2) "Lord, from now on, and until I attain enlightenment, I hold to this second vow, that I shall not allow any thought of disrespect toward the teachers (*guru*).

(3) "Lord, from now on, and until I attain enlightenment, I hold to this third vow, that I shall not allow any thought of anger and ill will toward sentient beings.

(4) "Lord, from now on, and until I attain enlightenment, I hold to this fourth vow, that I shall not allow any thought of jealousy toward the glory of others and the perfections of others.

(5) "Lord, from now on, and until I attain enlightenment, I hold to this fifth vow, that I shall not allow any thought of covetousness, no matter how meager the donated food.

(6) "Lord, from now on, and until I attain enlightenment, I hold to this sixth vow, that I shall not accumulate wealth for my own use, but shall deal with it to assist the poor and friendless.

(7) "Lord, from now on, and until I attain enlightenment, I hold to this seventh vow, that with the four articles of conversion[20] I

20 There are four articles of conversion, listed in the *Saṃgīti-sutta* of the *Dīgha-Nikāya*, which are considered to mature the sentient beings. They are: 1) giving, equal to the Mahāyāna "Perfection of Giving" (*dāna-pāramitā*); 2) fine, pleasant speech; 3) concordant acts; 4) oneself serving as an example. By the first one, the subject becomes a fit vessel, psychologically prepared to listen to the Doctrine. By the second one, faith is aroused in him toward the Doctine that is taught. By the third

shall benefit the sentient beings and not convert them for my own sake; indeed, I shall seek to convert the sentient beings with my mind unoccupied with material things, ever unsatisfied, and not retreating.

(8) "Lord, from now on, and until I attain enlightenment, I hold to this eighth vow, that when in the future I observe sentient beings who are friendless, trapped and bound, diseased, troubled, poor and miserable, I shall not forsake them for a single moment until they are restored. Lord, seeing them afflicted by suffering, I shall liberate them from each of those sufferings; having conferred goods upon them, I shall leave them.

(9) "Lord, from now on, and until I attain enlightenment, I hold to this ninth vow, that when I see persons with sinful occupations such as dealing in pigs, and those who violate the Doctrine and Discipline[21] proclaimed by the Tathāgata, I shall not take it lightly; and wherever my residence in towns, villages, cities, districts, and capitals, I shall destroy what should be destroyed and shall foster what should be fostered. Why so? Lord, by destroying and by fostering, the Illustrious Doctrine will long remain in the world, the bodies of gods and men will thrive, and evil destinies will fade. And the Lord, having turned the Wheel of the Doctrine, will continue to turn the Wheel of the Doctrine.

(10) "Lord, from now on, and until I attain enlightenment, I hold to this tenth vow, that, having embraced the Illustrious Doctrine,[22] I shall not forget it even in a single thought. Why so? Lord,

---

one, he is made to work in accordance with the Teaching. By the fourth one, he is led to continue training his mind accordingly. See Alex Wayman, "Buddhism," in *Historia Religionum*, II.

21 The terminology "Doctrine and Discipline" (*dharma-vinaya*) is the ancient comprehensive reference to the Buddhist scriptures. In Pāli, the two are the *vinaya* and the *dhamma*. In the First Council held the year after the Buddha's passing, Upāli rehearsed the *vinaya* and Ānanda the *dhamma*. With the growth of a new canon called in Sanskrit the Abhidharma, this class of writing was added to the former two to form what is called "the three baskets" (*tripiṭaka*). The *Śrī-Mālā*, by using the terminology "Doctrine and Discipline," may be expressing its adherence to the old tradition of only two divisions in the Buddhist scriptures. But the two Chinese translations mention only "Discipline."

22 Śāntideva, just prior to his quotation from the *Śrī-Mālā* in the *Śikṣāsamuccaya*, explains (Vaidya ed., p. 26) what is meant by "embrace of the Illustrious Doctrine": "It is this way:—He should guard his embodiment and so on, 'by not leaving the spiritual guide' and 'by constant perusal of the scriptures,' for the instructions of

if one forgets the Illustrious Doctrine, he forgets the Great Vehicle. If he forgets the Great Vehicle, he forgets the Perfections. If he forgets the Perfections, he discards the Great Vehicle. Lord, the Bodhisattva great-being who is uncertain about the Great Vehicle becomes averse to embracing the Illustrious Doctrine and is occupied with his own fancy; he reaps the fortune of entering the stage of the spiritually immature ordinary person. Lord, this I see to be a great disadvantage and harm. Lord, I foresee the perfection of aim yielding incalculable benefit for myself and future Bodhisattvas through embracing the Illustrious Doctrine; and so I take this vow to embrace the Illustrious Doctrine.

"Lord, I take those ten great vows in the presence of the Lord. For that, may the Master of the Dharma himself now be my witness! Although they be taken face to face with you the Teacher, some sentient beings with meager roots of virtue might think, 'Oh, those ten great vows are difficult to uphold,' and would have doubt or hesitation toward me. Lord, by so thinking they would incur for a long time much harm, suffering, and disaster. Lord, for the sake of helping precisely such persons, I wish to perform in the presence of the Lord this 'Blessing of Truth':[23]

"Lord, just as surely as I have taken exactly these ten great vows, and if they are just as stated by me, then, Lord, by dint of this, my

Bodhisattvas are principally seen in the scriptures. The Bodhisattva activities and Bodhisattva instructions are made known through words in this and that scripture. There should be constant diligence in perusing scriptures, lest by disregarding them there would be an intemperance due to ignorance amounting to a fall into sin. Hence, the phrase, 'by not leaving the spiritual guide,' and the phrase, 'by perusing the scriptures,' express all embrace of the Illustrious Doctrine." Later in the *Śikṣāsamuccaya* (Vaidya ed., p. 166) Śāntideva again quotes the *Ārya-Sāgaramati-sūtra* to show that the embrace of the Illustrious Doctrine is one of the three unrivaled ways to worship the Tathāgata: "When one arouses the thought of enlightenment, when one embraces the Illustrious Doctrine, and when one arouses the thought of great compassion toward the sentient beings."

23 For some recent studies on the Truth Act, cf. W. Norman Brown, "The Metaphysics of the Truth Act (**Satyakriyā*)," *Mélanges d'indianisme à la mémoire de Louis Renou*, pp. 171–77; Alex Wayman, "The Hindu-Buddhist Rite of Truth—An Interpretation," *Studies in Indian Linguistics*, pp. 365–69. In the case of Queen Śrīmālā, two causes are responsible for the supernatural phenomenon: her "roots of virtue" (*hetu*, the basic cause) and the "blessing" (*pratyaya*, the condition) of the Lord. She is awarded this "blessing" for her ritual verbalization of the truth.

word of truth, may a shower of heavenly flowers descend upon the group and may divine sounds be heard sounded!"

No sooner had Queen Śrīmālā uttered those words than there descended a shower of heavenly flowers, and heavenly sounds were heard in the air. The Lord said, "Queen, that is so! Just as you performed the 'Blessing of Truth,' so it happened, and in no other way." The entire retinue, having witnessed the marvelous supernatural phenomenon and having heard that conception through divine sounds,[24] were free from doubt and experienced the most intense joy. The whole retinue took a vow that they would be together with Queen Śrīmālā, and the Lord prophesied that they would accordingly not be separate from her.

CHAPTER TWO

Deciding the Cause

3. Three All-inclusive Aspirations

Then Queen Śrīmālā in the presence of the Lord formed three great aspirations:

(a) "Lord, by this blessing of truth and by the virtuous root[25] consisting of accumulated merit from bringing benefit to innumerable sentient beings, may I comprehend the Illustrious Doctrine in all my lives.

(b) "Lord, having obtained that comprehension of the Illustrious Doctrine, may I teach the Doctrine to the sentient beings without rest or weariness. This is my second great aspiration.

24 According to *Mkhas grub rje's Fundamentals of the Buddhist Tantras*, p. 55, "conception through divine sounds" apparently refers to a variety of promulgation technically called "promulgation through blessing of mind truth-force": "for example, the words of the Doctrine *(dharma)* which proceed from mountains, trees, walls, and so forth, through the force of having been uttered by the Bhagavat mentally with the power of truth *(satya-bala)*." The implication is that after Queen Śrīmālā had been awarded a supernatural phenomenon through the "blessing of truth," where the truth was hers, the Lord produced another phenomenon by the power of truth, where the truth was his.

25 As in n. 23 above, there are two causes, the basic one being the "virtuous root" (cf. n. 15, above) and the conditional one being the "blessing of truth."

(c) "Lord, while teaching the Illustrious Doctrine, then, without regard to my body, life force, or possessions,[26] may I seek to protect and to uphold the Illustrious Doctrine. This is my third great aspiration."

Then the Lord elucidated the great scope of Queen Śrīmālā's three great aspirations: "Queen, for example, if all forms were to be collected together in the realm of space, it would hold them all and extend beyond. In the same way, when all Bodhisattva aspirations as numerous as the sands of the Ganges are taken together within the three great aspirations, those three great aspirations include them and extend beyond."

4. Embrace of the Illustrious Doctrine

Then Queen Śrīmālā implored the Lord with these words: "Furthermore, when I am teaching in the scope of the great aspirations, may the Tathāgata's power make me eloquent." The Lord replied, "Queen, by permission of the Tathāgata, you shall be eloquent!" Queen Śrīmālā appealed to the Lord with these words: "Lord, the Bodhisattva aspirations as numerous as the sands of the Ganges are all collected and included in one great aspiration, namely, the embrace of the Illustrious Doctrine. Thus the embrace of the Illustrious Doctrine is of great scope." The Lord replied, "Queen, very good, very good! Your insight and means[27] are profound. Queen, whatever the sentient beings to whom you teach the Doctrine, they are rare who will comprehend the meaning: they are ones who for a long time generated the roots of virtue under many Buddhas. Queen, just as you embrace, teach, and explain the Illustrious Doctrine, in the same way the Tathāgatas of the past, present, and future embrace, teach, and explain the Illustrious Doctrine, have explained and will explain it. Queen, I also, having now attained

26 This terminology is repeated in the *Ratnagotravibhāga* (II, 63): "After embracing the Illustrious Doctrine, and after fulfilling the original vows (*ādipratijñā*) to benefit all sentient beings, he renounces body, life force, and possessions." In the summary verse of the *Ratnagotravibhāga* (II, 62), the embrace of the Illustrious Doctrine is indicated as "endlessness of cause" (*hetvānantya*), and the fulfillment of original vows as "imperishability of sentient-being realm" (*sattvadhātvakṣayatva*). According to these comments, the scope of the first two Aspirations serves as the cause (two causes) for the scope of the third Aspiration as the fruit.

27 The terminology "insight and means" is standard in Mahāyāna Buddhism for the six Perfections, where the first five, namely Giving, Morality, Forbearance, Striving, and Meditation, are the "means"; and the sixth, Insight, is the "insight."

the supreme Revelation-Enlightenment, embrace and teach the Illustrious Doctrine and explain it in many ways. Queen, while I now embrace, teach, and explain the Illustrious Doctrine in many ways, there is no end or limit to the merits of embracing the Illustrious Doctrine.[28] The insight and eloquence of the Tathāgata are also without end or limit. Why so? Queen, because this embrace of the Illustrious Doctrine has far-ranging meaning and great benefit." Queen Śrīmālā implored the Lord with these words: "Lord, may the Tathāgata's power make me also eloquent to teach the far-ranging meaning!" The Lord replied: "Queen, as you know that the time for it has come, may you preach eloquently!"

[a. Teaching in the Scope of the Great Aspirations]

Thereupon, with the Lord's permission, Queen Śrīmālā appealed to the Lord with these words:

"Lord, the embrace of the Illustrious Doctrine will perfect all the innumerable Buddha natures. The embrace of the Illustrious Doctrine includes the 84,000 doctrine gates.[29] For example, at the time of new

28 Immediately after Śāntideva's quotation in his *Śikṣāsamuccaya* (Vaidya ed., pp. 27–28) from the *Śrī-Mālā*, he quotes the *Ārya-Sāgaramati-sūtra* about these merits:

He is accepted by the Victors (i.e. the Buddhas), the gods, serpent deities, and Kinnaras (part man, part animal); accepted by reason of his merit (*puṇya*) and his knowledge (*jñāna*) after he has embraced the Illustrious Doctrine of the Tathāgatas. . . .

Never is he born in empty fields, for wherever he is born he sees a Victor, and beholding gains faith in him after he has embraced the Illustrious Doctrine of the Tathāgatas. He with the nature of a great soul (*mahātman*), remembers his previous births; and goes forth to the religious life again and again. He behaves with purity, his path the chief thing, after he has embraced the Illustrious Doctrine of the Tathāgatas. . . .

Having gained it, he is skilled in retaining it; its good auspice is not lost in a hundred ages. He becomes unhindered in eloquence, after he has embraced the Illustrious Doctrine of the Tathāgatas.

He is a Śakra, a brahmā, a world protector, a king of men, a universal emperor (*cakravartin*) on earth; he easily and pleasantly becomes awakened to enlightenment, after he has embraced the Illustrious Doctrine of the Tathāgatas.

The thirty-two characteristics arise in his body. He becomes splendid with faultless limbs. People never tire of seeing him, after he has embraced the Illustrious Doctrine of the Tathāgatas.

His mind of enlightenment is not confused; he does not stray in his practice of the Perfections; a hundred [men] cannot restrain his virtue, after he has embraced the Illustrious Doctrine of the Tathāgatas.

29 *Mkhas grub rje's Fundamentals of the Buddhist Tantras*, p. 57, mentions several theories for the 84,000 doctrines, and concludes, in agreement with Vasubandhu, that each one is the extent of doctrine sufficing to counteract one of the 84,000 defilements.

differentiation of the worlds there came a great cloud which poured down innumerable colors and poured down innumerable jewels. In the same way, this embrace of the Illustrious Doctrine pours down countless maturations of merit and pours down countless knowledge jewels. For example, at the time of new differentiation of the worlds, a great chiliocosm of worldly realms was the birthplace and from that arose myriad sets of four continents[30] of various shapes and colors and tremendous numbers of lesser satellite continents. In the same way, the embrace of the Illustrious Doctrine is the source yielding the Great Vehicle, and is the immeasurable womb giving rise to all the magical deeds of the Bodhisattva and the various entrances into the light of the Doctrine,[31] as well as to all mundane perfection, all mundane mastery, and all supramundane bliss not previously experienced by gods and men.[32]

30 *Śrī-Mālā*'s reference to "four continents of various shapes and colors" is intriguing. The Abhidharma literature (cf. *Abhidharma-kośa*, III, tr., pp. 145–46) consistently describes the four great continents in Buddhist cosmic geography as being in four shapes. Uttarakuru is square; Pūrvavideha has the shape of a half-moon; Aparagodānīya is round; and Jambūdvīpa is in wedge or triangular shape. However, the Abhidharma does not appear to ascribe colors to these shapes. In esoteric Buddhism (cf. F. D. Lessing, *Yung-ho-kung*, p. 151), except for the half-moon replaced by the crescent, those shapes happen also to be those of the four altars for the burnt offerings (*homa*), with characteristic colors, namely, white circle, yellow square, red crescent, black triangle. Also, the terminology "shapes and colors" agrees with the ancient explanation of "form" (*rūpa*) as having two aspects, "shape" (*saṃsthāna*) and "color" (*varṇa*).

31 The Sanskrit equivalent for "magical deeds" is *vikurvaṇa*. The explanations are usually with the word *ṛddhi*, one of the ten Bodhisattva powers (*vaśitā*) gained on the Eighth Stage (see n. 54, below). An excellent description is found in Har Dayal, *The Bodhisattva Doctrine*, pp. 112–16. Here we find that there are two kinds of *ṛddhi*. That called *pāriṇāmikā* (i.e. of the nature of transformation) covers all wondrous physical manifestations and revelations to others. That called *nairmāṇikī* (i.e. of the nature of creation) covers the creation of phantom bodies and voices. The "various entrances into the light of the Doctrine" (see Franklin Edgerton, *Buddhist Hybrid Sanskrit Dictionary*, pp. 281–82) are the basis of a chapter in the *Lalitavistara*, the "*Dharmālokamukhaparivarta*," where the future Buddha, of course a Bodhisattva on the Tenth Stage and ready to descend for his last life, preaches to the Tuṣita gods the 108 entrances into the light of the Doctrine. The first of these is faith (*śraddhā*) which serves for unassailable purpose.

32 The commentaries on the portion of our translation beginning "all mundane perfection" and ending "by gods and men" (that of Chi-tsang, p. 202; that of Hanayama's Shōtoku Taishi, p. 47; that of Saeki, p. 80) differ somewhat from each other, as do the two Chinese versions and the Tibetan for the segment itself. The commentaries seem agreed on one point: the segment should be understood to bear out the

"Lord, for example, the great earth supports four great burdens. What are the four? They are: the great ocean; all the mountains; all grass, herbs, shrubs, trees, and harvests; all the host of sentient beings. In the same way, a good son of the family or good daughter of the family who embraces the Illustrious Doctrine supports four great burdens even greater than those of the great earth. What are the four? As follows: 1. The good son of the family or good daughter of the family who for the sentient beings without spiritual guides,[33] not hearing [the Illustrious Doctrine], and lacking the Doctrine, turns them to virtuously apply themselves to the root of virtue of achieving the perfections of gods and men, supports a great burden greater than the earth's. 2. The good son of the family or good daughter of the family who acts to add certain sentient beings to the Vehicle of Disciples supports a great burden greater than the earth's. 3. The good son of the family or good daughter of the family who acts to add certain sentient beings to the

---

fourfold symbolism indicated previously by mention of four continents, and subsequently by earth's four burdens, and then the four kinds of jewels. Taking those commentaries as a point of departure, we believe the explanations can be worked out in the following manner. In the case of the four burdens supported by the good son or daughter of the family, there are key expressions "perfections of gods and men," "Vehicle of Disciples," "Vehicle of the Self-Enlightened," and "Great Vehicle." Therefore, "all mundane perfection"—the reading accepted from the Tibetan text—refers to "perfections of gods and men"; "all mundane mastery" refers to both "Vehicle of Disciples" and "Vehicle of the Self-Enlightened"; and "all supramundane bliss not previously experienced by gods and men" refers to "Great Vehicle."

33. The Sanskrit term for "spiritual guide" is *kalyāṇamitra*, literally, "a virtuous friend." The good son or daughter of the family here takes the role of the spiritual guide referred to by Śāntideva (see n. 22, above). From early times Buddhism has stressed the importance of relying on a spiritual guide; cf. Vajirañāṇa, *Buddhist Meditation in Theory and Practice*, chap. 8, "The Search for a Friend or Teacher." The *Śrī-Mālā* expects the utmost reverence for this guide, calling him "world mother of the Dharma" and promises for relying on him a great reward, called "infinite source of jewel treasure." Tsoṅ-kha-pa's *Lam rim chen mo* (Tashilumpo edition, f. 27b-3) attributes this passage to the *Gaṇḍavyūha-sūtra*: "O youth Sudhana, the spiritual guides protect one from all the evil destinies. They make one understand the equality of the *dharmas*. They teach what is a pleasant and what an unpleasant path. They exhort with the practice of Samantabhadra. They indicate the path to the city of omniscience. They conduct one to the place of omniscience. They make one set sail on the ocean of the *dharmadhātu*. They show the ocean of the knowable in the past, present, and future. They reveal the *maṇḍalas* of the noble host. The spiritual guides enhance all one's virtuous *dharmas*." Āryaśūra's *Jātakamālā* (XVII. "The Story of the Jar," verse 32), states in part: "But the speaker of the wholesome is to be honored by accepting his words and by taking them to heart."

Vehicle of the Self-Enlightened supports a great burden greater than the earth's. 4. The good son of the family or good daughter of the family who acts to add certain sentient beings to the Great Vehicle supports a great burden greater than the earth's. Those four are the four great burdens. The good son of the family or good daughter of the family who embraces the Illustrious Doctrine, and carries those four great burdens greater than earth's, carries an infinite burden, becomes for all sentient beings spontaneously friendly, compassionate, giver of solace, merciful, and is called 'world mother of the Dharma.'

"Lord, for example, this great earth is a source for the four kinds of jewels. Of what four kinds? A source for priceless jewels, for superior jewels, for medium-quality jewels, for inferior jewels. Just as the great earth is a source of the four kinds of jewels, so also the sentient beings who depend on the good son of the family or good daughter of the family who has embraced the Illustrious Doctrine gain four precious things superior to all jewels. What are the four? The sentient beings who depend on that good son of the family or good daughter of the family as a spiritual guide gain the treasure of merit that achieves the perfections of gods and men. They gain the acquirement of virtuous root for approaching the Vehicle of Disciples. They gain the acquirement of virtuous root for approaching the Vehicle of the Self-Enlightened. They gain the lofty collection of merit for approaching the Perfect Buddha (Samyaksaṃbuddha). Thus, the sentient beings who depend on the good son of the family or good daughter of the family with embrace of the Illustrious Doctrine gain four great precious things superior to all jewels. The expression 'infinite source of jewel treasure' refers to embrace of the Illustrious Doctrine.

[b. Teaching the Far-ranging Meaning]

"Lord, the embrace of the Illustrious Doctrine is called 'embracer of the Illustrious Doctrine.' The Illustrious Doctrine is not one thing and the embracer of the Illustrious Doctrine something else. That embracer of the Illustrious Doctrine is himself the Illustrious Doctrine. Neither is he different from the Perfections, nor are those different from the embracer of the Illustrious Doctrine. Lord, that embracer of the Illustrious Doctrine himself is the Perfections. For what reason?

"When the good son of the family or good daughter of the family who embraces the Illustrious Doctrine matures any sentient beings by giving (*dāna*)—if they are ones who can be matured by giving—then by the donation of his major or minor limbs,[34] they become matured. In that way, the matured ones are placed in the Illustrious Doctrine. This is his Perfection of Giving.

"When he matures any sentient beings by morality (*śīla*)—if these sentient beings can be matured through his guarding the six senses[35] and purifying the actions of body, speech, and mind—then by his dignified bearing[36] he protects and matures their minds. They having been thus matured are installed in the Illustrious Doctrine. This is his Perfection of Morality.

"When he matures any sentient beings by forbearance (*kṣānti*)—if these beings scold, insult, or threaten him—he shows no ill will but seeks to heal and thus to mature by the illustrious power of forbearance. By his maintaining facial composure, he protects and matures their minds. Being so matured they are installed in the Illustrious Doctrine. This is his Perfection of Forbearance.

"When he matures any sentient beings by striving (*vīrya*), he matures these beings by his not having a torpid mind, not being lazy, having great aspiration, and possessing great enterprise of striving. By his control of dignified bearing[37] he protects and matures their

34 The donation of major and minor limbs is a theme of some famous Jātakas or previous-birth stories of the Buddha. See, for example, the *Jātakamālā by Āryaśūra*, translated by J. S. Speyer, "The Story of the Tigress," and "The Story of the King of the Śibis." Tsoṅ-kha-pa's *Lam rim chen mo* (Bodhisattva section) makes it clear that in practice this extreme form of donation was carried on imaginatively, and quotes Śāntideva's *Bodhicaryāvatāra* (III, 10): "My embodiments, likewise my possessions, and all merit of past, present, and future, I renounce without regard [for reward], to accomplish the aim of all sentient beings." The particular meditation in which those things are given away is the topic of verses in Ārya-Śūra's *Pāramitāsamāsa* (I, 11B and I, 12) as now cited by Tsoṅ-kha-pa: " 'Why is this mine which is only yours? There is no pride of self in me with respect to it.' Whoever he be, having such marvelous reflections modeled on the state of a Buddha, the Buddhas who are the inconceivable beings call that outstanding Bodhisattva a great being."

35 The six senses are the five outer ones and the mind itself as the sixth sense.

36 Dignified bearing in the case of morality (*śīla*) means "possessed of good behavior and lawful resort" (*ācāra-gocara-saṃpanna*). According to Asaṅga, by this expression "there is explained the good-quality characteristic of the Prātimokṣa vow, which, making comparison with another, is so taken to heart." This characteristic pertains to the ability of the one with superior conduct to inspire men of like disposition to emulate him: cf. Alex Wayman, *Analysis of the Śrāvakabhūmi Manuscript*, p. 69.

37 Dignified bearing in the case of striving (*vīrya*) means, according to Asaṅga (*ibid.*, p. 108): "Among those, what is perfection of dignified posture? That when by day he spends time both by walking and by sitting—doing likewise in the first

minds. They having been thus matured are installed in the Illustrious Doctrine. This is his Perfection of Striving.

"When he matures any sentient beings by meditation (*dhyāna*), he matures them by having an undisturbed mind, his mind not straying outside and having no mistake of mindfulness. By not being sidetracked though he act for a long time or speak for a long time, he protects and matures their minds. They having been so matured stay in the Illustrious Doctrine. This is his Perfection of Meditation.

"When he matures any sentient beings by insight (*prajñā*), he matures them by responding confidently to their questions about meaning, and by explaining all technical treatises, sciences, and arts.[38] He protects and matures their minds by mastering problems of the sciences and the arts. They being thus matured abide in the Illustrious Doctrine. This is his Perfection of Insight.

"Lord, that being the case, the Perfections are not one thing, and the embracer of the Illustrious Doctrine something else. The embracer of the Illustrious Doctrine is himself the Perfections.

[c. Teaching the Great Meaning]

"Lord, may the Tathāgata's power make me also eloquent to teach the great meaning!" The Lord spoke: "Queen, by permission of the Tathāgata, you shall be eloquent!" Thereupon, Queen Śrīmālā appealed to the Lord with these words:

"Lord, the embracer of the Illustrious Doctrine is called 'embrace of the Illustrious Doctrine.' The embracer of the Illustrious Doctrine is not one thing and the embrace of the Illustrious Doctrine something else. The embracer of the Illustrious Doctrine is himself the embrace of the

watch of night; when in the middle watch he takes rest on his right side; and when in the last watch he quickly rises and spends time by walking and sitting; likewise when he sits on the acquired resting place as permitted by the Buddha—on a seat, stool, or grass mat, assuming the posture of crossed legs." It is also referred to as fourfold, namely as the four postures of walking, standing, sitting, and lying down.

38 This presentation of "insight" (*prajñā*) is close to the definition in Asaṅga's *Bodhisattvabhūmi* (Wogihara ed., p. 212): "Whatever analysis of natures (*dharma-pravicaya*) takes place for understanding any knowable, and, when one has understood any knowable, involves the five sciences, to wit, inner science (*adhyātma-vidyā*), logic, medicine, grammar, and the arts, this [analysis] is the intrinsic nature of the Bodhisattva's insight." *Mkhas grub rje's Fundamentals of the Buddhist Tantras* (p. 81) explains, "The treatises on Inner Science are those which show the means of vanquishing the obscurations of defilement and of the knowable that are on the inner thought." "Inner science" is the analysis of the Buddhist doctrine. The other four are profane.

Illustrious Doctrine. For what reason? The good son of the family or good daughter of the family who embraces the Illustrious Doctrine renounces three accessories for the sake of making [persons] embrace the Illustrious Doctrine. The three are body, life force, and possessions. Lord, the good son of the family or good daughter of the family by renouncing his body, thus obtaining the body of a Buddha, is equal to the uttermost limit of *saṃsāra*; thus obtaining freedom from old age, sickness, and death, is indestructible; thus being permanent, steadfast, calm, and eternal, is free from [ordinary] passing away and is endowed with boundless inconceivable merits; reaching the Dharmakāya of the Tathāgata.[39] Lord, the good son of the family or good daughter of the family by renouncing his life force, thus being stationed in the wondrous activity of the Buddha's Doctrine, is equal to the uttermost limit of *saṃsāra*; is free from [ordinary] passing away and is endowed with all the boundless, permanent, and inconceivable merits; achieving all the

39 According to our Introduction, this good son or daughter of the family is on the Eighth Bodhisattva Stage at the uttermost limit of *saṃsāra*, where the person has exchanged an ordinary body, subject to old age, sickness, and death, for the body of a Buddha, having the characteristics of the "embryo of the Tathāgata" which is permanent, steadfast, calm, and eternal, and having an inconceivable transference. The Guṇabhadra and Bodhiruci versions agree in closing the sentence with a phrase lacking in the Tibetan version, "reaching the Dharmakāya of the Tathāgata." In order to be consistent with the general position of the *Śrī-Mālā* and the *Ratnagotravibhāga*, the expression "Dharmakāya" should be understood here according to the tabulation in note 80. The "Dharmakāya" should mean "unconstructed *nirvāṇa*," which does not require possession of Buddha natures constituting the "constructed *nirvāṇa*." Therefore, it is not necessary to conclude that the *Śrī-Mālā* is opposed by the *Daśabhūmika-sūtra* in its section on the Eighth Stage, where it states (Rahder's edition, p. 65): "Prince, you should know concerning the Bodhisattva who has entered this Motionless (*acala*) Bodhisattva Stage, who stays, drawing upon the force of his former aspiration, in that stream which is the entrance to the natures (*dharma*), that for him the Buddha Lords make a providing of the Tathāgata's knowledge. And they speak thus to him: 'Very good, very good, son of the family! This absolute forbearance (*paramārthakṣānti*) is for the sake of approaching the Buddha natures. However, you should know, son of the family, that our perfection of Buddha natures consisting in the ten forces, the four confidences, and so forth—that is not in you. Engage yourself and begin to strive in searching for that perfection of Buddha natures! Do not turn away from the forbearance entrance!' " The term "forbearance" in this context usually refers to "forbearance of the unoriginated natures" (*anutpattikadharmakṣānti*), that is, not being upset by the stream of dream-like natures. However, the content of the above-cited *Daśabhūmika* passage appears to counter the recommendation of the *Mahāvastu*, as quoted in our Introduction, "Starting with the Eighth Stage the Bodhisattvas are to be honored with the honor due a Samyaksambuddha."

profound Buddha Dharma.[40] Lord, the good son of the family or good daughter of the family by renouncing possessions, thus being honored by all sentient beings, is equal to the uttermost limit of *saṃsāra*; is indestructible, devoid of discursive thought; and endowed with boundless, permanent, and inconceivable merits that are unshared with other sentient beings; being honored by all sentient beings.[41] Lord, in that way the good son of the family or good daughter of the family who embraces the Illustrious Doctrine and renounces these three accessories acquires those extraordinary three [sets of] merits; and [besides] is given a prophecy by all the Buddhas.

"Lord, at the time of decline of the Doctrine, when monks, nuns, male and female laymen quarrel with each other to break up into many sects, whatever good son of the family or good daughter of the family delighting in the Doctrine which is without deceit or falsehood, for the sake of maintaining the Illustrious Doctrine, creates a Bodhisattva group of those who have the Doctrine would certainly be the good son of the family or good daughter of the family to obtain a prophecy from all the Buddhas because of that activity.

"Lord, I suppose the embrace of the Illustrious Doctrine is thus the great striving (*mahāvīrya*). In this case, the Lord himself is the Eye,[42] is the Knowledge (*jñāna*),[43] is the root of all the Doctrines.[44] The Lord is omnipotent, is the resort."

40 According to our Introduction, this good son or daughter of the family represents the arising of the Jewel of Doctrine on the Ninth Bodhisattva Stage.

41 According to our Introduction, this good son or daughter of the family represents the arising of the Jewel of the Congregation on the Tenth Bodhisattva Stage.

42 Since the same remark occurs in the section of *Śrī-Mālā* entitled "Intrinsic Purity of the Mind," and in a context where the Lord alone can understand, it is plain that among the five eyes of Buddhist texts the "Buddha eye" is meant. This is also the position of Chi-tsang (pp. 123–24). According to the *Mahāvastu* (Basak ed., I, 190):

What is the Buddha-eye? The eighteen exclusive Buddha natures, as follows:—(1–3) The Tathāgata has unhindered knowledge and vision of the past; so of the future; so of the present. (4–6) All his acts of body are preceded by knowledge and attended with knowledge; so all his acts of speech; so all his acts of mind. (7–12) He has no loss of longing; or of striving; or of mindfulness; or of *samādhi*; or of insight; or of liberation. (13–18) He has no faltering; no harsh note; no forgetting; no unequipoised thought; no unpremeditated indifference; no idea of multiplicity. The knowledge in these eighteen exclusive Buddha natures is what is called "Buddha eye."

43 Chi-tsang (pp. 123–24): Among the eleven knowledges, his is the Knowledge of Thusness (*tathatā*).

44 *Ibid.*: "because [the Jewel of] the Dharma issues from [the Jewel of] the Lord." Saeki (p. 118): "The Illustrious Doctrine stands on the Buddha as a tree stands on roots."

Then the Lord, rejoicing at Queen Śrīmālā's explanation that the embrace of the Illustrious Doctrine is the great striving, said, "Queen, exactly so! Queen, the embrace of the Illustrious Doctrine is the great striving.

"Queen, for example, a small blow that pierces a sensitive spot of a strong man gives him pain. In the same way, even a little embrace of the Illustrious Doctrine that pierces the sinful Māras,[45] makes them suffer and groan. Queen, I do not notice any other virtuous doctrine so piercing the sinful Māras and making them suffer and groan as this little embrace of the Illustrious Doctrine.

"Queen, for example, the chief bull in height and breadth is superior to all the herd of cows and, shining, outshines. In the same way, even a little embrace of the Illustrious Doctrine of the Great Vehicle, because of its expanse, is superior to all the virtuous doctrines of the Vehicles of the Disciples and the Self-Enlightened.

"Queen, for example, Sumeru, king of mountains, in loftiness and breadth is superior to and towers above all mountain chains. In the same way, when the person of the Great Vehicle with no care for his body and life force, and with a generous mind,[46] has embrace of the Illustrious Doctrine, this, because of its expanse, is superior to all the virtuous natures of those newly entered in the Great Vehicle who still care for body and life force. How much more superior to the [virtuous natures of the] other two [Vehicles]!

"Queen, that being the case, you should install the sentient beings into the holding and embrace of the Illustrious Doctrine. You should make them rely upon it, extol it, rejoice in it, hold it aloft, and display it. Queen, the embrace of the Illustrious Doctrine is of great purpose, of great fruit, of great benefit. Queen, although I have already explained

45 Sometimes the word "sinful" is taken as part of the name, i.e. Māra Pāpimat, where "Pāpimat" means "sinful." B. C. Law, *Indological Studies*, Part II, p. 350, explains, "Māra was called pāpimā or the sinful one because he engaged himself in committing sins and led others to adopt the sinful path." For the various armies of Māra, see J. J. Jones, *The Mahāvastu*, II (London, 1952), 224–27.

46 In the light of the preceding, the expression "generous mind" can be understood as substituting for "renunciation of possessions." The *Mahāvastu* (Basak ed., I, 191, *mahīmaṇḍagato* taken as = *bodhimaṇḍagato*) says: "Equipped with eyes he gives away his dear possessions, while passing through a long succession of states with a serene mind. Then the Tathāgata, having proceeded by himself to the terrace of the earth [i.e. the terrace of enlightenment], awakens to the dear knowledge which is supreme."

for incalculable eons the merit and benefit of embracing the Illustrious Doctrine. I still have not come to the end of explaining the merit and benefit of embracing the Illustrious Doctrine. Queen, the embrace of the Illustrious Doctrine thus possesses infinite merit."

CHAPTER THREE

Clarifying the Final Meaning

5. One Vehicle

"Queen, you must preach eloquently the embrace of the Illustrious Doctrine that was held by all the Buddhas and was explained by me." Queen Śrīmālā replied to the Lord, "Very well." Having thought over the Lord's exhortation, she appealed to the Lord with these words:

[*re Vehicles of Disciples and the Self-Enlightened*]

"Lord, what is called 'Illustrious Doctrine' is a term for the Great Vehicle. Why so? Because all the vehicles of the Disciples and the Self-Enlightened and all the mundane and supramundane virtuous natures[47] are distributed by the Great Vehicle. For example, the four great streams

47 The interpretation of the phrase "mundane and supramundane virtuous natures" has been shown in our introduction ("One Vehicle") to differ from that of Asaṅga's Mahīśāsaka school, but some further data should be helpful. Tsoṅ-kha-pa cites the same *Saṃdhinirmocana-sūtra* passage in the *Lam rim chen mo* (beginning of Śamatha section, manuscript translation by Alex Wayman) in a way that clarifies that the mundane virtues are held to be the fruit of calming (the mind), and the supramundane virtues the fruit of clear vision. In contrast, the *Śrī-Mālā* takes the virtuous natures as mundane or supramundane according to whether a defiled or an undefiled consciousness views them. Yüan-ts'ê's great commentary on the *Saṃdhinirmocana-sūtra*, translated from Chinese into Tibetan (PTT, Vol. 106), has relevant comments in two places, p. 214–3, 4 and p. 230–3, 4 and points out many Chinese controversies over the meaning of the passage. For example, some said that the word "Disciples" includes the Pratyekabuddhas; and others included Pratyekabuddhas in the word "Bodhisattvas" (compare our discussion in the Introduction about two kinds of Pratyekabuddha). To solve the problem of what "mundane virtuous natures" belong to the Tathāgatas, Yüan-ts'ê (pp. 230–4) points out that mundane virtuous natures are usually fluxional but that there is also a category of nonfluxional mundane virtuous natures consisting of the consciousness associated

issue from Lake Anavatapta.[48] In the same way, all the vehicles of the Disciples and the Self-Enlightened and all the mundane and supramundane virtuous natures issue from the Great Vehicle. For example, whatever seeds there are, and plants, shrubs, herbs, trees, all of them, based on the great earth and resting on the great earth, sprout and grow. In the same way, whatever vehicles there be of Disciples and of the Self-Enlightened and whatever mundane and supramundane virtuous natures there be, they, based on the Great Vehicle, sprout and grow. Hence, Lord, when one is based on the Great Vehicle and embraces the Great Vehicle, he also has recourse to and embraces all the vehicles of Disciples and of the Self-Enlightened and all the mundane and supramundane virtuous natures.

"Lord, you explained six basic topics: preservation of the Illustrious Doctrine, decline of the Illustrious Doctrine, the Prātimokṣa, the Vinaya, the going forth to the religious life, and monk ordination; besides, these six topics stem from the purport of the Great Vehicle. For what reason? Lord, the expression 'preservation of the Illustrious Doctrine' has the purport of the Great Vehicle, since preservation of the Great Vehicle itself is the preservation of the Illustrious Doctrine. The expression 'decline of the Illustrious Doctrine' has the purport of the

with the "knowledge afterwards obtained" (*pṛṣṭhalabdha-jñāna*) (which is the consciousness of a person toward the world after a preceding lofty meditative state), and that the Lord has many mundane virtuous natures of the latter sort (unfortunately not specified). On 214-4 the information is given that the "Disciples" (meaning all disciples of the Lord) and the Tathāgatas have in common the virtues, presumably mundane, of the Eight Deliverances, etc., and do not have in common the virtues, presumably supramundane, of the (ten) powers, (four) confidences, (eighteen) exclusive natures, etc. The *Śrī-Mālā* avoids the *Saṃdhinirmocana-sūtra*'s problem by not qualifying the "mundane and supramundane virtuous natures" in terms of their possessors. By accepting that the supramundane virtuous natures are nonfluxional (*anāsrava*) (apparently the position of the *Vijñāptimātratāsiddhi*, I, 113), all the virtuous natures of the Arhats, Pratyekabuddhas, and Bodhisattvas who have attained power—in *Śrī-Mālā*'s terminology—could fit the category, and so would include the Bodhisattva natures listed in n. 54, below; and of course all the Buddha natures (nn. 42, 69, 75) would also fit the category.

48 Étienne Lamotte, *Le Traité de la Grande Vertu de Sagesse*, I, 385 (note), lists the four great rivers that issue from Lake Anavatapta as Gaṅgā, Sindhu (Indus), Vakṣu (Oxus), and Sītā (Tarim), as in *Abhidharma-kośa*, III, tr. pp. 147-48. The *Mahāparinirvāṇa-sūtra* names them the Gaṅgā, the Yamunā, the Sarayū, and the Hiṅgulā, according to Baron A. von Staël-Holstein, "On a Peking Edition of the Tibetan Kanjur Which Seems To Be Unknown in the West," *Harvard Sino-Indian Studies* (Peking, 1934), p. 7. The Lake Anavatapta (Pali, Anotatta), located in the Himālayas, figures in a number of Buddhist legends.

Great Vehicle, since decline of the Great Vehicle itself is the decline of the Illustrious Doctrine. The two Dharmas called Prātimokṣa and Vinaya[49] differ as words but have the same meaning. What is called 'Vinaya' is the instruction for persons in the Great Vehicle. The reason is that it is for Tathāgatahood and for the going forth to the religious life and monk ordination. That being the case, what are called 'Vinaya,' and 'the going forth to the religious life, and monk ordination' stand for the aggregate of strict morality of the Great Vehicle. Lord, going forth and monk ordination do not belong to the vehicles of the Disciples and the Self-Enlightened. Why so? Because going forth and monk ordination are not for the purpose of being a Disciple or a Self-Enlightened one. However, because there is Tathāgatahood, the Disciples and the Self-Enlightened ones go forth and have monk ordination.

[*re Arhats and Pratyekabuddhas*]

"Lord, the Arhats and the Pratyekabuddhas not only take refuge in Tathāgatahood, but also have fear. This is because both the Arhats and the Pratyekabuddhas hold to the idea of nonforbearing fear toward all constructions, for example, as though facing an executioner with uplifted sword. On that account, neither attains the deliverance that has endless bliss. But Lord, the refuge does not seek a refuge.[50] Just as sentient beings without a refuge are fearful of this and that and seek deliverance from this and that, so also the Arhats and the Pratyekabuddhas fear and, beset with fear, the Arhats and the Pratyekabuddhas take refuge in the Lord.

"Lord, not only do the Arhats and the Pratyekabuddhas have fear, but also, that being the case, both have a remainder of rebirth nature and are eventually reborn. They have a remainder of resort; hence they are not pure. They have not finished with *karma*; hence they have many needs. Besides, they have many natures to be eliminated; and because

49 The "Prātimokṣa" and the "Vinaya" are the chief words of the disciplinary code of Buddhism. The Vinaya is the most general term, and stands for the whole body of literature and practices of discipline for all the orders of laity and monks. The Prātimokṣa contains the list of prohibitions and those offenses for which confession must be made by the monk. *Mkhas grub rje's Fundamentals of the Buddhist Tantras*, pp. 55, 57, counts as "Vinaya-piṭaka" the text classes *nidāna* (instructive personal discourses), *avadāna* (parables), *itivṛttaka* (legends), and *jātaka* (the bodhisattva lives of the Buddha), from among the twelve groupings of the Sacred Word.

50 That is to say, the Lord, being the refuge, of course does not seek a refuge. In the last analysis, we cannot call anyone a refuge who himself is seeking a refuge.

those are not eliminated, the Arhats and the Pratyekabuddhas are far away from the Nirvāṇa-realm.

"Lord, what is called 'Nirvāṇa' is a means belonging to the Tathāgatas. A reason is that only the Tathāgata-Arhat-Samyaksambuddhas having attained Nirvāṇa possess all merits, while the Arhats and the Pratyekabuddhas do not have all merits.

"Lord, what is called 'Nirvāṇa' is a means belonging to the Tathāgatas. A reason is that only the Tathāgata-Arhat-Samyaksambuddhas having attained Nirvāṇa possess immeasurable merit, while the Arhats and the Pratyekabuddhas possess measurable merit.[51]

"Lord, what is called 'Nirvāṇa' is a means belonging to the Tathāgatas. A reason is that only the Tathāgata-Arhat-Samyaksambuddhas having attained Nirvāṇa possess inconceivable merit, while the Arhats and the Pratyekabuddhas possess conceivable merit.

"Lord, what is called 'Nirvāṇa' is a means belonging to the Tathāgatas. A reason is that only the Tathāgata-Arhat-Samyaksambuddhas having attained Nirvāṇa have eliminated all the faults to be eliminated and are completely pure, while the Arhats and the Pratyekabuddhas have a remainder of faults and are not completely pure.

"Lord, what is called 'Nirvāṇa is a means belonging to the Tathāgatas. A reason is that only the Tathāgata-Arhat-Samyaksambuddhas have indeed attained Nirvāṇa, while the Arhats and the Pratyekabuddhas are far away from the Nirvāṇa-realm.

"Lord, concerning the Arhats' and Pratyekabuddhas' realizing their liberation and gaining the four knowledges, thus reaching the stage of arrested breath,[52] the deep purport of the Lord analyzes and explains

51 This paragraph is added from the Guṇabhadra translation of the *Śrī-Mālā*, than which the Bodhiruci translation is briefer. Its inclusion is justified by the *Ratnagotravibhāga* (text, p. 56), which cites this verse:

> That liberation (*mokṣa*) characterized as inseparable from merits (*guṇa*) that have [the best of] all aspects, and that are immeasurable, inconceivable, and immaculate —is the liberation called "Tathāgata."

That is to say, the four merits of "all," "immeasurable," "inconceivable," and "immaculate" are key words in the four paragraphs which contrast the merits of the Tathāgata-Arhat-Samyaksambuddhas with the merits of the Arhats and the Pratyekabuddhas. For the meaning of "Tathāgata-Arhat-Samyaksambuddha" see Lamotte, *Le Traité de la Grande Vertu de Sagesse*, I, 126–28.

52 The terminology of four knowledges occurs later in the *Śrī-Mālā* in connection with the four Noble Truths (cf. n. 76 below). For the "stage of arrested breath," see n. 70, below.

that as 'attended with remainder' and 'not final meaning.' Why is that? Because there are two kinds of passing away—[the ordinary] discontinuous passing away and the passing away which is the inconceivable transference. The discontinuous passing away belongs to the sentient beings who have reconnection (*pratisaṃdhi*) [with sense organs].[53] The passing away which is the inconceivable transference belongs to the bodies made of mind (*manomaya-kāya*) of Arhats, Pratyekabuddhas, and Bodhisattva great beings who have attained power,[54] up to their reaching the terrace of enlightenment.

53 The important term *pratisaṃdhi* is apparently being employed here in its etymological sense of *saṃdhi* (connection, union), *prati* (again), hence implying discontinuity. Edgerton, *Buddhist Hybrid Sanskrit Dictionary*, p. 372, gives the primary sense as "rebirth," that is, connection again (with a new body). This would normally be the proper translation, for which see our Introduction, n. 98. However, the *Śrī-Mālā*, in the present context, contrasts the beings who are subject to *pratisaṃdhi* with certain individuals such as Arhats and denies that Arhats have avoided rebirth. Clearly, the rendition "rebirth" for *pratisaṃdhi* does not fit the *Śrī-Mālā*, which gives its own solution later on (Section 13, "Intrinsic Purity of the Mind"), when defining *saṃsāra* in terms of the Tathāgatagarbha and the taking hold anew of sense organs for perception. Asaṅga refers to the same topic in his *Śrāvakabhūmi* (Wayman, *Analysis*, p. 59): "That seed does not have the characteristics of difference as long as it stays apart from the six sense bases (*ṣaḍāyatana*)."

54 The standard Sanskrit for "attained power" in this context is *vaśitā-prāpta*. The "power" (*vaśitā*) in this connection should not be confused with the "power" (*bala*) belonging to the Tathāgata (n. 69, below), or belonging to the Bodhisattva in a different list. This "power" (*vaśitā*) of the Bodhisattva is of ten kinds and is attained, according to the *Daśabhūmika-sūtra*, on the Eighth Bodhisattva Stage. The ten powers are described in the *Mahāvastu* (Basak ed., I, 360):

> The Buddha, solar kinsman, has declared that ten Bodhisattva powers belong to the heroes. Listen now as I tell them. The wise Bodhisattva has dominion over his life-force as well as over eloquence. He has gained power over rebirth, over *karma*, over his consciousness (*citta*), and over the Doctrine. He has the power of magic (*ṛddhi*) and the power of purpose (*abhiprāya* = Aspiration). The wise Bodhisattva has dominion over time and place. These are the ten powers.

Another group of Bodhisattva powers, and here the word *bala* is employed, is assigned to the Ninth Bodhisattva Stage in Abhayākaragupta's *Muni* (p. 255-1), with thirteen items. It is obviously the same list with ten items and various differences as that found in the *Avataṃsaka-sūtra* (Śikṣānanda, LVI: D. T. Suzuki, *Studies in the Laṅkāvatāra Sūtra*, p. 425), as follows (with substitution of *Muni*'s comments when indicated): 1) the power of intention (*āśaya-bala*) (*Muni:* because there is no coursing of defilement); 2) the power of strong intention (*adhāśaya-bala*) (*Muni:* through the exercise of that Stage's wisdom [*jñāna*]); 3) the power of praxis (*prayoga-bala*) (*Muni*: by skill in the diverse practices of innumerable world realms); 4) the power of insight (*prajñā-bala*), the intuitive power to understand the mentalities of all beings; 5) the power of vow (*praṇidhāna-bala*) (*Muni*: because he does not abandon his application to any Buddha practice); 6) the power of practice (*caryā-bala*),

["Attended with Remainder" and "Not Final Meaning"]

"Lord, among those two kinds of passing away, it is the knowledge of having gained control over the discontinuous passing away that occurs to the Arhats and the Pratyekabuddhas, and they think, 'My births are finished.' Having accordingly resorted to a direct realization of the fruit attended with remainder, the Arhats and the Pratyekabuddhas think, 'It was my reliance on the pure life (*brahmacarya*).' Having resorted to eliminating all the defilements accompanying the activities of immature ordinary persons as well as of gods and men, and all the defilements accompanying the reconnections of the seven classes of trainees,[55] which they had not previously accomplished, the Arhats and the Pratyekabuddhas think, 'The duty is accomplished.'

"Lord, they think, 'There is nothing to be known beyond this.' It is because the Arhats and the Pratyekabuddhas have gained control over the defilements to be eliminated by the Arhat as well as control over the reconnections in *saṃsāra*, that it occurs to them, 'There is nothing to be known beyond this.' However, the person who thinks, 'There is nothing to be known beyond this,' has neither eliminated all defilements nor avoided all rebirth. Why is that? Because, Lord, in the

the power of working till the end of time; 7) the power of vehicle (*yāna-bala*), the power of creating all kinds of conveyances without giving up the Mahāyāna; 8) the power of magical transformation (*vikurvaṇa-bala*), to create an immaculate world in every skin pore; 9) the power of enlightenment (*bodhi-bala*), the power of awakening beings to enlightenment; 10) the power to set in motion the Wheel of the Doctrine (*dharmacakrapravartana-bala*). The above two lists of Bodhisattva powers are consistent with the discussion in our Introductory subsection "The Last Three Bodhisattva Stages," showing the arising of the Three Jewels (Buddha, Dharma, and Saṃgha) on the last three Stages. The *Avataṃsaka* list contains the item "the power to set in motion the Wheel of the Doctrine" as well as other items that agree with the arising of the Jewel of Doctrine on the Ninth Bodhisattva Stage.

55 The word "trainee" (*śaikṣa* or *śiṣya*) is not the usual designation for the seven that are meant here. Abhayākaragupta (*Muni*, p. 229-5) uses the expression "seven persons" (*pudgala*). In Pāli they are the "noble persons" (*ariya-puggala*). The terminology is based on the ancient Buddhist classification of path and fruit, with four paths of persons, and four persons with the respective fruits of those paths. There are four persons in path: 1) the one who has "entered the stream," 2) the "once-returner," 3) the "no-returner," 4) the Arhat. There are four persons in fruit, namely the fruits of those path-based persons, i.e. "the one with fruit of having entered the stream," etc. The group of seven is arrived at by omitting the eighth one, which is "the one with fruit of Arhatship." Saeki (p. 158) bears out this interpretation.

Arhats and the Pratyekabuddhas there are still uneliminated defilements as well as rebirth defilements that have not been searched out.

"Those defilements are of two kinds, static defilements and mobile defilements. The static kinds are of four varieties:[56] (1) the static kind based in a particular viewpoint; (2) the static kind in attraction to desire; (3) the static kind in attraction to form; (4) the static kind in attraction to [mundane] gestation. The four static defilements generate all the mobile defilements. The mobile ones are momentary, to wit, a moment of consciousness and its associate (a *dharma*).[57]

"Lord, the nescience entrenchment which has existed from beginningless time is unconscious. The great power among those four static kinds is the substratum of all the secondary defilements, but those four cannot bear comparison with the great power of the nescience entrenchment in terms of magnitude, portion, count, example, or cause. That being the case, the nescience entrenchment is the greatest power; it is also called 'static kind in attraction to [supramundane] gestation.' For example, the sinful Māras belong to the Paranirmitavaśavartin class of gods; still they surpass those gods in shape, color, radiance, power,

56 This group is obviously based on the Abhidharma subdivisions of the term *upādāna*, the ninth member of Dependent Origination (*pratītya-samutpāda*). According to *Abhidharma-kośa* III, tr. p. 86, the Sautrāntika view on the four kinds of *upādāna* is as follows:

kāma-upādāna = indulgence in the five strands of desire (the five sense objects).
dṛṣṭi-upādāna = indulgence in any of the 62 views of the *Brahmajālasūtra*.
śīlavrata-upādāna = indulgence in useless rules and vows.
ātmavāda-upādāna (understood as *ātmabhāva-upādāna*) = indulgence in embodiment.

When we compare the four static kinds of defilement, we notice:

1. static kind based in a particular viewpoint = *dṛṣṭi-upādāna*.
2. static kind in attraction to desire = *kāma-upādāna*.
3. static kind in attraction to form is a substitute for the old category *śīlavrata-upādāna*.
4. static kind in attraction to gestation = *ātmabhāva-upādāna*.

The old expression *śīlavrata-upādāna* seems to have lost meaning over the centuries. It is problematical whether the substitute expression "static kind in attraction to form" is intended to be equivalent to the old category, especially since the *śīlavrata-upādāna* can be subsumed under *dṛṣṭi-upādāna* (cf. Lamotte, *Le Traité*, I, 423), and thus disappear from explicit mention.

57 For this theory, see Th. Stcherbatsky, *The Central Conception of Buddhism and the Meaning of the Word "Dharma"* (reprint, Calcutta, 1961). Each moment of consciousness (a *citta*) appears simultaneously with a mental nature (a *citta-dharma*). The mental nature colors the consciousness or is reflected in it; the consciousness thus knows the mental nature.

retinue, and lordliness. In the same way, this nescience entrenchment called 'static kind in attraction to [supramundane] gestation' surpasses those four by way of entrenchment. It is the foundation exceeding the Ganges sands of secondary defilements. It has cohabited a long time with the four defilements. It cannot be erased by the knowledge of the Disciples and the Self-Enlightened. It is destroyed only by the enlightenment wisdom of the Tathāgatas.

"Lord, indeed the nescience entrenchment is of great power. For example, with indulgence as condition and fluxional action as basic cause, there arise the three kinds of gestation. In the same way, with nescience entrenchment as condition and nonfluxional action as basic cause, there arise the three bodies made of mind belonging to the Arhats, Pratyekabuddhas, and Bodhisattvas who have attained power. The nescience entrenchment is the condition for manifesting the nonfluxional *karma* and for the arising of these three bodies made of mind in three stages. Lord, there being a condition, a condition arises.[58] That being the case, the nescience entrenchment is the condition for nonfluxional action and for the three bodies made of mind. For this reason it has the same name as the static kind in attraction to [mundane] gestation. However, its action is not in common with the static kind in

58 This is a stock expression for the Buddhist doctrine of Dependent Origination (*pratītya-samutpāda*), which we have shown in our introductory subsection "Stages of the Bodies Made of Mind" to be fundamentally associated with *Śrī-Mālā*'s teachings about "nescience entrenchment," "*karma* without flux," and "bodies made of mind." Chi-tsang (pp. 169–70), while discussing the twelvefold Dependent Origination, mentions the old Buddhist teaching that "indulgence" (*upādāna*) (No. 9) is the cause of "motivations" (*saṃskāra*) (No. 2) and quotes (p. 170) from Nāgārjuna's *Madhyamaka-kārikā* (XXVI, "Surveillance of the Twelve Members," verse 7): "When there is indulgence (No. 9), the indulger's gestation (No. 10) evolves. If there were no indulgence, he would be liberated and have no gestation." Chi-tsang goes on to quote from the *Buddhagotraśāstra* (extant only in Chinese) concerning the four kinds of "indulgence" (*upādāna*) (see n. 56, above): The first two indulgences (in desires and in views) are nihilistic because they stick to the present and ignore the future; the last two indulgences (in useless rules and vows and in gestation) are eternalistic because they stick to the future. Besides, the first two especially concern ordinary persons, and the last two, the Disciples and the Self-Enlightened ones. Also, it is because of the first two that one "leaves home," i.e. enters the life of a monk; and it is because of the last two that one is a lay Buddhist. But how do the Arhats, Pratyekabuddhas, and Bodhisattvas who have attained power get reborn when they have eliminated "indulgence"? For this we move to Abhayākaragupta (*Muni*, p. 192–3), who quotes "Maitreya's Questions" (a section of the *Pañcaviṃśatisāhasrikā Prajñāpāramitā*): "Maitreya, I do not announce his rebirth under the control of *karma* and defilement; but I announce the Arhat's rebirth as the inconceivable transference of a 'manifestation' (**acintya-nirmita-pāriṇāmikīm*)."

attraction to [mundane] gestation, since the nescience entrenchment is indeed different from the four static kinds. It is to be eliminated by the Buddha stage and to be utterly eradicated by the enlightenment wisdom of the Tathāgata. The reason is that when the Arhats and the Pratyekabuddhas eliminate the four static kinds, they neither gain the power over the ending of fluxes nor do they manage to realize it directly.

"Lord, 'ending of fluxes' is a term applying to the nescience entrenchment. That being so, even the Arhats, the Pratyekabuddhas, and the Bodhisattvas in their last life, are obscured and prevented, are enwrapped and blinded by the nescience entrenchment. That is why they do not search and do not comprehend this and that nature (*dharma*). Not searching and not seeing this and that nature, they do not eliminate this and that nature which should be eliminated or purified. Since they do not eliminate or purify those natures to be eliminated, they are attended with remainder of liberation from faults, i.e. they are not liberated from all faults. They are subjects attended with remainder of purity since they are not subjects with complete purity. Their merits are attended with remainder because they do not have all merits. Lord, whoever are attended with a remainder of liberation from faults and so have not been liberated from all faults; who are subjects attended with remainder of purity and so are not subjects of complete purity; who are attended with remainder of merits and so do not have all merits are persons attended with remainder of suffering to search, attended with remainder of source of suffering to eliminate, attended with remainder of cessation of suffering to realize directly, and attended with remainder of path leading to the cessation of suffering to cultivate.

"Lord, whoever are attended with remainder of suffering to search, of source of suffering to eliminate, of cessation of suffering to realize directly, and of path leading to the cessation of suffering to cultivate are persons who have a fractional Nirvāṇa. Those who have attained a fractional Nirvāṇa, Lord, are called 'directed toward the Nirvāṇa-realm.' Those who search all suffering, who eliminate all sources of suffering, who realize directly the cessation of suffering, and who cultivate all the paths leading to the cessation of suffering attain the permanent, calm, and cooled[59] Nirvāṇa in the world destroyed by impermanence and

59 The Sanskrit is *śītībhūta*, which Edgerton's *Buddhist Hybrid Sanskrit Dictionary* (p. 529) records as noted only as an epithet of the Buddha, but which is here used as a description of Nirvāṇa. However, this could be considered as consistent with

ever sick, and become the protection and refuge of the world in a world without protection and without refuge. Why so? Because Nirvāṇa is not attained by those who distinguish superior and inferior natures:[60] it is attained by those for whom knowledge is equal; it is attained by those for whom liberation is equal; it is attained by those for whom pure knowledge and vision are equal. Therefore the Nirvāṇa-realm has a single taste (*ekarasa*). That is to say, the tastes of knowledge and liberation are identical.[61] Lord, whichever persons do not eliminate or purify the nescience entrenchment, are ones without the single taste of the Nirvāṇa-realm; that is to say, for them, knowledge and liberation taste different.[62] Why is it so? Because they who do not eliminate or purify the nescience entrenchment, do not eliminate or purify the natures to be eliminated that are more numerous than the sands of the Ganges; and when they do not eliminate or purify the natures to be eliminated that are more numerous than the sands of the Ganges, they do not reach, do not experience directly the virtuous natures more numerous than the sands of the Ganges.

"Lord, that being the case, the nescience entrenchment is the source from which arise all the [primary] defilements and secondary defilements, which should be eliminated by contemplation. From that [nescience entrenchment] there also arise the secondary defilements on

Edgerton's entry because in the *Śrī-Mālā* the Buddha's Enlightenment is identified with the Nirvāṇa-realm.

60 The Sanskrit citation in the *Ratnagotravibhāga* adds: "It is attained by those for whom *dharmas* are equal." The Chinese versions also have slight differences in this paragraph concerning what is "equal".

61 Cf. E. M. Hare, tr., *The Book of the Gradual Sayings*, IV, Vol. 139: "Pahārāda, just as the ocean has but one taste, the taste of salt; even so this discipline of Dhamma has but one flavour, the flavour of release . . . ." This is illustrated and explained in the *Ratnagotravibhāga* (I, 93, and commentary):

> The similarity to light, rays, and the solar disk comes from the brightness, radiance, and purity (respectively) of insight (*prajñā*), knowledge (*jñāna*), and liberation (*vimukti*); and [comes] from their nonseparateness.

Here, "insight" is what dispels the darkness; "knowledge" is the omniscience obtained after that dispelling; "liberation" of the innate mind (*cittaprakṛti*) is the basis of the foregoing two; their nonseparateness is from the (pure) Dharmadhātu and its merits (*guṇa*).

62 The *Śrī-Mālā* insists that this different taste is due to the presence of defilement. In terms of the foregoing citation of the *Ratnagotravibhāga*, it means there is no "liberation" of the innate mind, compared to the solar disk, which is the basis of both "insight" and its consequent "knowledge" compared to light and rays. Hence, when knowledge and liberation taste different, they are not the ultimate knowledge and liberation pertaining to the Nirvāṇa-realm.

thoughts, on calming, on clear vision, on meditation, on intense concentration, on equipoise, on *yoga*, on knowing, on the fruit, on understanding, on power, on fearlessness.[63]

"Lord, the secondary defilements which are more numerous than the sands of the Ganges are utterly eradicated by the enlightenment wisdom of the Tathāgatas; and all of them arise from the nescience entrenchment. The nescience entrenchment is the cause and condition for all the secondary defilements and their manifestations. Those manifestations are momentary, a moment of consciousness and its associate (a *dharma*). From time immemorial, the nescience entrenchment has been unconscious. The natures to be eliminated, more numerous than the sands of the Ganges and which are utterly eradicated by the enlightenment wisdom of the Tathāgatas, are all natures whose substratum and foundation is the nescience entrenchment. For example, whatever kind of seed it be, or grass, shrub, herb, or tree, all of them are founded on soil, germinate on soil, and grow on soil. If the great earth were shattered, should disintegrate, be displaced, and become nonexistent, then whatever kind of seed it be, or grass, shrub, herb, or tree, all of them would be shattered, would disintegrate, be displaced, and become nonexistent. Lord, in the same way, the natures to be eliminated, exceeding the sands of the Ganges River, which are all utterly eradicated

63 The *Śrī-Mālā* implies that all the faculties in the list are possible to each sentient being by having the "embryo of the Tathāgata" but are not manifested or realized by reason of the defilement that covers their potentiality. The Bodhiruci translation, but not the Guṇabhadra (and the Tibetan gives no indication), interposes between the terms for meditation and intense concentration the characters equivalent to the Sanskrit *yāvat* meaning "up to", a standard way of indicating textual omission in Buddhist texts. This suggests that Bodhiruci understood an omission which probably amounts to the term *vimokṣa* (liberation) to fill out a well-known group of meditation, liberation, intense concentration, and equipoise—in Sanskrit, the (four) *dhyānas*, the (eight) *vimokṣas*, the (three) *samādhis*, and the (two or nine) *samāpattis* (cf. *Abhidharma-kośa*, VII, tr. p. 69, n. 3). This observation facilitates the subdivision of the *Śrī-Mālā* list, as follows: 1. The defilement on "thoughts" or consciousness (*citta*) is mentioned first because this is the initial association with defilement according to the suggestion of n. 92, below; and of course this defilement is common to all persons with defilement. 2. The next set starts with "calming" (*śamatha*) and "clear vision" (*vipaśyanā*). The Abhidharma literature sets forth that these two are subject to the five hindrances of sensuous lust, ill will, torpor and sleepiness, mental wandering and regret, and doubt; which also would constitute hindrances to the attainment of the group beginning with "meditation." 3. The next set appears to be praxis (*yoga*), knowing (*jñāna*), the fruit (*phala*), and understanding (*adhigama*). 4. The final set is "power" (*bala*) and "fearlessness" (*vaiśāradya*), which refer to the ten powers and the four confidences (cf. *Abhidharma-kośa*, VII, verse 28a–b, tr. p. 66; and nn. 69 and 75, below).

by the enlightenment wisdom of the Tathāgata, are founded on the nescience entrenchment, are situated on the nescience entrenchment, germinate and grow [there]. If the nescience entrenchment were eliminated or purified and were to become nonexistent, the natures to be eliminated, exceeding the sands of the Ganges River, which are all utterly eradicated by the enlightenment wisdom of the Tathāgata, would all be eliminated or purified and become nonexistent."

["Final Meaning" and "One Vehicle"]

"Lord, when all the defilements and secondary defilements are eliminated, one obtains the inconceivable Buddha natures exceeding the sands of the Ganges River. Then, as a Tathāgata-Arhat-Samyaksambuddha, one gains the unhindered understanding of all natures; is omniscient and all seeing, free from all faults and possessed of all merits; King of the Doctrine and Lord of the Doctrine; and, having gone to the stage which is sovereign over all natures, utters the Lion's roar: 'My births are finished; the pure life fully resorted to; duty is done; there is nothing to be known beyond this.' That being so, the Lion's roar of the Tathāgatas has final meaning (*nītārtha*),[64] and explains this meaning straightforwardly.[65]

64 This is virtually a thesis attributed to the Mahāsāṅghika: "All the Sūtras promulgated by the Buddha have 'final meaning'" (Bareau, *Les sectes*, p. 67). A sūtra of "final meaning" contrasts with one of "provisional meaning" (*neyārtha*)—occurring in the *Śrī-Mālā* in the form "not final meaning" (**anītārtha*), that is, a sūtra whose utterance is not complete and final and therefore requires consultation of other sūtras. While it might appear here to be favoring the Mahāsāṅghika thesis, the *Śrī-Mālā* is only stressing the superiority of the "final meaning" scripture with its "One Vehicle" message, as is borne out in the next note, No. 65.

65 At this point there is no help from the commentaries, such as Chi-tsang, p. 191. The Tibetan translation for "straightforwardly," *mgo gcig tu*, could be equivalent to the Sanskrit *ekāṃśa*. G. M. Nagao's *Index to the Mahāyāna-Sūtrālaṃkāra* contains the item *an-ekāṃśa-vāda-parigraha*, Tib. *mgo gcig tu ma yin paḥi smra ba yoṅs su bzuṅ*, "denying the *ekāṃśa* school," translated into Chinese with the same characters for *ekāṃśa-vāda* that are used by both Guṇabhadra and Bodhiruci at this point in the *Śrī-Mālā*. Hence, there is no doubt that the original text of the *Śrī-Mālā* contained the term *ekāṃśa*, probably in the adverbial form *ekāṃśena* (Pāli, *ekaṃsena*). "Straightforwardly" is one of the four ways of explanation (*vyākaraṇa*) used to answer questions, as in the *Aṅguttara-Nikāya* (Book of Fours), *The Questions of King Milinda* (12th Dilemma), *Abhidharma-kośa* (Chapter Five, verse 22), and *Mahāvyutpatti* (Nos. 1657–1661). According to the *Abhidharma-kośa*, to such a question as "Do all beings die?" a straightforward or categorical answer is given, "They die." To such a question as "Will all beings be reborn?" a distinguishing (*vibhajya*) answer is given, "Beings with defilement will be reborn; beings devoid of defilement will not be reborn." To such

"Lord, there are also two kinds of knowing indicated by the statement 'There is nothing to be known beyond this.'

"The Tathāgata, having shattered and defeated the four Māras[66] by the incomparable victory of a Buddha, gained the Dharmakāya which is superior to all the worlds and which cannot conceivably be witnessed by any sentient being.[67] Having been made Lord of the Doctrine unhindered in all stages of the knowable, he rightly saw that there is no duty or stage beyond this to be left over or to be understood. Having properly entered the supreme incomparable stage[68] which is fearless and endowed with the power of the ten powers,[69] and having clearly seen

---

a question as "Is man superior or inferior?" a counter question is asked, "With respect to what?" with explanation depending on the response. To such a question as "Are the personality aggregates the same as the living being?" an explanation is refused because the "living being" is indeterminate ("nonexistent"). We reach the striking conclusion that the *Śrī-Mālā* associates the *ekāṃśa* type of explanation with the type of scripture called *nitārtha* (of final meaning). By implication, the scripture "of provisional meaning" (*neyārtha*) is associated with distinguishing (*vibhajya*) explanations. In fact, both the "straightforward" and the "distinguishing" kinds of explanation are found in the *Śrī-Mālā*: the "Lion's roar of the Tathāgata" illustrates the straightforward explanation; and the "two kinds of passing away", the distinguishing explanation.

66 Māra means "death" either metaphorically or concretely. There are four Māras: 1. The personality-aggregate Māra is the five grasping aggregates. Man dies among these. 2. The defilement Māra is the reason for man's birth and hence for his death. 3. The killing Māra fixes the time of death. 4. The son-of-the-gods Māra obstructs the yogin who is trying to transcend death. This Māra is king of the Paranirmitavaśavartin gods. According to Vasubandhu, the Buddha defeated the son-of-the-gods Māra at dusk beneath the Tree of Enlightenment by passing through the four "boundless states"—love, compassion, sympathetic joy, and indifference. At the time of enlightenment at dawn, he defeated both the defilement Māra and the personality-aggregate Māra. At Vaiśālī, three months before passing into Nirvana, he repressed the life motivation and thus defeated the killing Māra. This data is drawn from Wayman, "Buddhism," in *Historia Religionum*.

67 Abhayākara (*Muni*, p. 197–5) explains the expression "difficult to see" (an epithet of Nirvāṇa without remainder) as meaning "far transcending the domain of the fleshly and divine eyes." For these two kinds of eyes, see n. 104, below.

68 This stage according to the *Śrī-Mālā* is certainly the Nirvāṇa-realm and the Buddha-stage. The chief Buddha natures are indicated as going with this stage, to wit: "fearless" standing for the four confidences (see n. 75, below), "endowed with the power of the ten powers" standing for the ten of n. 69, below, and "having clearly seen all the knowable with unhindered knowledge," which points to the Buddha eye or the eighteen exclusive Buddha natures of n. 42, above.

69 This is a well-known list, but the *Mahāvastu* has the peculiar feature of identifying the ten with the "Dharma eye" of the Samyaksambuddha (Basak ed., I, 188–89), more technically as the "mental penetration" (*mano-vibhūtā*) of the ten powers (*adśa-bala*):

all the knowable with unhindered knowledge, he uttered the Lion's roar with the knowing, 'There is nothing to be known beyond this.'

"Lord, the Arhats and Pratyekabuddhas overcame the dangers of *saṃsāra* and promptly experienced the pleasure of liberation, rightly observing, 'Thus I have been liberated from the dangers of *saṃsāra* and will not again experience the sufferings of *saṃsāra*.' The Arhats and the Pratyekabuddhas, having realized, 'There is nothing to be known beyond this,' decided that they were in the supreme Nirvāṇa stage of the arrested breath.[70] Furthermore, when they so realized, they were

---

He discerns the possible and the impossible. This is the first power of the unlimited intellects. He knows every direction of the path. This is the second power. He knows the various realms in the world. This is the third power. He knows the diversity of faiths. This is the fourth power. He knows the addictions and merits of other persons. This is the fifth power. He recognizes the auspicious and inauspicious force of *karma*. This is the sixth power. He knows defilement and purification; knows meditation and equipoises. This is the seventh power. He knows the many modes of his former lives. This is the eighth power. There is the ninth power when he has the perfectly clear divine eye. There is the tenth power when he attains the destruction of all defilements.

Among those, the fifth power is substituted for "the power of knowing what is and is not the best sense organ" of the *Mahāvyutpatti* list; and the ninth power is more fully stated in other lists as "the power of knowing death, transfer, and rebirth." The expression "unlimited intellects" (*aprameya-buddhi*) stresses the discriminative faculty. In some Mahāyāna lists of "five eyes" the expression "knowledge eye" (*jñāna-cakṣus*) is substituted for the Dharma-eye, consistent with the stress on knowledge in the ten powers. The Pāli *Aṅguttara-Nikāya* (v. 32–36) also associates the lion's roar with the ten powers (cf. Ananda K. Coomaraswamy and I. B. Horner, *Gotama the Buddha*, pp. 222–24.). For the most extended treatment of the ten powers, see Lamotte, *Le traité*, III, 1505–66.

70 In the Fourth Dhyāna there is no inbreathing or outbreathing (cf. *Abhidharma-kośa*, VIII, tr. p. 161). Also, see J. J. Jones, tr., *The Mahāvastu*, II, 120–21, concerning the "breath-holding meditation" (*āsphānaka*). Furthermore, the *Abhidharma-kośa* (VI, tr. p. 177) states: "The Teacher and the Rhinoceros [i.e. the Pratyekabuddha] go up to enlightenment by way of an identical session in the last [i.e. the Fourth] Dhyāna." Also Pūrṇavardana in his commentary on the *Abhidharma-kośa* (the *ṭīkā-lakṣaṇānusāriṇī*, PTT Vol. 118, pp. 81–84) points out in comments on the eighth chapter that the Lord Buddha realized the incomparable rightly completed enlightenment by recourse to the Fourth Dhyāna. *Śrī-Mālā*'s passage seems to mean that the Fourth Dhyāna must be reached for the fractional Nirvāṇa as well as for the Tathāgata's Nirvāṇa-realm that is equivalent to the enlightenment. The unconstructed Nirvāṇa is the same for whichever saint reaches it; the difference is that the Tathāgata alone has this Nirvāṇa accompanied by the innumerable Buddha natures. The Arhats and the Pratyekabuddhas are quite right in deciding that they have reached the ultimate state, but for them it is not the "incomparable rightly completed enlightenment." Bareau (*Recherches sur la biographie*, p. 69) points out that all the sources represented by five different

subjects (*dharmin*) undeceived regarding that stage. Besides, they insisted on thinking, 'Without dependence on another, I have attained the [Nirvāṇa] stage with remainder;[71] I am certainly in the incomparable rightly completed enlightenment.'

"Why is that so? Because the vehicles of the Disciples and the Self-Enlightened ones are included in the Great Vehicle. Lord, 'Great Vehicle' is an expression for Buddha Vehicle. In that way, the three vehicles are counted as one vehicle (*ekayāna*). By realizing the 'one vehicle' one attains the incomparable rightly completed enlightenment. Lord, 'incomparable rightly completed enlightenment' is an expression for the Nirvāṇa-realm. 'Nirvāṇa-realm' is an expression for the Dharmakāya of the Tathāgata. The ultimate realization of the Dharmakāya is the One Vehicle. Lord, the Tathāgata is not one thing, and the Dharmakāya something else, but the Tathāgata is himself the Dharmakāya. The ultimate realization of the Dharmakāya is the ultimate of the One Vehicle. Lord, 'ultimate of the One Vehicle' is an expression for the absoluteness of the One Vehicle. Why so? Because, Lord, the Tathāgata does not dwell within the limits of time; the Tathāgata-Arhat-Samyaksambuddhas dwell at the uttermost limit. The Tathāgatas do not have a time limit for their compassion or for their pledge to heal the world. When people exclaim, 'Ah, for the world's benefit he has compassion without temporal limit, has the pledge without temporal limit,' they refer to the Tathāgata himself! When people exclaim, 'Ah, for the world's benefit he is the Refuge with imperishable nature, permanent nature, steadfast nature,' they refer to the Tathāgata himself! Lord,

---

traditions agree that the four meditations (the four Dhyāna) are the preparatory phase for the great enlightenment. *Mkhas grub rje's Fundamentals*, p. 27, mentions the legend that after Gautama had spent six years practicing austerities on the bank of the Nairañjanā River, he was equipoised in the great part of the "great Fourth Meditation" in the "unstirring *samādhi*" (*āniñjyo-nāma-samādhi*) and the "space-filling *samādhi*" (*āspharaṇaka-samādhi*) (apparently equivalent to the *āsphānaka-samādhi*). The Buddhas gathered from every direction, roused him from the *samādhi*, and informed him that this *samādhi* alone does not lead to Complete Buddhahood. They guided his "body made of mind" to the Akaniṣṭha heaven (in the pure abodes at the top of the realm of form), and there he became a Manifest Complete Buddha.

71 Nirvāṇa with remainder means cessation of all defilements (*kleśa*) while the personality aggregates (*skandha*) remain. According to Asaṅga's *Yogācārabhūmi*, this Nirvāṇa is free from all sufferings that would be due to one's own evolving perceptions but is not free from sufferings due to being alive such as result from hunger and thirst or are inflicted by hostile creatures (Wayman, "Buddhism," in *Historia Religionum*).

since that is the case, the Tathāgata-Arhat-Samyaksambuddhas in the world without refuge and without a protector are the imperishable refuge, the permanent refuge, the steadfast refuge at the uttermost limit.[72]

"Lord, 'Dharma' is an expression for teaching the path of One Vehicle. 'Saṃgha' is an expression for the host of the three vehicles. The second one of these refuges is the ancillary refuge of the first one and is not the highest refuge. Why is it so? Because the Dharma which teaches the path of One Vehicle is the ultimate realization of the Dharmakāya, and beyond this [the Dharmakāya] there is nothing whatever that concerns the Dharma which teaches the path of One Vehicle! The host of the three vehicles takes refuge, through fear, in the Tathāgata, then seeks the method of coming forth [in the religious life], studies and practices, and becomes directed toward the incomparable right completed enlightenment. Hence the second refuge is not the highest one; it is the refuge with temporal limitation.[73]

72 Abhayākaragupta (*Muni*, pp. 271–5 to 272–1): "He has the merit (*guṇa*) of dwelling at the limit of *saṃsāra* for the benefit and happiness of all sentient beings; because, after taking his post at the immaculate Dharmadhātu which is the limit of *saṃsāra*, at the time of candidates his doctrines of *sūtras* flow naturally in accordance with that uttermost limit and at that time he dwells in diverse ways." The *Ratnagotravibhāga* (text, p. 9) quotes the *Jñānālokālaṃkāra-sūtra* as follows: "Mañjuśrī, he the Tathāgata-Arhat-Samyaksambuddha is called 'Devoid of birth and cessation'"; and quotes (text, pp. 9–10) the same sūtra as follows: "Mañjuśrī, when the Tathāgata gained the Revelation-Enlightenment toward all natures of such sort, and observed the Dharmadhātu of the sentient beings as impure, not free from stain, and blemished, his Great Compassion named 'Playful' went forth toward the sentient beings."

73 The *Ratnagotravibhāga* discusses this viewpoint of the *Śrī-Mālā* in verses I, 19–21 and commentary (cf. Sanskrit text, pp. 17–20, and Takasaki, tr. pp. 180–85). Verse I, 20 summarizes the reasons for denying ultimate status to the Doctrine (*dharma*) and the Congregation (*saṃgha*):

> Because [the Doctrine] is to be left behind, is of deceptive nature, and is negation; and because [the Congregation] is possessed of fear—the two kinds of Doctrine, and the Noble Congregation, are ultimately not the supreme Refuge.

The two kinds of Doctrine are the Doctrine as the Teaching and the Doctrine as Higher Comprehension. The Doctrine as the Teaching is formed of the scriptures and is to be left behind by the Doctrine as Higher Comprehension. The Doctrine as Higher Comprehension is both the Truth of Path, which is of deceptive nature because it is provisional, and the Truth of Cessation, which is mere negation (*abhāva*) because it is described by absence of defilement and suffering. The Noble Congregation is the disciples in the three vehicles; with fear they take refuge in the Tathāgata. However, the *Śrī-Mālā* accepts the Doctrine as more worthy of refuge than the Congregation, because the Doctrine is the primary issuance from the Tathāgata. Even

"Lord, when those sentient beings to be tamed by the Tathāgata go to the Tathāgata for refuge, they have faith flowing from true nature (*dharmatā*).[74] Therefore, they also go to the Dharma and to the Saṃgha of monks for refuge. It is because of their faith flowing from true nature that they go for refuge to those two refuges. But when they go for refuge to the Tathāgata, they do not go for refuge by reason of faith flowing from true nature. Lord, the going to the Tathāgata for refuge is the actual going for refuge. To the extent the other two goings for refuge are also actual, one must understand them as ultimately the same as going to the Tathāgata for refuge. The reason is that the Tathāgata is not one thing, and the two refuges something else. Lord, the Tathāgata is himself the three refuges. This is because the Dharma which teaches the path of One Vehicle is the speech of the Tathāgata as Lord of bulls and is the Lion's roar of the Tathāgata which has the four kinds of confidence.[75] It is also because, whatever the beliefs, they are furnished for the sake of the Mahāyānists by the Tathāgata when he furnishes the means of both vehicles. When there is no terminology of two vehicles, this is the ultimate case where the One Vehicle is the genuine vehicle and incorporates the three vehicles.

---

so, the downgrading of the Doctrine and the Congregation refuges is done from the ultimate standpoint. When the *Śrī-Mālā* speaks earlier of "Embrace of the Illustrious Doctrine," it insists at length that one must rely on both the scriptures and a spiritual guide.

74 "Faith flowing from true nature" translates the Sanskrit *dharmatā-niṣyanda* (cf. Edgerton, *Buddhist Hybrid Sanskrit Dictionary*, p. 309). Their faith is a natural outcome, or an automatic consequence, of their going to the Tathāgata for refuge.

75 The association between the lion and the four confidences is set forth in the *Ratnagotravibhāga* (III, 10; comment in III, 32–34) by four key expressions (in italics):

> As the king of beasts in the forest is always free from fear and moves fearlessly amidst the beasts, so also the lion who is king of sages 'moves' amidst his flock, *unmolested* [by any danger], *self-reliant* [since even pure beings cannot compare], *abiding firm* [in *samādhi*], and *victorious* [over the nescience entrenchment].

The key expressions refer to the four confidences (with explanations here given according to Edgerton's *Buddhist Hybrid Sanskrit Dictionary*):

1. "Abiding firm": confidence that he is fully enlightened about all natures.
2. "Victorious": confidence in knowing the destruction of all defiling fluxes.
3. "Unmolested": confidence that he explains exactly and definitely the obstructive conditions (to the religious life).
4. "Self-reliant": confidence in the correctness of his path of salvation for realizing all (religious) success.

6. The Boundless Noble Truths

"Lord, when the Disciples and the Self-Enlightened ones have their one [-sided] knowledge which initially comprehends the four Noble Truths, they eliminate a certain amount of the static kinds [of defilement]. With that one [-sided] knowledge they realize directly the four merits of search and so on, and acutely discriminate the four objects according to their true nature. Lord, in the supramundane knowledge there is no progression of four knowledges and no progression of four meditative objects.[76] The supramundane knowledge which is diamond-like[77] is of nonprogressive nature. Lord, that being the case, all the Disciples and the Self-Enlightened ones actually know the first kind of knowledge of the Noble Truths which eliminates static kinds [of defilement], but they do not have the second kind of knowledge of the Noble Truths for eliminating the static kinds. Lord, the Tathāgata-Arhat-Samyaksambuddhas are outside the sensory domain of all disciples and Self-Enlightened ones, and eliminate all the defilement-stores by inconceivable voidness knowledge. The ultimate knowledge which disintegrates the entire defilement-store is entitled 'Right Knowledge.' The first kind of knowedge of the Noble Truths is not the ultimate knowledge but is the knowledge on the way towards the incomparable right completed enlightenment.

"Lord, the meaning of 'Noble' does not apply to any of the Disciples or Self-Enlightened ones. Both have a measurable merit, and because their merit is ancillary to that [Truth] the Disciples and the Self-Enlightened ones are called 'Noble' (*ārya*). The Noble Truths are not Truths belonging to the Disciples and the Self-Enlightened ones and are not merit belonging to them. Lord, these truths were first discovered by the Tathāgata-Arhat-Samyaksambuddhas; and after being fully

76 The *Śrī-Mālā* here refers to the four Noble Truths as the "four objects" and as the "four meditative objects." Each of these goes with one of the "four knowledges" or "four merits of search and so on." Thus, the Noble Truth of Suffering is to be searched out; the Truth of Source of Suffering is to be eliminated; the Truth of Cessation is to be directly realized; and the Truth of Path is to be contemplatively cultivated.

77 The reference is to the "adamantine *samādhi*" (*vajropama-samādhi*). According to Asaṅga (Wayman, *Analysis*, p. 134), "this *samādhi*, being among all learned *samādhis*, chief, best, most hard, most firm, overcomes all defilements and is not overcome by defilements of birth."

understood by them were revealed and taught to the world which is enclosed in the shell of nescience. That is the way one should understand the Noble Truths.

7. The Tathāgatagarbha

"Lord, the explanation of the meaning of the Noble Truths should be considered to be profound and subtle, difficult to understand, incapable of being judged, and not in the domain of logic. It takes a wise man to appreciate it.[78] It cannot be the concern of any worldly persons. Why is that? Because this profound teaching explains the Tathāgatagarbha (embryo of the Tathāgata). The Tathāgatagarbha is the domain of the Tathāgata. It is not the domain of any Disciple or Self-Enlightened one. Lord, the Tathāgatagarbha is the locus of this explanation of the meaning of the Noble Truths. Because the locus of the Tathāgatagarbha is profound, the meaning of the Noble Truths is considered to be profound and subtle, difficult to understand, incapable of being judged, and not in the domain of logic. It takes a wise man to understand it. It cannot be the concern of any worldly persons.

"Lord, whoever does not doubt that the Tathāgatagarbha is wrapped up in all the defilement-store, also does not doubt that the Dharmakāya of the Tathāgata is liberated from all the defilement-store. When anyone's mind reaches the ultimate purport of the Tathāgatagarbha, the Dharmakāya of the Tathāgata and inconceivable realm of the Buddha, he has implicit trust and the conviction in two kinds of explanation of the meaning of the Noble Truths. The two kinds of explanation of the meaning of the Noble Truths are difficult to know and difficult to understand.

"Lord, what are the two kinds of explanation regarding the meaning of the Noble Truths? The Create and the Uncreate explanations regarding the meaning of the Noble Truths.[79] The Create explanations of

78 The language used here by *Śrī-Mālā* goes back to stock phraseology of the *Brahmajālasutta* (in *Dīgha-Nikāya*, Vol. I): "Monks, there are other doctrines, profound, difficult to discern, difficult to understand, peaceful, not in the domain of logic, subtle, to be appreciated only by a wise man. These the Tathāgata has realized by himself and penetrates with direct experience."

79 The "Create" explanation involves aiming at "Cessation of Suffering" but not fully achieving it. The "Uncreate" explanation involves aiming at "Cessation of Suffering" accompanied by innumerable Buddha natures, and fully achieving it. The Sanskrit for "Uncreate" is *akṛta*, according to *Ratnagotravibhāga* (text, p. 12, line 11). Therefore, *kṛta* is the Sanskrit for "Create."

the meaning of the Noble Truths present the four Noble Truths with intellectual limitation. Why so? Because when one depends on another person, one does not seek out all suffering, eliminate all sources of suffering, directly realize the cessation of all suffering, cultivate all the path leading to the cessation. That being the case, not only are there both the constructed and the unconstructed *saṃsāra*, but also there are both the constructed and the unconstructed *nirvāṇa*.[80] Lord, the Uncreate explanations of the meaning of the Noble Truths present the Noble Truths without intellectual limitation. Why so? Because in dependence on oneself, one seeks out all deepfelt suffering, eliminates all deepfelt sources of suffering, directly realizes the deepfelt cessation of all suffering, cultivates all the deepfelt path leading to the cessation. That being the case, those explanations by the Tathāgata of the four Noble Truths become eight kinds (four Create and four Uncreate) of Noble Truths.

"Lord, the Tathāgata-Arhat-Samyaksambuddhas perfect those four Uncreate explanations of the meaning of the Noble Truths. The Disciples and the Self-Enlightened ones do not perfect them, for the reason that one cannot understand the realm of Nirvāṇa by understanding natures as superior, middling, and inferior. Then how is it that the Tathāgata-Arhat-Samyaksambuddhas perfect the Uncreate explanations of the meaning of the Noble Truths? It is because all the Tathāgata-Arhat-Samyaksambuddhas completely know all future suffering, eliminate every source of suffering which incorporates any defilement

80 Our Introduction ("Vehicle and Nirvāṇa") gives more material. We may summarize here in tabular form:

	Nirvāṇa	Saṃsāra
Unconstructed:	"Cessation of Suffering"	"Suffering"
Constructed:	Buddha natures	Defilement-stores

Here "Suffering" is the Tathāgata-garbha; and "Cessation of Suffering" is the Dharmakāya. The two kinds of Nirvāṇa and Saṃsāra are apparently mentioned by the *Śrī-Mālā* at this point to rationalize the "Create" and "Uncreate" explanations of the Noble Truths. The tabulation neatly suggests the possible combinations. The ordinary person has the "Suffering" and defilement-stores. The saint combines "Cessation of Suffering" with defilement-stores. The Tathāgata has "Cessation of Suffering" with Buddha natures. With compassion he returns to the world, applying the Buddha natures to "Suffering." In the position of the *Śrī-Mālā*, the constructed is extrinsic to the unconstructed. Cf. the later sentences of the *Śrī-Mālā*: "The one Truth—Cessation of Suffering—excludes the realm with the characteric of suffering" and "The Tathāgatagarbha excludes [*vyativṛtta*] the realm with the characteristic of the constructed."

or secondary defilement, and realize the cessation of all suffering amounting to the cessation of the entire mind aggregate.[81]

8–9. The Dharmakāya and the Meaning of Voidness

"Lord, the cessation of suffering is not the destruction of Dharma. Why so? Because the Dharmakāya of the Tathāgata is named 'cessation of suffering,'[82] and it is beginningless, uncreate, unborn, undying, free from death; permanent, steadfast, calm, eternal; intrinsically pure, free from all the defilement-store; and accompanied by Buddha natures more numerous than the sands of the Ganges, which are nondiscrete, knowing as liberated, and inconceivable. This Dharmakāya of the Tathāgata when not free from the store of defilement is referred to as the Tathāgatagarbha.[83]

81 Saeki (p. 230) explains "mind" as "body made of mind" and "aggregate" as "the five aggregates of flux." This comment refers to the body made of mind accompanied by the five personality aggregates in their defiled form. Chi-tsang (p. 225) states that the suffering of the body made of mind is the future suffering for Arhats and Pratyekabuddhas. If they can understand this kind of suffering, they can understand all (= "entire") sufferings. Hanayama's Shōtoku Taishi (p. 117) explains "entire" as the suffering covering the three worlds. Chi-tsang's comment readily accords with *Śrī-Mālā*'s thesis that the Arhats and the Pratyekabuddhas have a remainder of rebirth.

82 From "Lord" down to "cessation of suffering" the translation is completely from Tibetan since it makes better sense in this context than the two Chinese translations. Regarding the terminology "cessation of suffering," the *Ratnagotravibhāga* (text, p. 12, 3–5) has this explanation: " 'Imagination' (*vikalpa*) means the 'improper mental orientation' (*ayoniśo-manasikāra*) which is the cause for the arising of action (*karma*) and defilement (*kleśa*). That ultimate nonarising of suffering when there is no coursing of the imagination of duality after one has penetrated the intrinsic cessation of that [imagination]—this is called 'Cessation of Suffering.' "

83 The last sentence is translated according to Johnston's editing of the *Ratnagotravibhāga* (text, p. 12.14): *ayam eva ca bhagavaṃs tathāgatadharmakāyo 'vinirmuktakleśakośas tathāgatagarbhaḥ sūcyate*, which is apparently the reading adopted in both Chinese translations of the *Śrī-Mālā*. The Tibetan interprets the sentence without the *avagraha*: "The Tathāgatagarbha when free from the store of defilement is referred to as the Tathāgata's Dharmakāya," which is somewhat forced. The *avagraha* appears quite in order, since it preserves the Dharmakāya as the topic of discussion, as it has been throughout the paragraph. Doctrinally, this remark does not identify the Dharmakāya and the Tathāgatagarbha; in fact, this is the closest the *Śrī-Mālā* ever comes to doing so. Elsewhere the *Śrī-Mālā* insists that the Tathāgatagarbha is not a self and that the Dharmakāya is self. The parallelism of Nirvāṇa and Saṃsāra (see n. 80, above) depends on the contrast of the Dharmakāya and the Tathāgatagarbha. However, they approach through the terminology of "Thusness" (*tathatā*), which undefiled is the Dharmakāya and defiled is the Tathāgatagarbha.

"Lord, the knowledge of the Tathāgatagarbha is the voidness knowledge[84] of the Tathāgatas. The Tathāgatagarbha is something not seen before or understood before[85] by any Disciple or Self-Enlightened one.[86] It has been seen directly and understood by the Lord. The voidness knowledge of the Tathāgatagarbha is of two kinds. The two are as follows:

"Lord, the Tathāgatagarbha is void of all the defilement-stores, which are discrete and knowing as not liberated.

"Lord, the Tathāgatagarbha is not void of the Buddha *dharmas* which are nondiscrete, inconceivable, more numerous than the sands of the Ganges, and knowing as liberated.

"Lord, these two kinds of voidness knowledge of the Tathāgatagarbha arouse trusting faith in the Lord, even by the great Disciples.[87] Lord, the voidness knowledge of all the Disciples and Self-Enlightened

84 "Voidness" is explained this way in the *Ratnagotravibhāga* (text, p. 76): *yad yatra nāsti tat tena śūnyam iti samanupaśyati*, "Whatever is lacking in some place, one observes that thing as the void of it." For example, "self" is the void of the five personality aggregates, otherwise stated as the "non-self" realization of Buddhism. In the *Śrī-Mālā*, the defilement-stores are the void of the Tathāgatagarbha. This scripture further speaks of "voidness knowledge" which knows that the Tathāgatagarbha is void of all the defilement-stores and is not void of the Buddha *dharmas*. For further information about the meaning of "voidness" here, see Ruegg, *La théorie*, pp. 319 f.

85 The *Ratnagotravibhāga* (text, p. 72) cites an unidentified scripture: "Therefore, the element of Tathāgata occurs as the state of embryo arisen in all sentient beings, but those sentient beings do not understand it." In this tradition, "do not understand it" means that those beings do not have the "perfection of insight" (*prajñāpāramitā*) that observes the void. This insight, according to the material in n. 94, below, takes after the "self" (i.e. the Dharmakāya) while procreating the Buddha natures. But those who take the Tathāgatagarbha as a "self" do not understand it. This position is well stated by Ueda Yoshifumi, "The Status of the Individual in Mahāyāna Buddhist Philosophy," in Charles A. Moore, ed., *The Status of the Individual in East and West*, p. 88: "The reason why he is non-self is the reason why he 'knows' his true self without conceptualizing it, and, at the same time, it is the reason why he can "'know' everything as it is (suchness, *tathatā*)."

86 Sanskrit, Tibetan, and Bodhiruci Chinese agree on the reading here accepted, "Disciple or Self-Enlightened one." Guṇabhadra shifts to the other set, "Arhat, Pratyekabuddha, or Bodhisattva who has attained power."

87 Saeki (p. 245) says that these are not disciples of the Hīnayāna, but Bodhisattvas in the Mahāyāna. Hence they are not meant to be disciples of a standard list, such as the ten great disciples in the *Vimalakīrtinirdeśa-sūtra*. Shōtoku (p. 123) says they are Bodhisattvas ranking "middle" in advancement. Chi-tsang does not comment. Possibly they are the Eighth Stage Bodhisattvas later called "Bodhisattvas possessed of the Great Doctrine."

ones involves the four wayward objects.[88] That being so, none of the Disciples or Self-Enlightened ones have ever seen before or understood before the cessation of all suffering. The Lord has experienced it directly and understood it. Also he has overcome all the defilement-store and cultivated all the path leading to the cessation of suffering.

10. The One Truth

"Lord, among those four Noble Truths, three Truths are impermanent and one Truth is permanent. Why so? Because the three Truths belong to the characteristic of the constructed, and anything belonging to the characteristic of the constructed is impermanent. Anything impermanent has an illusory nature. Everything with illusory nature is untrue, impermanent, and not a refuge. Therefore, the Noble Truths of Suffering, Source of Suffering, and Path leading to the Cessation of Suffering are actually untrue, impermanent, and not a refuge. Lord, among those [four], the one Truth—Cessation of Suffering—excludes the realm with the characteristic of the constructed. Anything excluding the realm with the characteristic of the constructed is permanent. Whatever is permanent lacks an illusory nature. Anything that lacks an illusory nature is true, permanent, and a refuge. Therefore, the Truth—Cessation of Suffering—is in reality true, permanent, and a refuge.

11–12. The One Refuge and Wayward Stage

"Lord, the Truth—Cessation of Suffering, being beyond the object of perception of all sentient beings, is inconceivable and is not the domain of knowledge of any Disciple or Self-Enlightened one. For example, just as a blind person cannot see forms, or as a seven-day-old infant cannot see the sun, so also the Truth, Cessation of Suffering, is neither the perceptual object of any immature ordinary person, nor the knowledge domain of any Disciple or Self-Enlightened one. Lord, 'perception of any immature ordinary person' is terminology for the wayward views of the two extremes. 'Knowledge of any Disciple or

88 The "four wayward objects" are specifically mentioned subsequently in the *Śrī-Mālā* as the four beginning with "they have the idea that the impermanent is permanent." The Disciples and Self-Enlightened ones rightly regard the "impermanent" of *saṃsāra* as "impermanent," and likewise the other three. But they fail to regard the "permanence" of the Dharmakāya, and so their voidness knowledge does not lead to the cessation of all suffering.

Self-Enlightened one' is terminology for pure knowledge.[89] 'Views of the two extremes' is terminology for the reasonings of the immature ordinary persons with egoistic attachment to the [five] grasping personality aggregates.[90] Lord, his 'extreme views' are two; and what are the two? The nihilistic view and the eternalistic view. If he would observe, 'The constructions are impermanent,' that would be his nihilistic view; that would not be his right view. If he would observe, 'Nirvāṇa is permanent,' that would be his eternalistic view; that would not be his right view. Why is that? Lord, when someone observes that body, sense organs, feelings, and volitions deteriorate in the present life, and he cannot understand or find their transmigration, then his viewpoint with such reasons, being a confused view, is the nihilistic view. Lord, when someone is confused regarding the stream of consciousness and cannot understand the momentary perishing of consciousness, his viewpoint with such reasons, being the view that the domain of perception does not alter, is the eternalistic view. Lord, in that way the reasoning views declare such to be the case; they insist on nihilism or insist on eternalism because their view goes too far from the meaning, or their view falls short of the meaning, or their view is mixed with a different character.[91] Lord, the sentient beings

89 As in n. 88, the Disciples and Self-Enlightened ones are said to have "pure knowledge" because when they observe, "The constructions are impermanent," it is indeed the impermanent of which they have knowledge. That is to say, they are free from the four wayward objects in the mundane sense.

90 There are five personality aggregates (Skt. *skandha*), namely, form or material aggregate (*rūpa*), feelings (*vedanā*), ideas (*saṃjñā*), motivations (*saṃskāra*), and perceptions (*vijñāna*). The *Śrī-Mālā* explains below that the sentient beings go astray in the four wayward objects, as applied to the five personality aggregates.

91 Chi-tsang (pp. 243–45): Their nihilistic view goes too far, because when they view the destruction of the personality aggregates, they infer (erroneously) that there is no continuation in the future. Their eternalistic view falls short, because when they do not observe the momentary perishing and rebirth in the stream of consciousness, they infer (erroneously) that it is permanent. Or their view is mixed with a different character, when they view something permanent and mix it with an impermanent character, or view something impermanent and mix it with a permanent character. Chi-tsang reports (p. 244) that someone used the rope and snake analogy: When you mistake a rope for a snake, you have gone too far; when you mistake a snake for a rope, you have fallen short. Saeki (p. 263) remarks on the difficulty of observing the momentariness in the stream of consciousness: one "moment" consists of 900 disappearances and appearances; one snap of the fingers consists of 64 moments. Without expressing it, the *Śrī-Mālā* is actually pointing to the Middle Doctrine which avoids the extremes of eternalism and nihilism. See in this connection Lamotte, *Le traité*, I, 422, where the classification of false views as two amounts to the eternalistic

go astray regarding the five grasping personality aggregates; they have the idea that the impermanent is permanent, suffering is pleasure, nonself is self, the impure is pure.[92]

"Lord, the domain of omniscient knowledge which is the Dharmakāya of the Tathāgata has never been seen before,[93] even by the pure knowledge of the Disciples and the Self-Enlightened. When sentient beings have faith in the Tathāgata and those sentient beings conceive [him] with permanence, pleasure, self, and purity, they do not go astray. Those sentient beings have the right view. Why so? Because the Dharmakāya of the Tathāgata has the perfection of permanence, the perfection of pleasure, the perfection of self, the perfection of purity. Whatever sentient beings see the Dharmakāya of the Tathāgata that way, see correctly. Whoever see correctly are called the sons of the Lord born from his heart, born from his mouth, born from the Dharma, who behave as manifestation of Dharma and as heirs of Dharma.[94]

---

and nihilistic views. Here the eternalistic view is a forbearance of consciousness (*cittakṣānti*) which takes the five personality aggregates as eternal; the nihilistic view is a forbearance of consciousness which takes the five aggregates as perishable. The Bodhisattva who can eliminate these two false views from sentient beings can eliminate the other views (amounting in all to sixty-two) from sentient beings and thus establish those beings in the Middle Path.

92 This is found in the *Aṅguttara-Nikāya* (Book of Fours): there are four waywardnesses each of ideas (*saññā*, Skt. *saṃjñā*), of consciousness (*citta*), and of views (*diṭṭhi*, Skt. *dṛṣṭi*). The *Śrī-Mālā* principally mentions the "idea" type of the four. Notice that Yüan-ts'ê (PTT, Vol. 106, p. 211–2) explains their order as 1) idea of the four, 2) view which is attached to the idea, and 3) consciousness with secondary defilements going with the view attachment.

93 The *Ratnagotravibhāga* (text, p. 30.21) quotes this passage and adds at this point "with voidness knowledge" (*śūnyatājñānena*), an expression that agrees with *Śrī-Mālā*'s position but is not in Tibetan or Chinese. Furthermore, the *Ratnagotravibhāga* II, 31–32, details the intractability to understanding. This is Verse II, 31: "Buddhahood, the domain of omniscient knowledge, is inconceivable and incapable of being understood by those with knowledge bodies, since it is not the domain of the three knowledges." Verse II, 32, mentions the three knowledges that fail to understand Buddhahood. Because of its subtlety, supreme meaning, and profundity of nature, it is respectively inaccessible to the knowledges derived from learning, pondering, and mundane contemplation.

94 This terminology was applied to Śāriputra (Pāli, Sāriputta), the Buddha's celebrated disciple, in *Majjhima-Nikāya* (III, 28–29), translated in Coomaraswamy and Horner, *Gotama the Buddha*, p. 201: "even so, in speaking aright of Sāriputta, he would say: 'He is the lord's own son, born of his mouth, born of *dhamma*, heir of *dhamma*, not heir of material things.'" Likewise, there is the passage in the *Saṁyutta-Nikāya* (II, 221): "son of the Lord, born from his heart and from his mouth, born from the *dhamma*, manifested by the *dhamma*, heir to the *dhamma*." Again, in the

"Lord, 'pure knowledge' is the knowledge perfection of all Disciples and Self-Enlightened ones, and accordingly is pure knowledge. Since the Truth—Cessation of Suffering—is neither the domain nor the object of pure knowledge, how much more is the Truth—Cessation of Suffering—not the domain, not the object, of those having [merely] the knowledge of the four resorts![95] Why is that? It was so that the beginners in the three vehicles would as undeluded subjects comprehend the meaning and fully understand the meaning that the Lord pointed out and explained the four resorts. These four resorts are mundane. Lord, this single resort, the Truth—Cessation of Suffering—is the best of all resorts and supramundane. That is said to be the genuine resort, and it is the refuge.

Ratnagotravibhāga (I, 34):

Whose seed is conviction in the highest vehicle;
Whose mother is Insight (*prajñā*) for procreation of the Buddha natures;
Whose womb is the felicity of meditation (*dhyāna*);
And whose nurse is compassion,
They are the sons, taking after the Munis.

They take after the Munis, because according to the *Ratnagotravibhāga* (text, pp. 31–32), the conviction takes after purity, the Insight after self, the meditation after pleasure, and the compassion after permanence; that is, they take after the four perfections of the Dharmakāya.

95 The four resorts are included in the *Mahāvyutpatti*, Nos. 1545–1549:

1. One should cultivate by resort to the meaning (*artha*), not by resort to the letter (*vyañjana*).
2. One should cultivate by resort to doctrines (*dharma*), not by resort to personalities (*pudgala*).
3. One should cultivate by resort to knowledge (*jñāna*), not by resort to perception (*vijñāna*).
4. One should cultivate by resort to a scripture of final meaning (*nitārtha*), not by resort to a scripture of provisional meaning (*neyārtha*).

See de La Vallée Poussin, *L'Abhidharmakośa*, Chap. IX, pp. 246–48, for the canonical references. Ratnākaraśānti's *Prajñāpāramitopadeśa* (PTT, Vol. 114, p. 237–3) explains the resorts according to the *Sūtrālaṃkāra* and other texts. For the most obscure set—*jñāna* and *vijñāna*—when we combine the references in de La Vallée Poussin (especially from the *Bodhisattvabhūmi*) with Ratnākaraśānti's explanations, we arrive at the following:

jñāna is supramundane insight (*prajñā*), devoid of discursive thought, namely, insight consisting in creative contemplation (*bhāvanāmayī prajñā*).

vijñāna is mundane insight, with discursive thought, namely, insight consisting in hearing (*śrutamayī prajñā*) and insight consisting in pondering (*cintāmayī prajñā*).

The *Śrī-Mālā* rejects this particular distinction of supramundane and mundane, and declares all four resorts to be mundane. Only the Truth "Cessation of Suffering" is supramundane. By this position, the *Śrī-Mālā* avoids entering into some hot disputes of Mahāyāna Buddhism, especially the arguments over the *nītārtha* and *neyārtha* sūtras.

13. Intrinsic Purity of the Mind

"Lord, *saṃsāra* is based on the Tathāgatagarbha. It was with reference to the Tathāgatagarbha that the Lord pointed out and explained, '[It is] without limit in the past.' Since there is the Tathāgatagarbha, there is a reason for speaking of 'cyclical flow' (*saṃsāra*). Lord, as to 'cyclical flow,' no sooner do the sense organs for perception pass away than it [the Tathāgatagarbha] takes hold of sense organs for perception, and that is 'cyclical flow.'[96] Lord, the two natures, 'passing away' and 'rebirth', are conventional terminology for the Tathāgatagarbha. Lord, 'perished' and 'born' are conventional terminology for the world (*loka*). 'Perished' is the loss of the senses. 'Born' is the renewal of the senses. But, Lord, the Tathāgatagarbha is not born, does not die, does not pass away to become reborn. The Tathāgatagarbha excludes the

96 The purport of *Śrī-Mālā*'s passage is expanded in the *Ratnagotravibhāga* (text, p. 55), including a quotation presumably from the lost *Ṣaḍāyatana-sūtra* (identification from Chinese made by Takasaki, p. 260):

> There is the meaning that the substrate lineage (*gotra*) has been passed down in an inconceivable manner. With reference to this point, it is said: "Derived from True Nature and passing from one existence to another since beginningless time, it is specialized by the six sense bases, becoming similar."

Since we have shown that the *Śrī-Mālā* is a Mahāsāṅghika work, it is reasonable to expect the passage in its text, which amounts to the Mahāsāṅghika thesis that there is no intermediate state (*antarābhava*) (Bareau, *Les sectes*, p. 68). What is more significant is the Buddhist sects or works that agree with this thesis. Bareau (*Les sectes*, p. 283) mentions, besides the Mahāsāṅghikas, the Theravādin, the Vibhajyavādin, the Mahīśāsaka, and the work *Śāriputraparipṛcchāsūtra*. In contrast (Bareau, *idem*), the sects that maintain that there is an intermediate state are the Pūrvaśaila, Sammatīya, Sarvāstivādin, Vātsīputrīya, and the Later Mahīśāsaka. It is of considerable interest that the sects which deny the intermediate state are precisely those which modern research has lumped together as the sects more or less meant by the term "Vibhajyavādin" (included independently in the group) which the rival Sarvāstivādin employs in an adverse sense and not in the sense of the word given in n. 65, above. T. Kimura, in *Shūkyō kenkyū*, II (1925), 839–70, decided that the Mahāsāṅghika group of mountain sects (which, however, includes the Pūrvaśaila), to which he applied a term meaning "reserve forces" or "loose affiliation," is included in the Vibhajyavādin group. In the same volume, pp. 705–26, C. Akanuma decided that the Vibhajyavādin is just the Mahīśāsaka. Demiéville (*Origine de sectes bouddhiques*) made known to Western scholars the conclusions of these two Japanese scholars. Bareau (*Les sectes*, pp. 167–71) ably discusses the difficult question of the "Vibhajyavādin," which he understands to mean (in this adverse usage) "those who maintain distinct [i.e. heretical] theories." It appears that the literal meaning of the expression "Vibhajyavādin" might throw light on why the connotation is what Bareau has determined. The Sarvāstivādins would have a vehement reason for calling its rivals

realm with the characteristic of the constructed. The Tathāgatagarbha is permanent, steadfast, eternal. Therefore the Tathāgatagarbha is the support, the holder, the base of constructed [Buddha natures] that are nondiscrete, not dissociated, and knowing as liberated from the stores [of defilement]; and furthermore is the support, the holder, the base of external constructed natures that are discrete, dissociated, and knowing as not liberated.

"Lord, if there were no Tathāgatagarbha, there would be neither aversion towards suffering nor longing, eagerness, and aspiration towards Nirvāṇa. What is the reason? Whatever be these six perceptions, and whatever be this [other] perception, these seven natures[97] are unfixed, momentary, and lack experience of suffering; hence these natures are unfit for aversion towards suffering or for longing, eagerness, and aspiration towards Nirvāṇa. Lord, the Tathāgatagarbha has

"Vibhajyavādin" ("those who maintain the [unwarranted] division") because those rivals made subdivisions in the old sixth *vijñāna*, the "*mano-vijñāna*," which in its undivided form is all the Sarvāstivādin accepts outside of the five sense *vijñānas*. We notice that the Mahāsāṅghikas have a thesis of a "root *vijñāna*" and later of a Tathāgatagarbha, the Theravādins and the Vibhajyavādins a thesis of a "subconscious [*bhavāṅga-*] *vijñāna*," the Mahīśāsakas, in their illustrious Yogācāra son Asaṅga, a thesis of seventh and eighth *vijñānas* called "defiled mind" (*kliṣṭa-manas*) and "*ālaya-vijñāna*," all of which additions split up the old *mano-vijñāna* to give a resultant group of a new "*mano-vijñāna*" and one or more other elements. This literal interpretation is consistent with Bareau's connotational explanation because those Vibhajyavādins are led to espouse distinct theories (held by their rivals to be untenable), for example, that there is no intermediate state.

97 The six perceptions (*vijñāna*) are the five outer-door perceptions, i.e. eye-perception, ear-perception, nose-perception, tongue-perception, body- (i. e. skin-) perception; plus the mind-perception (*mano-vijñāna*). The other, added as a seventh perception, forces the sixth one, the mind-perception, to be simply the mental reflex of the five outer sense perceptions. Saeki (p. 291) explains the seventh to be the basis of the sixth perception, and to perceive intellectually or emotionally; it is a momentary stream like a stream of running water and sometimes perceives directly, at other times metaphorically with false imputation. Chi-tsang (p. 265) presents two theories which he rejects. The second theory uses the eight-*vijñāna* system (the eighth being the *ālaya-vijñāna*). However, a part of the second theory, claiming that the seventh perception knows *dharmas*, seems consistent with Saeki's explanation, and consistent with the earlier sentence in *Śrī-Mālā*, "Those manifestations are momentary, a moment of consciousness and its associate [a *dharma*]." The implication is that *Śrī-Mālā*'s seventh perception as a momentary stream is constituted by moments of consciousness, each of which know a *dharma* (a nature). Hence this seventh perception could also be called the "defiled mind" as in our introductory subsection "The Tathāgatagarbha and the *ālayavijñāna*." It might also be the "root consciousness" (*mūla-vijñāna*) among the Mahāsāṅghika theses (Bareau, *Les sectes*, p. 72).

ultimate existence without beginning or end, has an unborn and undying nature, and experiences suffering; hence it is worthy of the Tathāgatagarbha to have aversion towards suffering as well as longing, eagerness, and aspiration towards Nirvāṇa.

"Lord, the Tathāgatagarbha is neither self nor sentient being, nor soul, nor personality. The Tathāgatagarbha is not the domain of beings who fall into the belief in a real personality, who adhere to wayward views, whose thoughts are distracted by voidness. Lord, this Tathāgatagarbha is the embryo of the Illustrious Dharmadhātu, the embryo of the Dharmakāya, the embryo of supramundane *dharma*, the embryo of the intrinsically pure *dharma*.

"Lord, this intrinsic purity of the Tathāgatagarbha stained by adventitious secondary defilements is the domain of the Tathāgata, who is the inconceivable master. Why so? The virtuous consciousness, being momentary, is not defiled by defilements; and also the unvirtuous consciousness, being momentary, is not defiled by defilements. Lord, since neither do defilements touch that consciousness nor does that consciousness touch defilements, in that case, how does consciousness, having a noncontacting nature, get defiled? Lord, there is both the defilement and the defiled consciousness. Therefore, the meaning of the defilement on the intrinsically pure consciousness is difficult to understand.[98] The Lord alone has the Eye, the Knowledge for it. The Lord is the root of all Doctrines. The Lord is the omnipotent being. The Lord is the resort."

The Lord, having heard Queen Śrīmālā explain matters difficult to understand, sympathetically rejoiced and said, "Queen, exactly so! It is difficult to understand the meaning of the intrinsically pure consciousness in a condition of defilement. Queen, these two Doctrines are

98 The *Ratnagotravibhāga* (text, pp. 14.16 to 15.2) expands upon the *Śrī-Mālā* passage as follows: "Now, these two, the intrinsic brightness of consciousness and the defilement upon it, are of utmost difficulty to penetrate; indeed in the nonfluxional realm both the virtuous and the unvirtuous consciousness live alone, for which reason neither one contacts the other one." Obermiller (p. 139, note) translates Rgyal tshab rje's comment on this, which we paraphrase as follows: The difficulty stems from the fact that to interpret the situation we would ordinarily say that the two kinds of consciousness are either real or unreal. If real, they should be concomitant and contacting; if unreal, there is no cogency in the cause and effect relation implied in the prior purity and subsequent defilement. Rgyal tshab rje, whose main commentaries are on Buddhist logical works, leads us to conclude that only when we are free from such positing of reality or unreality can we understand it.

difficult to understand: the consciousness intrinsically pure is difficult to understand; and the defilement of that consciousness is difficult to understand. Queen, you as well as the Bodhisattvas possessed of the great Doctrine[99] are able to hear[100] these two Doctrines. Queen, the rest, the Disciples,[101] accept the two Doctrines only through faith in the Tathāgata."

CHAPTER FOUR

Entering the One Vehicle Path

14. The True Son of the Tathāgata

"Queen, whatever disciples of mine are possessed of faith and [then] are controlled by faith, they by depending on the light of faith have a knowledge in the precincts of the Dharma, by which they reach certainty in this.[102] Queen, 'knowledge in the precincts of the Dharma' is (a) vision of sensory representation in the range of the mind, (b) vision of the maturation of *karma*, (c) vision of the sleep of the Arhats, (d) vision

99 This is made clear by the *Ratnagotravibhāga* (I, 14–16) in the context where it quotes the *Śrī-Mālā* about the two Doctrines:

> The host (*gaṇa*) of nonregressing wise ones is accompanied with supreme merits because of their purity of introspective knowledge and vision within the phenomenal and the noumenal.
>
> Because they understand the peaceful nature of the world, there is the noumenal from the time they view the original privation of defilement on account of intrinsic purity.
>
> They have intelligence concerning the phenomenal limit of the knowable from the time they have the vision that there is the nature of omniscience in all sentient beings.

The *Ratnagotravibhāga* Sanskrit commentary mentions in the case of this intelligence of phenomenal limit that it starts from the First Bodhisattva Stage. That forces the intelligence of the noumenal to start from the Eighth Bodhisattva Stage at which stage the Bodhisattva becomes "nonregressing." Therefore, the "Bodhisattva possessed of the Great Doctrine" is the Bodhisattva who has attained power in the Eighth Stage.

100 Cf. the early passage in the *Śrī-Mālā*: "having heard that conception through divine sounds. . . ."

101 The *Ratnagotravibhāga* (p. 22.3–4) when quoting this passage adds "and the Self-Enlightened ones."

102 The Chi-tsang and Saeki commentaries point out that four successive stages of the disciple are meant, in two groups of two. This also can be inferred dimly from the grammar of the Tibetan translation of the sentence. These true sons of the

of the joy and pleasure in the meditation of those who control their mind, (e) vision of the magical power of the nobles[103] which belongs to the Arhats, Pratyekabuddhas, and to the Bodhisattvas who have attained power. Queen, in regard to having this skill in the five kinds of vision,[104] those who now and, after my passing, in future times are my disciples possessed of faith and [then] are controlled by faith, they by depending on the light of faith have a knowledge in the precincts of the Dharma, by which they reach certainty in the intrinsic purity and in

---

Tathāgata are 1) possessed of faith, and then 2) controlled by faith; they then 3) by depending on the light of faith gain a knowledge in the precincts of the Law and finally 4) reach certainty "in this." According to Chi-tsang (p. 278), there are two levels of faith: the disciples begin with faith in the teaching, and then advance to faith with understanding. (In the *Abhidharma-kośa*, "faith with understanding" is of four kinds, toward the Buddha, his Doctrine, and the Congregation, and toward the moral rules dear to the noble ones.) Then there are two levels of Dharma-knowledge: the disciples by depending on the light of faith gain a knowledge in the precincts of the Dharma, which is their breadth of knowledge; then they reach certainty, which is their depth of knowledge. Saeki (p. 305) tries to correlate the four levels with the Bodhisattva Stages: the one with simple faith precedes the Bodhisattva stages; the next one who adds understanding is on the First, Second, and Third Stages; the one who gains the knowledge in the precincts of the Dharma is on the Fourth, Fifth, and Sixth Stages; the one who reaches certainty is on the Seventh or higher Stage. In terms of the *Śrī-Mālā*'s subsequent three kinds of good son or daughter of the family, the one "who shrinks from gaining the knowledge of the profound Dharma by himself" is on the first two levels of discipleship. The one with the knowledge in the precincts of the Dharma is of course on the third level; and the one who has the profound Dharma through introspection is on the fourth or final level.

103 According to *Abhidharma-kośa* VIII (tr. p. 210) the "magical power of the nobles" is the supernatural power by which a saint transforms or empowers substance, and renounces life force.

104 Chi-tsang (pp. 278–81) presents many theories about the four levels of disciples, including the way in which they correspond with the five visions, and mentions a theory taking the first two visions with the first two levels, the third vision with the third level, the fourth vision with the fourth level, and assigning the fifth vision to a level beyond the fourth, namely to the Buddhahood fruit. However, this correspondence seems to violate the *Śrī-Mālā* text itself, which clearly assigns all five visions to "knowledge in the precincts of the Dharma," which the Chi-tsang commentary ascribes to the third level of discipleship. A possible solution that occurs to us stems from the *Mahāvastu*, a feasible source here because the *Śrī-Mālā* is so obviously colored by Mahāsāṅghika views. The *Mahāvastu* has a theory of the "five eyes" that differs in various ways from the descriptions of these eyes found in other traditions, such as in Sthiramati's subcommentary on the *Mahāyāna-Sūtrālaṃkāra*. The *Mahāvastu* (I. 187) states: "After they have come to the Tree of Enlightenment, but before they attain Omniscience (*sarvākārajñatā*), they [i.e. the Buddhas] become

the defilement of consciousness. Queen, that very certainty of theirs is a cause for installing [persons] in the path of the Great Vehicle. That being the case, because with faith in the Tathāgata they do not abandon the profound Doctrine, they are a great benefit to the living beings."

15. The Lion's Roar of Queen Śrīmālā

Then Queen Śrīmālā implored the Lord with these words: "May the Tathāgata's power make me eloquent for still further explanations of the faultless meaning!" The Lord replied: "Queen, you shall be eloquent!"

---

endowed with the five eyes." Briefly speaking (cf. J. J. Jones's translation of Vol. I, p. 123 ff.), the first eye is a superior eye of flesh, which by implying a superior set of all six senses appears to agree with the first vision, "of sensory representation which is the range of the mind." The second eye, called the "divine eye," has a standard meaning in Buddhist texts of seeing the beings passing to different destinies as a fruit of *karma*, mentioned as the second vision. It is of interest that the *Mahāvastu* says that this eye is concerned with forms made-of-mind (*tat pravṛttaṃ manomayeṣu rūpeṣu*). The *Mahāvastu* (I, 188) explains that the eye of insight (*prajñā-cakṣus*) is the one which the eight persons (see n. 55, above) up to the Arhat possess, but in the Buddha's case is clearer. In this connection, we should notice that the Chi-tsang commentary (p. 280) preserves the account of a scholar in China who, upon being asked about the obscure "vision of the sleep of the Arhats," examined some manuscripts of the *Śrī-Mālā* and suggested that "sleep" is a (graphical) corruption for "eye" or "light." It may be that the passage in question could be better translated, "vision belonging to the Arhats in their 'sleep' " with the suggestion that this "sleep" is the "Nirvāṇa of arrested breath" mentioned earlier in the *Śrī-Mālā*, and so their "sleep" would be a cessation of ordinary consciousness which nevertheless allows an insight that is the highest for the "eight persons." Those three eyes seem to agree reasonably well with the first three visions among the five visions. The last two eyes, the Dharma-eye and the Buddha-eye, descriptions of which have been translated in notes 69 and 42, respectively, do not obviously agree with the last two visions, nor obviously disagree. For purposes of accommodating the visions to "eyes," the fourth and fifth might be better translated "vision belonging to the joy and pleasure in the meditation of those who control their mind" and "vision of the magical power of the nobles belonging to the Arhats, Pratyekabuddhas, and Bodhisattvas who have attained power." Since the *Mahāvastu* credits the Buddha with a clearer vision in each case of an eye, the argument to be used if we wish to make those two eyes agree with the last two visions would be that the Dharma-eye is the same but clearer than the fourth vision, and that the Buddha-eye is the same but clearer than the fifth vision. Of course, if this explanation is considered reasonably cogent, we must revise Saeki's allocation of Bodhisattva stages to the four levels of discipleship. The five visions would pertain to experiences at the Tree of Enlightenment, and so "the knowledge in the precincts of the Dharma" should be allocated to the Eighth Stage, with the Jewel of Dharma arising on the Ninth Stage.

Queen Śrīmālā appealed to the Lord: "Lord, there are three kinds of good son of the family and good daughter of the family who guard themselves to be unblemished and unspoiled regarding the profound Dharma; and these generate much merit and also have entered the path of the Great Vehicle. Who are the three? Lord, (a) any good son of the family or good daughter of the family who has the profound Doctrine through introspection; (b) any good son of the family or good daughter of the family who has the knowledge in the precincts of the Dharma; (c) any good son of the family or good daughter of the family who shrinks from gaining the knowledge of the profound Doctrine by himself, thinking, 'I cannot possibly know it; this meaning can only be understood by the Tathāgata himself,' and so keeping the Lord in mind, obtains the mental presence of the Lord. Lord, those are the three kinds of good son of the family or good daughter of the family.

"Lord, there are sentient beings, differing from those three kinds of good son of the family or good daughter of the family, who occupy themselves seriously with the profound Dharma, but are attached to mistaken ideas and pose as teachers, talking much. Lord, may I defeat in the manner of a royal decree those persons who have turned their backs on the Illustrious Doctrine and who have the rotten seed of the heretics. May I utterly overcome those rotten seeds by the scope of command among gods, men, and demigods."[105]

When Queen Śrīmālā had appealed with those words, her retinue joined her in bowing to the feet of the Lord. The Lord then said to Queen Śrīmālā, "Excellent, most excellent, timely and opportune is your explanation of the means for properly guarding oneself in the profound Doctrine and your explanation of overcoming the enemies of the Illustrious Doctrine! Queen, the worship of a hundred thousand Buddhas is less a marvel than your explanation of the meaning."

Then the radiant Lord illumined the bodies of the entire retinue and ascended skyward to a height of seven *tala*.[106] By the magical power

105 The translation "demigods" is based on the Tibetan *lha ma yin*, indicating an original Sanskrit of *asura*. The inclusion here of the *asura* class suggests that the *Śrī-Mālā* follows the "six destinies" tradition, where the *asura* is added to the other five classes of gods, men, animals, hungry ghosts, and hell beings. Cf. Paul Mus, *La Lumière sur les Six Voies*.

106 Chi-tsang (p. 286) says that one *tāla*-tree is forty-nine feet high, so seven *tāla* make 343 feet. Cf. Coomaraswamy and Horner, *Gotama the Buddha*, pp. 48–49 (from *Dīgha-Nikāya*, III, 27): "When I had taught, roused, incited, and gladdened the assembly with talk on *dhamma*, I entered into the condition of fire and rose above the

of levitation he proceeded in the direction of Śrāvastī. Meanwhile Queen Śrīmālā and her retinue, with hands folded at their heads, were gazing enraptured and unblinking at the Lord. When the Lord passed out of sight, Queen Śrīmālā and her retinue showed utter transport in their faces. One by one and again and again they praised the merits of the Tathāgata. Not losing their attentive mindfulness of the Buddha, they returned to the city of Ayodhyā.

Back in the palace, Queen Śrīmālā converted King Yaśomitra to the Great Vehicle. She converted all the women in the capital seven years or older to the Great Vehicle. King Yaśomitra converted all the men in the capital seven years or older to the Great Vehicle. In the same manner the whole state was brought over to the Great Vehicle.

EPILOGUE

On his part, the Lord arrived at the Jetavana and called the venerable Ānanda.[107] He also remembered Devendra Śakra.[108] In an instant, Devendra Śakra, surrounded by the retinue of gods, appeared in front of the Lord. Then the Lord extensively explained this Scripture to Devendra Śakra and the venerable Ānanda:

"Kauśika, retain this scripture! Kauśika, explain it to the thirty-three gods! Ānanda, retain this scripture! Ānanda, explain it to the fourfold retinue—monks, nuns, male and female laymen!"

---

ground to the height of seven palm-trees, and after having produced a flame to burn and smoke to the height of another seven palm-trees, I came down again at the Gabled Hall in the Great Wood."

107 Ānanda was a first cousin of the Buddha and one of his principal disciples. According to tradition he was born on the same day as the Buddha. During the last twenty-five years of the Buddha's life, Ānanda was his constant attendant. He had a remarkable verbal memory, and in the First Council following the Buddha's death at the age of eighty, Ānanda although himself very aged recited the entire Sūtra canon. For a legendary explanation of Ānanda's name, see Étienne Lamotte, *Le Traité de la Grande Vertu de Sagesse de Nāgārjuna*, I, 225–31.

108 Śakra, powerful one of the gods (*devendra*), is a title of Indra. Kauśika, another of his names, is used in the *Śrī-Mālā* for direct address of Indra by the Buddha. In Indian mythology, Indra is the most powerful one of the thirty-three gods, is located in the East, and is regent of offerings. Buddhist mythology has reinterpreted Indra as a protector of Buddhism and includes the thirty-three gods as one group of the "six passion deities" in the realm of desire.

Then Devendra Śakra asked the Lord: "Lord, what is the name of this scripture and how is it to be retained?" The Lord replied: "Kauśika, this scripture has infinite merits. If all the Disciples and Self-Enlightened ones are unable to know, to discern, or to understand the entire meaning of this scripture, then how much less can other sentient beings! Kauśika, just so, this scripture is profound and a source of great merit. Therefore, I shall tell you the titles which convey the merits of the scripture. Listen well and retain them in mind!" Devendra Śakra and Ānanda urged the Lord, saying "Excellent! We will listen to what you teach." The Lord spoke as follows: "Retain this as 'Praises of the true and infinite merit of the Tathāgata.' Also retain it as 'The inconceivably great vows.' Also retain it as 'The great aspiration which includes all aspirations.' Also retain it as 'Teaching the inconceivable embrace of the Illustrious Doctrine.' Also retain it as 'Teaching the entering in one vehicle.' Also retain it as 'Teaching the boundless Noble Truths.' Also retain it as 'Teaching the Tathāgatagarbha.' Also retain it as 'Teaching the Dharmakāya.' Also retain it as 'Teaching the hidden purport of the meaning of voidness.' Also retain it as 'Teaching the one truth.' Also retain it as 'Teaching the permanent, steadfast, calm, eternal; and the one refuge.' Also retain it as 'Teaching what is the wayward stage.' Also retain it as 'Teaching the hidden purport that the mind is intrinsically pure.' Also retain it as 'Teaching the true son of the Tathāgata.' Kauśika, also retain it as 'Lion's roar of Queen Śrīmālā.' Also retain all explanations contained in this scripture as 'Eliminating all doubts, deciding the cause, clarifying the final meaning, and entering the One Vehicle path.'[109] Kauśika, I entrust to your hands this scripture that teaches the Lion's roar of Queen Śrīmālā. For as long as the Illustrious Doctrine lasts in the world, so may you recite and teach it in all the worlds of the ten quarters."[110]

109 The title as here given is the result of combining the Tibetan with the Chinese versions. The Tibetan *rgyu ba bcad pa daṅ / ṅes paḥi don daṅ / rton pa gcig pa źes bya bar* means "deciding the cause, [also] the final meaning, and the sole resort." The Chinese versions mean: "Eliminating all doubts, deciding the final meaning, and entering the One Vehicle Path." As is explained in the Introduction, "Structure of Śrī-Mālā," we have combined the two versions to reach the title which furnished the four major headings of the scripture: "Eliminating all doubts, deciding the cause, clarifying the final meaning, and entering the One Vehicle."

110 The ten quarters means the four cardinal directions and the four intermediate directions, plus the zenith and nadir.

Then Devendra Śakra exclaimed to the Lord, "Excellent!" Having embraced this scripture in the presence of the Lord, and having learned it by heart, Devendra Śakra, the venerable Ānanda, others who had assembled there, and gods, men, demigods, and heavenly musicians all rejoiced and praised what the Lord had pronounced.

APPENDIX I

The Chinese Section Titles of *Śrī-Mālā* and Japanese Diagram Analyses of Four Classical Commentaries

The accompanying table shows that the fifteen chapter titles found in the Guṇabhadra translation (T. No. 353) are based on the first fifteen of the sixteen titles found in the Epilogue of the scripture. Bodhiruci's translation (T. No. 310/48) of the sixteen titles is so close to Guṇabhadra's (as compared with the numerous differences between the two elsewhere in the scripture) as to indicate that Bodhiruci had Guṇabhadra's translation before him and decided at this point to accept it for the most part. Guṇabhadra's chapter headings are adhered to faithfully by Hui-yüan, and there are only two minor divergences in K'uei-chi's titles. Chi-tsang's headings adhere to the Epilogue's titles except for minor divergence from two titles. Six of Shōtoku Taishi's headings are slightly altered from Guṇabhadra's, but Shōtoku Taishi's amount only to fourteen, thus counting the fourteenth and the fifteenth as one chapter and understanding the fifteenth Epilogue title to be part of the Sūtra title. The agreement to accept those fifteen titles of the Epilogue as indications of sections in the whole scripture, but not to include the sixteenth title as such a sectional indication, forced another interpretation for the sixteenth title. As far as its translation is concerned, Guṇabhadra and Bodhiruci are identical: "Eliminating all doubts, deciding the final meaning, and entering into the One Vehicle Path."

The expressions in the sixteenth title obviously apply to the entire scripture, but do not provide much help for grouping the fifteen sections. The four classical commentaries by Hui-yüan, Chi-tsang, K'uei-chi, and Shōtoku Taishi have variously applied those expressions for grouping purposes. Modern Japanese Buddhist scholars have analyzed the grouping indications of those commentaries into diagrams. The accompanying diagrams are based on information in Ono's Dictionary (pp. 359–60), Kanaji (pp. 208–10), Hirakawa ("Ronshū," p. 106), Saeki (pp. 36–37). The analyses can easily mislead one regarding affiliation. On the surface there are two affinities: a) that of Hui-yüan and K'uei-chi, where the first four sections are labeled "means" or "cause," answering to the words "Eliminating all doubts"; where the fifth section "One Vehicle" is labeled the "fruit," or "fruit of One Vehicle," answering to the terminology

Table: The Chinese sectional titles of *Śrī-Mālā*

	Guṇabhadra titles 經名十六 (No. 353) (from sūtra epilogue)	Bodhiruci titles 經名十六 (No. 310) (from sūtra epilogue)	15 chapter headings by Guṇabhadra (d. A.D. 468)
1.	歎如來眞實第一義功德	讚歎如來眞實功德	如來眞實義功德章第一
2.	不思議大受	說不思議十種弘誓	十受章第二
3.	一切願攝大願	以一大願攝一切願	三願章第三
4.	說不思議攝受正法	說不思議攝受正法	攝受章第四
5.	說入一乘	說入一乘	一乘章第五
6.	說無邊聖諦	說無邊諦	無邊聖諦章第六
7.	說如來藏	說如來藏	如來藏章第七
8.	說法身	說佛法身	法身章第八
9.	說空義隱覆眞實	說空性義隱覆眞實	空義隱覆眞實章第九
10.	說一諦	說一諦義	一諦章第十
11.	說常住安隱一依	說常住不動寂靜一依	一依章第十一
12.	說顚例眞實	說顚例眞實	顚例眞實章第十二
13.	說自性清浄心隱覆	說自性清浄心煩惱隱覆	自性清浄章第十三
14.	說如來眞子	說如來眞子	眞子章第十四
15.	說勝鬘夫人師子吼	說勝鬘夫人正師子吼	勝鬘章第十五
16.	斷一切疑決定了義入一乘道	斷一切疑決定了義入一乘道	——

15 chapters by 慧遠 (Hui-yüan, A.D. 523-592)	15 chapters by 吉藏 (Chi-tsang, A.D. 549-623)	14 chapters by 聖徳太子 (Shōtoku Taishi, A.D. 574-622)	15 chapters by 窺基 (K'uei-chi, A.D. 632-682)
(Identical with Guṇabhadra, Column 3)	(Identical with 15 names in No. 353, Column 1, except for 5 and 8)	佛歎眞實功徳章	(Identical with Guṇabhadra, Column 3, except for 14 and 15)
		十大受章	
		三大願章	
		攝受正法章	
	5. 說一乘章第五	一乘章	
		無邊聖諦章	
		如來藏章	
	8. 說如來法身章第八	法身章	
		空義隱覆章	
		一諦章	
		一依章	
		顚例眞實章	
		自性清浄章	
		眞子章	14. 如來眞子章第十四
		—	15. 勝鬘獅子吼章第十五
—	—	—	

"deciding the final meaning"; and where sections six through thirteen are labeled "doctrine of One Vehicle" or "doctrine," answering to the words "entering into the One Vehicle Path"; b) that of Chi-tsang and Shōtoku Taishi, where the first three sections are called respectively "means for the Illustrious Doctrine" and "practice for oneself," answering to "Eliminating all doubts"; where sections four and five are respectively "practice of the One Vehicle" and "practice for others," answering presumably to "deciding the final meaning," a consistency which Mahāyāna Buddhism certifies; and where six through thirteen are the plane of One Vehicle, hence the "entering into the One Vehicle path." Since the three terms of the Epilogue's sixteenth title are in each of the four solutions exhausted in grouping sections one through thirteen, the final two sections are left over, which accounts for their different interpretation in each of the commentaries. Against the affiliation of the Hui-yüan and K'uei-chi commentaries, Ono's Dictionary (360d) points out that K'uei-chi quotes more from the *Mahāyānasaṃgraha* and other Vijñaptimātratā texts. Against the affiliation of the Chi-tsang and Shōtoku Taishi commentaries, Hirakawa ("Ronshū," p. 106) points out that these two commentaries differ in the treatment of the first five and the last two sections. In May, 1970, Professor Akira Fujieda told Mr. Wayman that after most of the Hui-yüan commentary had been pieced together (see Introduction, n. 21) it became obvious that Chi-tsang borrowed heavily from that commentary. The recent discovery that the *Shêng-man i-su pên-i* is the prototype of the Shōtoku Taishi commentary (see Introduction, n. 31) further complicates the relationships. Therefore, at the present time we cannot define decisively the relation of the four solutions.

Alex Wayman's solution of the grouping (see Introduction, "Structure of *Śrī-Mālā*") is based upon a fresh interpretation of the Epilogue's sixteenth title reached by combining the Tibetan and Chinese parts of this title. This new method of grouping, stemming from four terms instead of three as in the Chinese tradition, gives rise in our translation to the four new chapter titles under which the standard fifteen sections are grouped. As this solution understands the first four sections as "cause," it appears to be more consistent with the Hui-yüan and K'uei-chi than with the Chi-tsang and Shōtoku Taishi diagram analyses. However, this consistency is limited to the sectional groupings, and admittedly we have not conducted the thorough comparison of the four classical commentaries that would be necessary for a more definitive conclusion.

It is of interest to note that of the four grouping diagrams, only K'uei-chi's avoids the term "Vehicle" (*yāna*) in the explanation of grouping attributed to his commentary. This probably is due to K'uei-chi's affiliation with the Vijñaptimātratā school of his teacher Hsüan-tsang, for this school has three vehicles (of

Śrāvakas, Pratyekabuddhas, and Bodhisattvas) without teaching that ultimately there is only a single vehicle. The other three diagrams stress the Vehicle (meaning "One Vehicle") terminology to the extent of interpreting this as the central message of *Śrī-Mālā*. If K'uei-chi actually had little regard for this feature of *Śrī-Mālā*, it is a significant testimonial to this scripture's popularity in China that K'uei-chi would lecture on it anyway. This point is also open to future study.

Another observation we can make concerns the usage in those diagrammatic analyses of the standard pairs of Mahāyāna Buddhism, namely, "practice" and "doctrine"; "practice for oneself" and "practice for others"; "cause" and "fruit"; "practice" and "goal"; "practice" and "persons (practicing)"; "first seven stages" and "last three stages." The application of such pairs varies from true relevance to mere artificiality. We wonder why each commentator would not notice categories based on the actual content of these sections, in particular, that sections five through thirteen concern discrimination between contrasting alternates, such as "the ultimate and the temporary," the "boundless and the limited Noble Truths," "Dharmakāya and Tathāgatagarbha," "the perfectly pure and the wayward," "the purity and the defilement of the mind." In short, for these sections (5–13), our own chapter heading "Clarifying the Final Meaning" implies the discrimination throughout of "the final meaning and the provisional meaning." But the diagram based on the Shōtoku Taishi commentary has a perceptive division of sections six through thirteen as "generalities" and "particulars" of four sections each. For, if one reads those sections with such a division in mind, it does appear that section six is continued in section ten, seven in thirteen, and eight-nine in eleven-twelve. They constitute two groups of four sections that doctrinally clarify section five, "One Vehicle."

If one judges only the relevance of ascriptions to the content of the sections throughout the *Śrī-Mālā*, one may conclude that the Chi-tsang commentary surpasses the others. However Ui (*Saiiki butten no kenkyū*, p. 305) points out that the earlier *Shêng-men i-chi* (see Introduction, n. 20) by its simplicity is sometimes more convenient than the Chi-tsang commentary.

Finally, the four classical commentaries all agree that the *Śrī-Mālā* does have a well-defined structure, and the diagrams show them to be reasonably close to each other in regard to the major divisions.

Diagram Analyses of Four Classical Commentaries

A. Hui-yüan's *Shêng-man ching i-chi.* 慧遠 勝鬘經義記

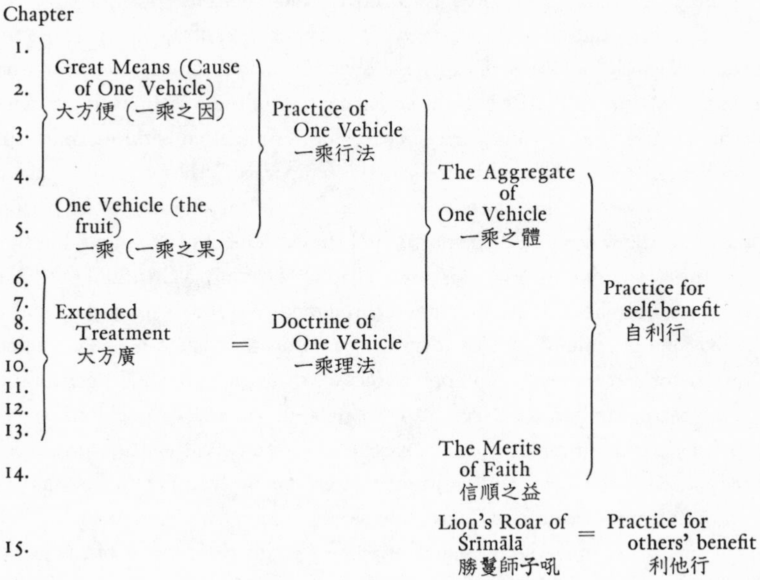
Chapter
1.
2.
3.
4.
5.
6.
7.
8.
9.
10.
11.
12.
13.
14.
15.
Great Means (Cause of One Vehicle)
大方便（一乘之因）
One Vehicle (the fruit)
一乘（一乘之果）
Practice of One Vehicle
一乘行法
Extended Treatment
大方廣
=
Doctrine of One Vehicle
一乘理法
The Aggregate of One Vehicle
一乘之體
The Merits of Faith
信順之益
Practice for self-benefit
自利行
Lion's Roar of Śrīmālā
勝鬘師子吼
=
Practice for others' benefit
利他行

B. K'uei-chi's *Shêng-man ching shu-chi.* 窺基 勝鬘經述記

Chapter			
1.	Practice (Cause) 行	Clarification of Doctrine (*dharma*) 明法	All-embracing Practice 修萬行 and Practice for self-benefit 自利行
2.	Practice (Cause) 行	Clarification of Doctrine (*dharma*) 明法	All-embracing Practice 修萬行 and Practice for self-benefit 自利行
3.	Practice (Cause) 行	Clarification of Doctrine (*dharma*) 明法	All-embracing Practice 修萬行 and Practice for self-benefit 自利行
4.	Practice (Cause) 行	Clarification of Doctrine (*dharma*) 明法	All-embracing Practice 修萬行 and Practice for self-benefit 自利行
5.	Fruit 果	Clarification of Doctrine (*dharma*) 明法	All-embracing Practice 修萬行 and Practice for self-benefit 自利行
6.–13.	Doctrine 教理	Clarification of Doctrine (*dharma*) 明法	All-embracing Practice 修萬行 and Practice for self-benefit 自利行
14.		Persons skilled in advocating 辨人	All-embracing Practice 修萬行 and Practice for self-benefit 自利行
15.		Persons of practice 修行者	= Practice for others' benefit 他利行

C. Chi-tsang's *Shêng-man ching pao-k'u.* 吉藏 勝鬘經寶窟

Chapter			
1.	The Mind of Enlightenment 菩提心	Means for the Illustrious Doctrine 起說方便	Illustrious Teaching 正說
2.–3.	Bodhisattva Practice 修菩薩行		
4.	Explaining the Great Birth 辨廣大出生	Practice of (One) Vehicle 乘行	
5.	Integration into One Vehicle 無二收入		
6.–9.	(6) Limited versus Unlimited Truth 量無量諦	Realm of (One) Vehicle 乘境	
10.–13.	(10) The Three Truths 三諦		
14.			Instilling Faith 勸信
15.			Upholding the Doctrine 護法

D. Shōtoku Taishi's *Shōmangyō gisho.* 聖徳太子 勝鬘經義疏

Chapter

- Scope of the Illustrious School 正宗體
  - Aggregate of (One) Vehicle 乘之體
    - 1.–3. Practice for oneself, up to Seventh Stage 自分行（七地迄）
    - 4.–5. Practice for others, Eighth through Tenth 他分行（八一十地）
  - Realm of (One) Vehicle 乘之境
    - 6.–9. Generalities 總明
    - 10.–13. Particulars 別明
  - 14. Persons installed in One Vehicle 御乘人

Epilogue Titles

- Full Title of the Sūtra 一經通名
  - 15. The teaching in terms of personal name 通以人名標教
  - 16. All Doctrines incorporated into the Sūtra 總取說理目經

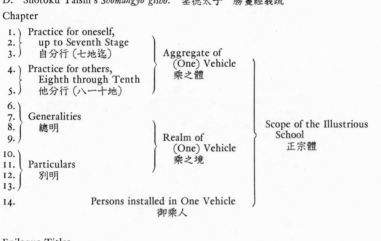

APPENDIX II

Works Cited in Chi-tsang's Commentary (Bunkyō Sakurabe's List Expanded by Shinjō Kawasaki).

Professor Bunkyō Sakurabe, in his Japanese edition (the *Hōkutsu*) of Chi-tsang's commentary on the *Śrī-Mālā-sūtra*, has rendered the valuable service of appending a register of works cited by Chi-tsang with their number of occurrences. In the course of his edition Sakurabe frequently locates the citations in the respective works as found in the *Kokuyaku Issaikyō* canon. This list is important for these reasons: a) it demonstrates the great lengths to which Chinese Buddhist scholars resorted in order to clarify the relationships of the *Śrī-Mālā* to other scriptures; b) it has its own interest as a list of viable Buddhist works with which Chi-tsang, the celebrated commentator on the San-lun (J. Sanron) school, was presumably familiar. Chi-tsang could not refer to the *Mahāvastu*, which we have observed to be important for the *Śrī-Mālā*, because the *Mahāvastu* was never translated into Chinese.

Professor Sakurabe gives individual titles of works, when recognizable as such, even if difficult to identify, and includes at the end of the list the number of citations of the type "As it is stated in the sūtras," and so on, which obviously do not include identifiable titles. Mr. Shinjō Kawasaki has added further data, such as the more standard Chinese title in some cases, romanization of the title when the work is identifiable, the Sanskrit title as known, author in case of a commentary, the date(s) of translation into Chinese, and Taishō reference. We have edited the material and added the number of occurrences in the *Hōkutsu* in parentheses at the end of the entry. Professor Burton Watson has made some further corrections.

The intention of the identifications is to indicate no more works than could be consulted by Chi-tsang. For this reason, translations are indicated only up to his generation, even though in a number of cases the works in question have been translated several times, and a later translation may have become authoritative in Chinese Buddhism.

1. 阿含 A-han. S. Āgama. T, Vols. 1 and 2. (2)
2. 阿弥陀佛經 A-mi-t'o fo ching. S. Sukhāvatyamṛtavyūha-sūtra (smaller Sukhāvatīvyūha *or* Sukhāvatī-vyūho nāma mahāyānasūtram). Tr. A.D. 402. T12, pp. 346 ff. (1)
3. 溫室經 (溫室洗浴衆僧經) Wên-shih hsi-yü chung-sêng ching. Tr. 148–170. T16, pp. 802 ff. (1)
4. 起信論 (馬鳴) (大乘起信論) Ta-ch'eng ch'i-hsin lun. Tr. A.D. 550. T32. 575 (5)
5. 俱舍論 (阿毘達磨俱舍論) A-p'i-ta-mo chü-shê lun. S. Abhidharmakośa-śāstra. By 天親 Vasubandhu. Tr. by Paramārtha 563–567. (3)
6. 賢愚經 Hsien-yü ching. S. Damamūka (nidāna-sūtra). Tr. A.D. 445. T4. 349 (1)
7. 賢劫經 Hsien-ch'ieh ching. S. Bhadrakalpita-sūtra. Tr. A.D. 291 or A.D. 300. T14.425 (1)
8. 華嚴經 Hua-yen ching. S. Buddha-avataṃsaka-nāma-mahāvaipulya-sūtra. Tr. 418–420. T9.395 (16)
9. 金剛仙論 Chin-kang-hsien lun. This is a commentary on the Vajracchedikā Prajñāpāramitā sūtra, presumably either composed by or translated by Bodhiruci of the Northern Wei, in A.D. 535. Published in canonical supplement, T25.798 (2)
10. 金剛般若 (金剛般若波羅蜜經) Chin-kang pan-jo po-lo-mi ching. S. Vajracchedikā Prajñāpāramitā. Tr. 402–412 *or* 509 *or* 558–569. T8, pp. 748, 752, 762. (1)
11. 金剛般若論 Chin-kang pan-jo lun. S. Vajracchedikā-sūtra-śāstra. By 無著 Asaṅga. Tr. 605–616. T25.757 (2)
12. 金光明經 (金光明最勝王經) Chin-kuang-ming tsui-shêng-wang ching. S. Suvarṇaprabhāsottama-rāja-sūtra. Tr. by Paramārtha 552–557. (3)
13. 雜心論 (雜阿毘曇心論) Tsa-a-p'i-t'an hsin lun. S. Samyukta-abhidharmahṛdaya-śāstra. By 僧伽跋摩 Saṅghavarman. Tr. 434 or 435. T28. 869 (10)
14. 三界義 San-chieh-i. Explanation of the Three Realms. No information. (The same characters form the title of a later Japanese work, the San-gai-gi). (1)
15. 四分律 Ssŭ-fên lü. (Prātimokṣa of the Dharmagupta sect.) Tr. A.D. 408. T22.567 (1)
16. 十二遊經 (佛說十二遊經) Fo-shuo shih-êrh-yu ching. (Regarding the twelve-year activities of Śākyamuni after his enlightenment.) Tr. A.D. 392. T4.145 (1)
17. 十二門論 Shih-êrh-mên lun. S. Dvādaśamukha-śāstra. By 龍樹 Nāgārjuna. Tr. A.D. 409. T30.159 (1)

18. 十誦律 Shih-sung lü. (Vinaya of the Sarvāstivāda sect.) Tr. by Puṇyatāra and Kumārajīva. (1)

19. 十住論 (十住毘婆沙論) Shih-chu p'i-p'o-sha lun. S. Daśabhūmi-vibhāṣa-śāstra. By 龍樹 Nāgārjuna. Tr. 344–413. T26.20 (1)

20. 十地經 (地經) Shih-ti ching. S. Daśabhūmika-sūtra. Tr. A.D. 516 by 菩提流志 (Bodhiruci). (5)

21. 十地論 (十地經論) Shih-ti ching lun. S. Daśabhūmi-vyākhyāna. By 天親流志 Vasubandhu. Tr. 508–535. T26.123 (9)

22. 首楞嚴經 (首楞嚴三昧經) Shou-lêng-yen san-mei ching. S. Sūraṃgama-samādhi-nirdeśa. Tr. 402–412. T15.629 (1)

23. 肇論 Chao lun. By 僧肇 Sêng-chao (384–414). T45.150 (5)

24. 勝天王般若波羅蜜經 Shen-t'ien-wang pan-jo po-lo-mi ching. Tr. A.D. 565. T8.687 (1)

25. 攝論 (攝大乘論) Shê ta-ch'eng lun. S. Mahāyānasaṃgraha. By 無著 Asaṅga. Tr. 499–569. T31.113 (20)

26. 闍王懺悔經 Shê wang ch'an-hui ching (阿闍世王經) A-shê shih-wang ching. This may well be the scripture with Sanskrit title Ajātaśatru-kaukṛtya-vinodana (Sūtra of repentance of the King Ajātaśatru), probably T15.406 (1)

27. 成實論 Ch'êng-shih lun. S. Satyasiddhiśāstra. By 訶梨跋摩 Harivarman. Tr. 402–412. T32.239 (11)

28. 善生經 (善生子經) Shan-shêng-tzŭ ching. S. Śigālovāḍa-sūtra (from the Dīrghāgama). T1.252 (1)

29. 僧祇律 (摩訶僧祇律) Mo-ho sêng-chih lü. (Collection of Vinaya.) By 佛陀跋陀羅 Buddhabhadra. Tr. 416-418. T22.227 (1)

30. 像法決疑經 Hsiang-fa chüeh-i ching. T85.1335 (1)

31. 提謂經 (提謂波利經) T'i-wei po-li ching. (Translation missing; possibly was known to Chi-tsang only in quotation). (1)

32. 大品般若 (摩訶般若波羅蜜經) Mo-ho pan-jo po-lo-mi ching. S. Pañcaviṃ-śatisāhasrikā Prajñāpāramitā. Tr. 344–413. T8.217 (19)

33. 大集經 (大方等大集經) Ta-fang-têng ta-chi ching. S. Mahā-vaipulya-mahā-saṃnipāta-sūtra. Tr. 414–426. T13.1 (3)

34. 第一義法勝經 Ti-i-i fa-shêng ching. S. Paramārtha-dharma-vijaya-sūtra. Tr. A.D. 542. T17.879 (1)

35. 中論 Chung lun. S. Madhyamaka-śāstra (=Mūla-madhyamaka-kārikā). By 龍樹 Nāgārjuna. Tr. A.D. 409. T30.1 (15)

36. 中論疏 (中觀論疏) (曇影) Chung-kuan lun su. A Chinese work by 曇影 T'an-ying, a disciple of Kumārajīva. (1)

37. 中邊論 (辨中邊論) Pien chung-pien lun. S. Madhyānta-vibhāga-ṭīkā. By 天親 Vasubandhu. Presumably tr. 499–569. T31.451 (1)

38. 智度論 (大智度論) (龍樹) Ta-chih-tu lun. S. Mahāprajñāpāramitā-śāstra. By 龍樹 Nāgārjuna. Tr. 402–406. T25.57 (23)

39. 中阿含 Chung-a-han, S. Madhyamāgama. Tr. 397–398. T1.421 (1)

40. 中本起經 Chung-pên-ch'i ching. (Treats the first turning of the wheel to the end of Śākyamuni's life.) Tr. A.D. 207. T4.147 (1)

41. 注維摩經 (注維摩詰經) Chu wei-mo-chieh ching. (Commentary on the Vimalakīrtinirdeśa.) By 僧肇 Sêng-chao (384–414.) T38.327 (9)

42. 地持經 (論) (菩薩地持經) P'u-sa ti-ch'ih ching. S. Bodhisattvabhūmi. Tr. 414–426. T30.888 (12)

43. 灯論 (天親) Têng lun. Professor Sakurabe attributes this work to Vasubandhu. But no further information is available. (1)

44. 同性經 (大乘同性經) Ta-ch'êng t'ung-hsing ching. S. Mahāyāna-abhisamaya-sūtra. Tr. A.D. 570. T16.640 (1)

45. 泥洹經 (大般泥洹經) Ta-pan ni-yüan ching. S. Mahāparinirvāṇa-sūtra. Tr. 416–418. T12.853 (1)

46. 仁王經 (仁王般若波羅蜜經) Jên-wang pan-jo po-lo-mi ching. (Sūtra on national guardianship, said to be of Chinese origin.) Tr. 344–413. T8.825 (6)

47. 涅槃經 (大般涅槃經) Ta-pan nieh-p'an ching. S. Mahāparinirvāṇa-sūtra. Tr. 416–423. T12.365–603 (55)

48. 涅槃論 (涅槃無名論) Nieh-p'an wu-ming lun. Attributed to Vasubandhu. T26.277 (1)

49. 婆娑 P'o-sha. S. Bhāṣā. Abbreviated reference to unidentified work, possibly Dharmatrāta's Samyukta-abhidharma-hṛdaya, tr. A.D. 426, which comments on the next item (No. 50), as the basis of the Chinese Abhidharma school called P'i-t'an (毘曇). (9)

50. 毘曇 (阿毘曇心論) A-p'i-t'an hsin lun. S. Abhidharmahṛdaya-śāstra. By Dharmottara. Tr. A.D. 391 or 376. T28.809 (4)

51. 浮荼不多羅經 (Transcription from Sanskrit; possibly the Pitāputra-sūtra, although the first character is romanized Fou.) (1)

52. 普賢觀經 (觀普賢菩薩行法經) Kuan P'u-hsien p'u-sa hsing-fa ching. S. Samantabhadra-bodhisattva-dhyānacaryādharma-sūtra. Tr. 424–441. T9.389 (2)

53. 佛性論 Fo-hsing lun. S. Buddhagotraśāstra. Attributed to Vasubandhu. Tr. 557–569. T31.787 (13)

54. 分別功德論 Fên-pieh kung-tê lun. Commentary on the Ekottarāgama. Tr. *c.* A.D. 220. T25.30 (1)

55. 法華經 (妙法蓮華經) Miao-fa lien-hua ching. S. Saddharmapuṇḍarīka-sūtra. Tr. A.D. 406. T9.1 (23)

56. 法華疏 (道融) This is a commentary on the Saddharmapuṇḍarīka by 道融 Tao-jung. It no longer exists. (1)

57. 法華疏 (吉藏) Fa-hua su. (Chi-tsang's commentary on the Saddharma-puṇḍarīka-sūtra.) T34.451 (See item No. 58.)

58. 法華玄論 Fa-hua hsüan lun. (Chi-tsang's work on the Saddharmapuṇḍarīka-sūtra.) T34.361. (Together with the foregoing work, cited 9 times.)

59. 法華序 (法華宗要序)(慧觀) Fa-hua tsung yao-hsü. This is an introduction to the Saddharmapuṇḍarīka by 慧觀 Hui-kuan, and may have been known to Chi-tsang only by quotation. (1)

60. 法華論 (妙法蓮華經憂波提舍) Miao-fa lien-hua ching yu-po-t'i-shê. (The only Indian commentary on the Saddharmapuṇḍarīka-sūtra.) By 天親 Vasubandhu. Tr. 508–535. T26.1 (22)

61. 法鼓經 (大法鼓經) Ta-fa-ku ching. S. Mahābherīhāraka-parivarta. Tr. by Guṇabhadra. 435–443. T9.290 (1)

62. 法身無浄土論 Fa-shen wu-ching-t'u lun. (This work is not present in the canon. It may have been known to Chi-tsang only in quotation.) (1)

63. 寶性論 (究竟一乘寶性論) Chiu-ching i-ch'êng pao-hsing lun. S. Mahāyā-nottaratantra-śāstra-vyākhyā. Tr. A.D. 508. T31.813 (4)

64. 梵網 (梵網經) Fan-wang ching. S. Brahmajāla-sūtra (from Dīrghāgama). (1)

65. 來曾有經 (未曾有因緣經) Wei-ts'êng-yu yin-yüan ching. S. Adbhuta-dharma-paryāya. Tr. 479–502. T17.575 (1)

66. 無量義經 Wu-liang-i ching. S. Ananta-nirdeśa. Tr. A.D. 481. T9.383 (1)

67. 無量寿經 (大無量寿經) (觀無量寿佛經) Ta-wu-liang-shou ching, Tr. A.D. 252. T12.265. OR: Kuan-wu-liang-shou-fo ching. Tr. 424–442. T12.340. This is the Sukhāvatī-vyūha (the larger Sukhāvatī-vyūha). (1)

68. 文殊十禮經 (文殊師利菩薩無相十禮經) Wên-shu-shih-li p'u-sa wu-hsiang shih-li ching. (Tun-huang manuscript in Pelliot Collection.) T85.1296 (2)

69. 文殊問般若經 (文殊師利所說般若波羅蜜經) OR: (文殊師利問經) Wên-shu-shih-li so-shuo pan-jo po-lo-mi ching. S. Ārya-Saptaśatikā-nāma-Prajñāpāramitā-sūtra. Tr. 503 *or* 506–520. T8.726 or T8.732 OR: Wên-shu-shih-li-wên ching. (Questions of Mañjuśrī). Tr. A.D. 518. T14.492 (1)

70. 維摩經 (浄名經 維摩詰所說經) Wei-mo-chieh-so-shuo-ching. S. Vimalakīrti-nirdeśa-nāma-mahāyāna-sūtra. Tr. A.D. 406. T14.537 (15)

71. 遺教經 (佛垂般涅槃略説教誡經) Fo-ch'ui pan-nieh-p'an lüeh-shuo chiao-chieh ching. (The sūtra of the Buddha's last instruction.) Tr. 344–413. T12.1110 (1)

72. 瓔珞經 (菩薩瓔珞本業經) P'u-sa ying-lo pên-yeh ching. (The sūtra of the Bodhisattva's diadem.) Tr. 376–378. T24.1010 (13)

73. 立世毘曇 (立世阿毘曇論) Li-shih a-p'i-t'an lun. S. Loka-utthāna-abhidharma-śāstra? Tr. A.D. 558 or 559. T32.173 (1)

74. 楞伽經 (大乘入楞伽經) Ta-ch'eng ju leng-ch'ieh ching. S. Laṅkāvatāra-sūtra. Tr. by Guṇabhadra A.D. 443. T16.480 (also Tr. A.D. 513, T16.514) (7)

75. 經 (unspecified sūtras) (4)

76. 論 (unspecified śāstras) (2)

77. 世俗の書 (詩經, 白虎通, . . .) Secular works (4)

GLOSSARY

This list does not include names given in the bibliography of Chinese and Japanese works.

ch'an 禅
Ching-t'u 浄土
Chŏng'u 靖邁
Dharmakṣema 曇無讖
Ennin 圓仁
Enryakuji 延暦寺
Fa-yao 法瑤
gisho 義疏
Gyōson 堯尊
Honchō kōsō den 本朝高僧傳
Hōryūji 法隆寺
Hoke *or* Hokke 法華
Hui-kuan 慧觀
Hyeja (J. Eji) 恵慈
jibungyō 自分行
jijōju 自成就
Jikaku daishi 慈覺大師
jiriki 自力
Jōgū Shōtoku hō ō tei setsu 上宮聖徳法王帝說
Junna 淳和
Kaimyō 誡明
Kawaguchi Ekai 河口慧海
Kawasaki Shinjō 川崎信定
Kenshin Tokugyō 顯眞得業
Koguryŏ 高句麗
Koizumi Enjun 古泉圓順
Kumārajīva 鳩摩羅什
Liu Sung 劉宋
Nihon shoki 日本書紀
North Wei 北魏
Pao-yün 寶雲
Paramārtha 眞諦
sangyō 三經
Sêng-tsung 僧宗
Shêng-man (J. Shōman) 勝鬘
Shinran shōnin 親鸞上人
Shōkō mandara 聖皇曼荼羅
Shōryōin 聖靈院
Shōsōin 正創院
Silla 新羅
South Liang 南梁
Suiko 推古
tabungyō 他分行
Tada Tōkwan 多田等觀
T'ang 唐
T'an-pin 曇斌
tariki 他力
T'ien-t'ai 天台
Tollyun 遁倫
Tun-huang 敦煌
Umayado no ōji 厩戸皇子
Wŏnhyo 元曉
Wu-ti 武帝
Yōmei 用明
Yüan 元
Yuima 維摩
Yung-ho-kung 雍和宮

BIBLIOGRAPHY

A. Chinese and Japanese Works.*

Bodhiruci 菩提流志. Shêng-man fu-jên hui 勝鬘夫人會. T11.672, No. 310(48).

Chi-tsang 吉藏 (Chia-hsiang ta-shih 嘉祥大師). Shêng-man ching pao-k'u 勝鬘經寶窟. T37.1, No. 1744; Kyōshobu, 1–90 pages.

Fujieda Akira 藤枝晃. Hokuchō ni okeru "Shōmangyō" no denshō 北朝における「勝鬘經」の傳承. Tōhōgakushū 40, Kyoto, 1969.

Guṇabhadra 求那跋陀羅. Shêng-man shih-tsŭ-hou i-ch'êng ta-fang-pien fang-kuang ching 勝鬘師子吼一乘大方便方廣經. T12.217, No. 353.

Hanayama Shinshō 花山信勝. Shōtoku Taishi gyosei, Shōmangyō gisho 聖徳太子御製 勝鬘經義疏. Iwanami bunko 3740–3741, Tokyo, 1948.

Hasuzawa Jōjun 蓮澤成淳. Shōman shishiku ichijō daihōben hōkō kyō 勝鬘師子吼一乘大方便方廣經. Kokuyaku Issaikyō, Hōjakubu 7, Tokyo, 1932.

Hirakawa Akira 平川章. "Shōmangyō gisho yori mita jūdaiju sandaigan to nyoraizō" 勝鬘經義疏より見た十大受三大願と如來藏. Shōmangyō gisho ronshū 勝鬘經義疏論集. Kyoto, 1965.

Hui chang yün 慧掌蘊. [? Copier,] Shêng-man i-chi 勝鬘義記. T85.253, No. 2761; also Stein No. 2660.

Hui-yüan 慧遠. Shêng-man ching i-chi 勝鬘經義記. Svastik ed. of Chinese Buddhist canon, 1–30–4.

Iyenaga Saburō 家永三郎. Jōdai Bukkyō shisōshi kenkyū 上代佛教思想史研究, Tokyo, 1950.

Kanaji Isamu 金治勇. Shōtoku Taishi kyōgaku no kenkyū 聖徳太子教學の研究 Kyoto, 1962.

Kimura Taiken 木村泰賢. "Funbetsu ronsha to buha no shozoku ni tsuite" 分別論者と部派の所屬に就て, Shūkyō kenkyū 宗教研究, Vol. 11–5, 1925.

K'uei-chi 窺基. Shêng-man ching shu-chi 勝鬘經述記. Svastik ed., 1–30–4.

Ming-k'ung 明空. Shêng-man ching i-su ssŭ-ch'ao 勝鬘經義疏私鈔. Svastik ed., 1–30–4.

Mochizuki Shinkō 望月信亨. Bukkyō daijiten 佛教大辭典. Vol. 111, Kyoto, 1957, p. 2775, entry on "shōmangyō gisho" 勝鬘經義疏.

* The abbreviation T employed here and in the Appendixes refers to the Taishō collection mentioned under Takakusu, editor.

Mori Mikisaburō 森三樹三郎. Ryō no Butei: Bukkyō ōchō no higeki 梁の武帝—佛教王朝の悲劇. Kyōto, 1961.

Nihon Bukkyō gakkai 日本佛教學會. Shōtoku Taishi kenkyū 聖徳太子研究. Kyoto, 1964.

Nihon Bukkyō genryū kenkyūkai 日本佛教源流研究會. Shōmangyō gisho ronshū 勝鬘經義疏論集. Kyoto, 1965.

Nishi Giyū 西義雄. "Yuimagyō gisho senjutsu no ito" 維摩經義疏撰述の意圖. Shōtoku Taishi kenkyū 聖徳太子研究. Kyoto 1964.

Ono Genmyō 小野玄妙. Bussho kaisetsu daijiten, sha-sho 佛書解說大辭典シャーショ. Tokyo, 1933, pp. 358–63.

Saeki Jōin 佐伯定胤. Shōmangyō kōsan 勝鬘經講讃. Osaka, 1939.

Sakaino Kōyō 境野黃洋. Shōman shishiku ichijō daihōben hōkō kyō 勝鬘師子吼一乘大方便方廣經. Kokuyaku Daizokyō, Kyōbu 3, Tokyo, 1918.

Sakurabe Bunkyō 櫻部文鏡. Shōman hōkutsu 勝鬘寶窟. Kokuyaku Issaikyō, wakan senjutsu 3, Kyōshobu 11.

Shōtoku Taishi 聖徳太子. Shōmangyō gisho 勝鬘經義疏. T6.1, No. 2185.

Takakusu Junjirō 高楠順次郎, editor, Taishō Shinshū Daizōkyō 大正新修大藏經. Tokyo, 1914–22. 85 vols.

Tun-huang manuscript. Shêng-man i-su pên-i 勝鬘義疏本義. The Toyo Bunko, Tokyo, Japan.

Ui Hakuju 宇井伯壽. Bukkyō jiten 佛教辭典. Tokyo, 1938.

———. Hōshōron kenkyū 寶性論研究. Tokyo, 1959.

———. Saiiki butten no kenkyū 西域佛典の研究, Tokyo, 1969, pp. 273–309.

Uryūzu Ryūshin 瓜生津隆眞. "Shōmangyō no chibettoyaku to kūshisō" 勝鬘經のチベット譯と空思想. Shōmangyō gisho ronshū, Kyoto, 1965.

Wang Chung-min 王重民. Tun-huang i-shu tsung-mu so-yin 敦煌遺書總目索引. Shanghai, 1962.

B. Sanskrit, Pāli, and Tibetan Texts Consulted.*

Aṅguttara Nikāya (Catukkanipāta and Pañcakanipāta), ed. Bhikkhu J. Kashyap (Varanasi, 1960).

* The abbreviation PTT refers to The Tibetan Tripitaka, Peking edition . . . , reprinted under the supervision of the Otani University, Kyoto, ed. by Daisetz T[eitaro] Suzuki, vols. 1-168 (Tokyo-Kyoto, Tibetan Tripitaka Research Institute, 1955-1961), the set at The University of Wisconsin. Narthang refers to the Narthang edition of the Tibetan canon at Columbia University. Tibetan sūtras usually begin with "Ḥphags pa" (S. Ārya-), omitted from the titles here given.

Bodhicaryāvatāra by Śāntideva, ed. Vidhushekara Bhattacharya (Calcutta, 1962).
Bodhisattvabhūmi by Asaṅga, ed. Unrai Wogihara, Part 2 (Tokyo, 1936).
Brahmajālasutta, in Dīgha-nikāya, I, ed. Bhikkhu J. Kashyap (Varanasi, 1958).
Chos mṅon paḥi mdzod kyi ḥgrel bśad mtshan ñid kyi rjes su ḥbraṅ ba, tr. of Abhidharmakośa-ṭīkā-lakṣaṇānusāriṇī by Pūrṇavardhana, PTT, Vol. 118.
Daśabhūmika-sūtra, ed. J. Rahder (Paris, 1926).
Dgoṅs pa ṅes par ḥgrol pa, tr. of Saṃdhinirmocana-sūtra, PTT, Vol. 29.
Dgoṅs pa zab mo ṅes par ḥgrel paḥi mdoḥi rgya che ḥgrel pa, PTT, Vol. 106, tr. from the Chinese commentary on the Saṃdhinirmocana-sūtra, by Wen tsheg (Yüan-ts'ê), Chap. 6, Rnal ḥbyor rnam par ḥbyed paḥi leḥu.
Gaṇḍavyūha-sūtra, ed. Daisetz Teitaro Suzuki and Hokei Idzumi (Kyoto, 1949).
Lalitavistara, ed. Dr. S. Lefmann (Halle, 1902).
Lam rim chen mo, by Tsoṅ-kha-pa (native blockprint, Tashilumpo monastery).
Laṅkāvatāra-sūtra, ed. Bunyiu Nanjio (Kyoto, 1956).
Lha mo dpal phreṅ gi seṅ geḥi sgra źes bya ba theg pa chen poḥi mdo, tr. of Śrīmālādevīsiṃhanāda-nāma-mahāyānasūtra, PTT, Vol. 24, and Narthang Kanjur, Dkon brtsegs, Vol. Cha.
Madhyamakakārikā by Nāgārjuna, in the Prasannapadā commentary by Candrakīrti, ed. Louis de La Vallée Poussin (Japanese photographic reprint).
Mahāvastu Avadāna, ed. Dr. Radhagovinda Basak (Calcutta, 1963), Vol. I.
Mahāvyutpatti, ed. Ryōzaburō Sakaki, 2 vols. (2d ed., Tokyo, 1962).
Mahāyāna-Sūtrālaṃkāra, ed. Sylvain Lévi (Paris, 1907).
Mdo sdeḥi rgyan gyi ḥgrel bśad, tr. of Sūtrālaṃkāra-vṛtti-bhāṣya, by Sthiramati, PTT, Vols. 108 and 109.
Pāramitāsamāsa by Āryaśūra, ed. A. Ferrari, in Annali Lateranensi, Vol. X (1946).
Ratnagotravibhāga Mahāyānottaratantraśāstra, ed. E. H. Johnston (Patna, 1950).
Rṅa bo che chen poḥi leḥu źes bya ba theg pa chen poḥi mdo, tr. of Mahābherīhārakaparivarta-nāma-mahāyānasūtra, Narthang Kanjur, Mdo, Vol. Tsa.
Rnam par mi rtog par ḥjug pa źes bya baḥi gzuṅs, tr. of Avikalpapraveśadhāraṇī. Narthang Kanjur, Mdo, Vol. Da.
Rnam par mi rtog par ḥjug paḥi gzuṅs kyi rgya cher ḥgrel pa, tr. of Avikalpapraveśadhāraṇīṭīkā by Kamalaśīla, Narthang Tanjur, Mdo tshogs ḥgrel pa, Vol. Ji.
Rnal ḥbyor spyod paḥi sa las mñam par bźag paḥi sa, tr. of Samāhitabhūmi by Asaṅga, PTT, Vol. 109.
Rnal ḥbyor spyod paḥi sa rnam par gtan la dbab pa bsdu ba, tr. of Yogācārabhūmi-viniścayasaṃgrahaṇī by Asaṅga, PTT, Vols. 110 and 111.

Rten ciṅ ḥbrel par ḥbyuṅ ba daṅ po daṅ rnam par dbye ba bśad pa, tr. of Pratītyasamutpādādi-vibhaṅga-nirdeśa by Vasubandhu, PTT, Vol. 104.

Saṃgīti-sutta, in Dīghanikāya, III, ed. Bhikkhu J. Kashyap (Varanasi, 1958).

Saṅs rgyas thams cad kyi yul la ḥjug paḥi ye śes snaṅ baḥi rgyan źes bya ba theg pa chen poḥi mdo, tr. of Sarvabuddhaviṣayāvatāra-Jñānālokālaṃkāra-nāma-mahāyānasūtra, Narthang Kanjur, Mdo, Vol. Ga.

Śes rab kyi pha rol tu phyin paḥi man ṅag, tr. of Prajñāpāramitopadeśa by Ratnākaraśānti, PTT, Vol. 114.

Śikṣāsamuccaya of Śāntideva, ed. P. L. Vaidya (Darbhanga, 1961).

Sor moḥi phreṅ ba la phan pa źes bya ba theg pa chen poḥi mdo, tr. of Aṅgulimālīya-nāma-mahāyānasūtra, Narthang Kanjur, Mdo, Vol. Ma.

Thub paḥi dgoṅs paḥi rgyan, tr. of Munimatālaṃkāra by Abhayākaragupta, PTT, Vol. 101.

Zab lam nā-roḥi chos drug gi sgo nas ḥkhrid paḥi rim pa "Yid ches gsum ldan," by Tsoṅ-kha-pa, PTT, Vol. 161.

C. Western Language Sources.

Bagchi, Prabodh Chandra. *Le canon bouddhique in Chine*, 2 vols. Paris, 1927, 1938.

Bareau, André. *Les sectes bouddhiques du Petit Véhicule*, Saigon, 1955.

———. *Recherches sur la biographie du Buddha dans les Sūtrapiṭaka et les Vinayapiṭaka anciens*, Paris, 1963.

Bendall, Cecil, and W. H. D. Rouse, trs. *Śāntideva's Śikṣāsamuccaya*, London, 1922.

Brough, John. " 'Thus Have I Heard . . .'," *Bulletin of the School of Oriental and African Studies*, XIII (Part 2, 1950), 416–26.

Brown, W. Norman, "The Metaphysics of the Truth Act (*Satyakriyā)," *Mélanges d'indianisme à la memoire de Louis Renou* (Paris, 1968), pp. 171–77.

Chang, Chung-Yuan. *Original Teachings of Ch'an Buddhism*, New York, 1969.

Coomaraswamy, Ananda K., and I. B. Horner. *Gotama the Buddha*, London, 1948.

Dayal, Har. *The Bodhisattva Doctrine*, London, 1932.

Demiéville, P. "L'origine des sectes bouddhiques d'après Paramārtha," *Melanges chinois et bouddhiques*, Vol. I (1931–32).

Edgerton, Franklin. *Buddhist Hybrid Sanskrit Dictionary*, New Haven, 1953.

Fang, Thomé H. "The World and the Individual in Chinese Metaphysics," *Philosophy East and West*, XIV, no. 2 (July, 1964).

Fujieda, Akira. "The Tunhuang Manuscripts," Part II, *Zinbun*, No. 10 (Kyoto University, 1969).

Giles, Lionel. *Descriptive Catalogue of the Chinese Manuscripts from Tunhuang in the British Museum*, London, 1957.

Guenther, Herbert V. *Sgam. Po. Pa: The Jewel Ornament of Liberation*, London, 1959.

Hakeda, Yoshito S. *The Awakening of Faith, Attributed to Aśvaghosha*, New York, 1967.

Hanayama, Shinsho. *A History of Japanese Buddhism*, Tokyo, 1960.

Hare, E. M., tr. *The Book of the Gradual Sayings IV*, London, 1955.

Hirakawa, Akira. "The Rise of Mahāyāna Buddhism and its Relationship to the Worship of Stupas," *Memoirs of the Research Department of the Toyo Bunko*, No. 22 (Tokyo, 1963).

Jayasundere, A. D. *The Book of the Numerical Sayings*, Madras, 1925.

Jones, J. J., tr. *The Mahāvastu*, 2 Vols. London, 1949, 1952.

Kern, H., tr. *Saddharma-Puṇḍarīka or The Lotus of the True Law*, Oxford, 1884; Dover, New York, 1968.

Lamotte, Étienne, tr. *La Somme du Grand Véhicle d'Asaṅga*, Louvain, 1938–39.

———. *Le Traité de la Grande Vertu de Sagesse*, Vols. I and III, Louvain, 1944, 1970.

———. *L'Enseignement de Vimalakīrti*, Louvain, 1962.

La Vallée Poussin, Louis de, tr. *L'Abhidharmakośa de Vasubandhu*, 6 vols. Paris, 1923–31.

———. *La Siddhi de Hiuan-tsang*, 2 vols. Paris, 1928–29.

Law, Bimala Churn. *Indological Studies*, Parts III and IV, Allahabad, 1954, 1962.

Lessing, Ferdinand D. *Yung-ho-kung*, Stockholm, 1942.

———. and Alex Wayman, eds. and trs. *Mkhas grub rje's Fundamentals of the Buddhist Tantras*, The Hague, 1968.

Lin Li-kouang. *L'Aide-Mémoire de la Vraie Loi*, Paris, 1949.

Malalasekera, G. P. *Dictionary of Pāli Proper Names*, 2 vols. London, 1960.

Mus, Paul. *La Lumière sur les Six Voies*, Paris, 1939.

Nakamura, Hajime. "A Critical Survey of Mahāyāna and Esoteric Buddhism Chiefly based upon Japanese Studies," *Acta Asiatica*, No. 7 (Tokyo, 1964).

Obermiller, E. *The Doctrine of Prajñā-pāramitā as exposed in the Abhisamayālaṃkāra of Maitreya*, reprint from *Acta Orientalia*, Vol. XI (1932).

Obermiller, E., tr. *The Sublime Science of the Great Vehicle to Salvation* [*Uttaratantra*], *Acta Orientalia*, Vol. IX (1931).

Pachow, W., and Ramakanta Mishra. *The Prātimokṣa-sūtra of the Mahāsāṅghikas*, Allahabad, 1956.

Rhys Davids, Caroline, tr. *The Book of Kindred Sayings*, Part I, London, 1917.

Rhys Davids, T. W., tr. *The Questions of King Milinda*, 2 Parts, Oxford, 1890, 1894.

Rowland, Benjamin. *The Art and Architecture of India*, Baltimore, 1953.

Ruegg, David Seyford. *La theorie du Tathāgātagarbha*, Paris, 1969.

Samtani, N. H. "The Opening of the Buddhist Sūtras," *Bhāratī* (Bulletin of the College of Indology, No. 8, Part II, 1964–65), pp. 47–63.

Sastri, Nilakanta. *A History of South India*, Madras, 1963.

Speyer, J. S., tr. *The Jātakamālā by Āryaśūra*, London, 1895.

Staël-Holstein, Baron A. von. "On a Peking Edition of the Tibetan Kanjur Which Seems to be Unknown in the West," *Harvard Sino-Indian Studies*, Peking, 1934.

Stcherbatsky, Th. *The Central Conception of Buddhism and the Meaning of the Word "Dharma"*, London, 1923; reprint, Calcutta, 1961.

Suzuki, D. T. *Studies in the Laṅkāvatāra Sūtra*, London, 1930.

Takakusu, J. "The Life of Vasubandhu by Paramārtha (A.D. 499–569)," *T'oung pao*, Ser. II, Vol. V (1904).

Takasaki, Jikido. *A Study on the Ratnagotravibhāga*, Rome, 1966.

Vajirañāṇa Mahāthera, Paravahera. *Buddhist Meditation in Theory and Practice*, Colombo, 1962.

Waley, Arthur, tr. *The Analects of Confucius*, London, 1938.

Watters, Thomas. *On Yuan Chwang's Travels in India*, Vol. II, London, 1905.

Wayman, Alex. *Analysis of the Śrāvakabhūmi Manuscript*, Berkeley, 1961.

———. "The Bodhisattva Practice According to the Lam-Rim-Chen-Mo," *The Tibet Society Newsletter*, 1:2 (July-Dec., 1967), 85–100.

———. "Buddhism," in *Historia Religionum*, Vol. II, Leiden, 372–464.

———. "The Hindu-Buddhist Rite of Truth—An Interpretation," *Studies in Indian Linguistics* (Volume presented to Prof. M. B. Emeneau on his sixtieth birthday year) (Poona, 1968), pp. 365–69.

———. "Notes on the three myrobalans," *Phi Theta Annual* (Oriental Languages Honor Society, Berkeley), V (1954–55), 63–77.

———. "The Sacittikā and Acittikā Bhūmi and the Pratyekabuddhabhūmi (Sanskrit texts)," *Journal of Indian and Buddhist Studies* (Tokyo), VII, no. 1 (1960), 375–79.

Yamamoto, Kosho, tr. *The Kyogyoshinsho*, Tokyo, 1958.

Yampolsky, Philip B., tr. *The Platform Sutra of the Sixth Patriarch*, New York, 1967.

Yoshifumi, Ueda. "The Status of the Individual in Mahāyāna Buddhist Philosophy," in Charles A. Moore, ed., *The Status of the Individual in East and West* (Honolulu, 1968), pp. 77-89.

INDEX

TRANSLATIONS FROM THE ORIENTAL CLASSICS

Major Plays of Chikamatsu, tr. Donald Keene 1961

Records of the Grand Historian of China, translated from the Shih chi of Ssu-ma Ch'ien, tr. Burton Watson, 2 vols. 1961

Instructions for Practical Living and Other Neo-Confucian Writings by Wang Yang-Ming, tr. Wing-tsit Chan 1963

Chuang Tzu: Basic Writings, tr. Burton Watson, paperback ed. only 1964

The Mahābhārata, tr. Chakravarthi V. Narasimhan 1965

The Manyōshū, Nippon Gakujutsu Shinkōkai edition 1965

Su Tung-p'o: Selections from a Sung Dynasty Poet, tr. Burton Watson 1965

Bhartrihari: Poems, tr. Barbara Stoler Miller. Also in paperback ed. 1967

Basic Writings of Mo Tzu, Hsün Tzu, and Han Fei Tzu, tr. Burton Watson. Also in separate paperback eds. 1967

The Awakening of Faith, attributed to Aśvaghosha, tr. Yoshito S. Hakeda 1967

Reflections on Things at Hand: The Neo-Confucian Anthology, comp. Chu Hsi and Lü Tsu-ch'ien, tr. Wing-tsit Chan 1967

The Platform Sutra of the Sixth Patriarch, tr. Philip B. Yampolsky 1967

Essays in Idleness: The Tsurezuregusa of Kenkō, tr. Donald Keene 1967

The Pillow Book of Sei Shōnagon, tr. Ivan Morris, 2 vols. 1967

Two Plays of Ancient India: The Little Clay Cart and the Minister's Seal, tr. J. A. B. van Buitenen 1968

The Complete Works of Chuang Tzu, tr. Burton Watson 1968

The Romance of the Western Chamber (Hsi Hsiang chi), tr. S. I. Hsiung 1968

The Manyōshū, Nippon Gakujutsu Shinkōkai edition. Paperback text edition. 1969

Records of the Historian: Chapters from the Shih chi of Ssu-ma Ch'ien. Paperback text edition, tr. Burton Watson 1969

Cold Mountain: 100 Poems by the T'ang poet Han-shan, tr. Burton Watson. Also in paperback ed. 1970

Twenty Plays of the Nō Theatre, ed. by Donald Keene. Also in paperback ed. 1970

Chūshingura: The Treasury of Loyal Retainers, tr. Donald Keene 1971

The Zen Master Hakuin: Selected Writings, tr. P. B. Yampolsky 1971

Chinese Rhyme-Prose, tr. Burton Watson 1971

Kūkai: Major Works, tr. Yoshito S. Hakeda 1972

The Old Man Who Does as He Pleases: Selections from the Poetry and Prose of Lu Yu, tr. Burton Watson 1974

The Lion's Roar of Queen Śrīmālā, tr. Alex & Hideko Wayman 1974

COMPANIONS TO ASIAN STUDIES

Approaches to the Oriental Classics, ed. Wm. Theodore de Bary 1959
Early Chinese Literature, by Burton Watson 1962
Approaches to Asian Civilizations, ed. Wm. Theodore de Bary and Ainslie T. Embree 1964
A Guide to Oriental Classics, ed. Wm. Theodore de Bary and Ainslie T. Embree 1964
The Classic Chinese Novel: A Critical Introduction, by C. T. Hsia 1968
Chinese Lyricism: Shih Poetry from the Second to the Twelfth Century, tr. Burton Watson 1970
A Syllabus of Indian Civilization, by Leonard A. Gordon and Barbara Stoler Miller 1971
Twentieth-Century Chinese Stories, ed. by C. T. Hsia and Joseph S. M. Lau 1971
A Syllabus of Chinese Civilization, by J. Mason Gentzler, 2d ed. 1972
A Syllabus of Japanese Civilization, by H. Paul Varley, 2d ed. 1972

INTRODUCTION TO ORIENTAL CIVILIZATIONS

WM. THEODORE de BARY, EDITOR

Sources of Japanese Tradition	1958	Paperback ed., 2 vols.	1964
Sources of Indian Tradition	1958	Paperback ed., 2 vols.	1964
Sources of Chinese Tradition	1960	Paperback ed., 2 vols.	1964

STUDIES IN ORIENTAL CULTURE

1.	The Ōnin War: History of Its Origins and Background, with a Selective Translation of the Chronicle of Ōnin, by H. Paul Varley	1967
2.	Chinese Government in Ming Times: Seven Studies, ed. Charles O. Hucker	1969
3.	The Actors' Analects (Yakusha Rongo), ed. and tr. by Charles J. Dunn and Bunzō Torigoe	1969
4.	Self and Society in Ming Thought, by Wm. Theodore de Bary and the Conference on Ming Thought	1970
5.	A History of Islamic Philosophy, by Majid Fakhry	1970
6.	Phantasies of a Love Thief: The Caurapancasika Attributed to Bihana, by Barbara S. Miller	1971
7.	Iqbal: Poet-Philosopher of Pakistan, ed. by Hafeez Malik	1971
8.	The Golden Tradition, by Ahmed Ali	1973
9.	Conquerors and Confucians, by John W. Dardess	1973